BEHOLD YOUR GOD

BOOKS BY AGNES SANFORD

BEHOLD YOUR GOD

THE HEALING LIGHT

LOST SHEPHERD

A PASTURE FOR PETERKIN

HEALING GIFTS OF THE SPIRIT

HEALING POWER OF THE BIBLE

MELISSA AND THE LITTLE RED BOOK

SEALED ORDERS

CREATION WAITS

Behold

Your God

By Agnes Sanford

MACALESTER PARK PUBLISHING COMPANY

Saint Paul, Minnesota

BEHOLD YOUR GOD

Fourteenth Printing 1986

*Published in the United States of America
by Macalester Park Publishing Company,
1571 Grand Avenue, Saint Paul,
Minnesota 55105*

ISBN 0-910924-63-5

TABLE OF CONTENTS

DEDICATION

TO THOSE WHO HAVE MASTERED
THE TEACHINGS OF MY OTHER BOOKS,
AND WHO HAVE LONGED TO VEN-
TURE FARTHER IN AN UNDERSTAND-
ING OF THE SPIRITUAL KINGDOM, THIS
BOOK IS DEDICATED

1. God is Our

Loving Father

Some years ago I saw a miracle. It was a small thing as miracles go—merely a little child who went to sleep when a minister prayed for him, and who awoke and was well. That miracle made for me a new heaven and a new earth. It showed me that God is real, and that His Word still goes forth to accomplish His Will upon the creation of His making. So it awoke in me hope and faith and a renewed purpose for living.

I had seen with my eyes that God's power could work through an individual. But I did not know how an individual could become a channel for God's power. Before many months I wanted to know this, because I saw about me suffering and darkness that only God could help, and I saw that people were shut off from God so that His help could not reach them. How could one reconnect them with Him, so that His will could be done in them? There was no one to tell me. The minister who had prayed for my baby could channel the power, but could not explain it in words that I was able to comprehend. True, I learned from him many useful things about the care of my own body and mind. But when I asked, "What is this power and how does one use it for others?" he only replied, very truly, "It is a power of the super-mind."

Yes, but what was the "super-mind" and how could one put it into action?

There are many books today that try to explain this matter. But at the time I knew none of them. Therefore, I decided to find the answer in two ways: first, by studying the words of Jesus

Christ, and second, by trying what He said and seeing whether it worked or not.

This sounds very simple, but it did not prove to be so. First of all, I found that what He said went directly contrary to many of the explanations concerning religion that I had been taught since my youth. For instance, I had been told that the age of miracles was past—yet I had seen a miracle. I had been told that God no longer worked through an individual—yet I had seen Him work through an individual.

If I had at that time tried to reconcile all the teachings of today and make them conform to the words of Jesus, I would never have started any healing work. I knew this. I also knew that there was no use in trying to understand what I had not experienced. Therefore, I set myself to find an *experience of* God's power.

In order to do this, I laid aside temporarily all that I had been taught concerning Christianity. I did not disbelieve it, I merely laid it on the table to be considered later. And that is what all of us must do if we are to learn.

To learn—What? To learn two things: how to know the working of God's power in ourselves and how to pass it through us to others. This is experiencing God. Religion is an *experience* of God. Theology is merely an attempt to explain the experience. As man's experience of God changes through the ages, the explanation concerning that experience must of necessity also change. To limit the experience within the bounds of what one learned in Sunday School or in Seminary would preclude any further growth in grace and any further revelation from that very Spirit of Truth whom Jesus sent to lead us into all truth.

Christianity is already swinging away from the great nineteenth century heresy[1], the statement that God no longer does works of power—that His hand is shortened, that it cannot save (Isa. 59:1)—that this is a new dispensation, one in which everything must be done by man's mind and hands—that Jesus Christ came to give us less abundant life and that the works that He did we should not do. Many people are re-discovering the eternal truth: that God is both able and eager to help us (Matt. 10:29-31); that the works that Jesus did, we should do too (John 14:12); that the greatest things are accomplished not by men's hands

---

[1] *A Reporter Finds God,* Emily Gardiner Neal. Morehouse, Gorham, N. Y. 1957

and minds, but by the Spirit of God abiding in them (Zech. 4:6); that Jesus came to give us more abundant life (John 10:10)— more joy (John 16:22), more power (Acts 1:8), more guidance (John 16:13), more opportunity to sacrifice for His sake (Matt. 5:10-11).

For many years I stepped out on these promises without understanding. Time and again I found myself frustrated and baffled by the contradictions between popularly accepted ideas of Christianity and the actual things that happened. This frustration and confusion was a strain on my faith and a hindrance to my work. So I began to seek for understanding—to re-think the basic beliefs of our religion in the words of today, and to measure them according to the actual workings of the power of God. I found that each new gleam of understanding increased the power and released the joy of the new life. So it is my hope to pass on in this book an expanded concept of God and of His workings through Jesus Christ Our Lord. It is my hope that the reader will, for the present, consider these matters with an open mind and that he will not try to make them conform to his present concepts until he has finished the book.

For instance, faith is the tool by which God's works are done. But when I tried to help myself in prayer, I met with an immediate obstacle—namely, I could not believe that God really wanted to heal me. It was just as apt to be His will, I thought, that I should go on suffering. In other words, I did not believe that God felt toward me as my father felt. My father was a good father. So is God. A good father loves his children. Do we believe that God loves us as a good father loves his child?

Not long ago I had a letter from the mother of a spastic child, one of many letters pathetically alike. She believed that her child had been born spastic as punishment for some sin of hers or of her husband's, though what that sin might be she did not know, and neither do I, for her letter breathed goodness. They had searched themselves, she and her husband, they had repented of every error that they could find within themselves and they had prayed for the child's recovery. They knew that God could heal the child at any moment and they were just waiting upon His will. But the years had passed and their hearts had grown old with waiting and the child was not healed. Nevertheless, they still trusted God and knew that in His own good time He would heal their child.

Surely these dear people were mistaken in their estimate of

the nature of God! Come now and let us reason together. Is that the way a good father would act? You have known a good father or mother. Perhaps you are such a one. Would you act in that manner toward your child? Would you condemn a little baby to be born a spastic in order to punish someone else? Or if you did so, would you withhold a healing even after the sinner had repented? Yes, I am shocking you. I challenge you to answer that question out of a truthful heart.

You would not. If the parents had sinned and repented, you would forgive the sin. You would rush to heal that child. Yet Jesus said, "If ye then, being evil" (as we all are in comparison with the perfect love of God) "know how to give good gifts unto your children, how much more shall your Father which is in heaven give good things to them that ask him (Matt. 7:11)?" Not only once did Jesus say this, but time after time. "Oh, but He means only spiritual things," we say, ignoring the fact that He never failed to pour out physical healing as well as spiritual to those who came to Him. Never once did He say, "God does not want to heal your body, but He will forgive your sins." Not once did He say, "I am not sure that it is God's will to heal you—" not once. Search the Scriptures and prove this for yourselves! Nor did He limit his prayer-work to the forgiveness of sins, as some like to claim, and let the healing follow as a matter of course. Some illnesses are the natural result of breaking God's laws, as we shall see in a later chapter, and in order to remain in health the sinner must learn to keep those laws. But other illnesses have nothing to do with the sin of the individual. It was not his own sin that caused a man to be born blind (John 9.2), nor a woman to be bound by Satan eighteen years (Luke 13:16), nor a baby to be born a spastic. There is nothing to indicate that the illness of Jairus' daughter (Mark 5:23) and of the centurion's servant (Luke 7:2) was psychosomatic. Christianity, praise be to God, is a religion not only of the soul but also of the body. And Jesus, who knew the will of the Father as no one else has ever known it, insisted always that God desired us to be perfect, even as He himself is perfect (Matt. 5:48). If He had not been clear and firm on this point, He could never have healed the imperfect and infirm who came to Him. Nor can we. And He taught us first of all that God is a Father (Matt. 6:8-9), because that concept first of all releases in us the faith to accept His healing.

What then can we say to parents such as those mentioned

above? I am apt to write them something like this: "I do not believe that God caused your baby to be born spastic. It is one of the mistakes of a nature that has gone far away from God. I cannot feel that it is a punishment for your sins or for the child's sins, for God loves you and your child as a father loves his children. But it does have something to do with the sins of a world that could so forget God as to open a door to Satan. Therefore, I would continue in faith and prayer for the child, rejoicing in all improvement even though it may be slow. And I would offer my present suffering to God as a sacrifice willingly given for the sins of the world, and thus would turn it into power. Finally, I would look forward always to the Kingdom of Heaven, when God's will shall be done on earth as it is in heaven and tragedies like these shall be no more."

This I would write in the firm belief that sorrows such as this are the result of the fall of man and thus are the work of Satan and not the will of God.

Jesus explained this in one of His trenchant stories. "The kingdom of heaven is likened unto a man which sowed good seed in his field," He said. "But while men slept, his enemy came and sowed tares among the wheat, and went his way (Matt. 13:24-25)." And when His disciples asked Him to explain this story He said in so many words, "The enemy that sowed them is the devil (Matt. 13:39)."

As we try to believe in a God who is a Father, brooding over us with a truly parental love, we come immediately to the devil. This is an impossible concept to those who believe that God is good and that God made all and therefore all is good. But there is one trouble with this picture of life: obviously all is not good. Some people circumvent this obstacle by closing their eyes to evil and saying that as it is not the ultimate reality, therefore it does not really exist. I have no quarrel with this point of view. Its aim is both clear and worthy; it is to help the individual to focus his attention upon the good. My sympathy and appreciation go forth to those who are able to satisfy themselves with this theory. But I am not writing for them. Since they are satisfied, they will not need to read this book. I am writing for those—shall we say less fortunate ones?—who must needs ask themselves and God, "Why? Why? Why? Why are children born with afflictions which science is unable to cure? Why is the world torn apart with wars when all of us so earnestly want peace? Why are the nations filled with murder and violence? Why? Why? Why?"

Jesus told us that the enemy who sowed these seeds of destruction is the devil.

We who claim to follow Him did much better when we believed these words of His. St. Paul said, "Put on the whole armour of God, that ye may be able to stand against the wiles of the devil (Eph. 6:11)." And he added, "For we wrestle not against flesh and blood, but against principalities, against powers, against the rulers of the darkness of this world, against spiritual wickedness in high places (Eph. 6:12)."

It did not depress St. Paul to know this. It encouraged him. He would have been far more upset to think that all of the evil that he saw around him came out of the imagination of men's hearts alone. It cleared his spiritual eyes to see his "adversary the devil," who "as a roaring lion walketh about seeking whom he may devour (I Peter 5:8)." It made him a more victorious and a more effective soldier of Our Lord to know whom he was fighting.

But in the last few centuries, the church has been through a phase that must have delighted the heart of that same character, the devil. Quite possibly indeed, this phase was inspired by him. C. S. Lewis says that the devil's cleverest trick is to make us believe that there is no devil. Those who exaggerate the power of our own thinking like to feel that if they believe that there is no power of evil, then there is none. But this, while holding a shred of truth that we will later examine, is not wholly true. If one walks upon the edge of a cliff upon a dark night and believes that there is no cliff there, his belief does not cause the cliff to disappear. On the whole, he is safer if he sees the cliff and avoids it.

We have not desired to see the devil and avoid him. We have somehow acquired the thought that it is unscientific to believe that there might be a devil or, indeed, angels and archangels and all the host of heaven. In spite of the fact that we sing in church, "Therefore with angels and archangels and with all the host of heaven we laud and magnify Thy glorious name[1]," we have nevertheless hugged to our bosoms the smug thought that after all, there cannot really be any living beings in the universe except ourselves and those humble animals that we see with our eyes. In spite of the fact that our babies are baptised

---

[1] *The Book of Common Prayer*

with the power of the Trinity so that they may have the strength to fight manfully under the banner of Jesus Christ against sin, the world, and the devil, and have loudly said "Amen", we have meant just the opposite of Amen, because we have not believed this thing at all.

Is it really unscientific, then, to believe that there may be other living creatures in the universe than those upon the earth? How amazing and how amusing it is that science, as it plods its way toward knowing, makes it more and more possible for us to believe what the Bible told us long ago: that there are beings who have never lived on earth[1]! We know now that the stars are suns, like ours, millions of them, among whom our sun is but one insignificant heavenly candle. For generations, however, astronomy assured us that there were no planets about any other sun but ours, and that living creatures could not exist upon our sister planets. But recently science states that in all probability there are planets around other suns after all, as indeed why should there not be? The laws of life that produced planets around our sun are more than likely to produce the same manifestations around other suns.

Moreover, now science informs us that there may be living creatures upon them! Indeed, we are even contemplating the possibility of inventing fantastic rocket-ships so that we may go and call upon these beings!

In my children's book, *Let's Believe,* I summed up the matter thus:

> *"Are there really angels*
> *With blue and purple wings?*
> *Are there really seraphim*
> *And other shiny things?*
>
> *The sky is full of lots of worlds!*
> *How funny God would be*
> *If nothing lived and moved on them*
> *But people just like me."*

---

[1] References to angels, or to "men" who are obviously not men of this earth: Gen. 3:24, Job 38:7, Psalms 29:1 & 2, 89:7, 80:1, 99:1, 148:2 & 5, Isa. 6:1-3, Dan. 8:16, 10:5, 6 & 13, Matt. 4:6 & 11, 13:9, 16:24, 25:31, 26:53, Mark 12:25, Luke 1:19, 12:8 & 9, 15:10, 22:43, John 20:12, Acts 8:26, 12:7-9, 27:23, I Cor. 4:8, Eph. 6:10, II Thess. 1:7-10, I Tim. 3:16, 5:21, Heb. 1:4, 2:16, Jude 9, Rev. 5:11 & 12, 12:7.

Is it so frightfully stupid for Christians to believe what the Bible tells us, namely that there are other living creatures beside mankind in the world, when even science contemplates the possibility?

Assuming then that God may have given life to other beings than human beings, let us go on to the next question: how could God have made an evil being, since God is good?

The answer to that is very simple, and is plainly stated in the Bible.

God did not create an evil being. St. Jude speaks of the angels which kept not their first estate but left their own habitation, whom he hath reserved in everlasting chains under darkness (Jude 6). Ezekiel laments upon the King of Tyre, and upon the "anointed cherub" who fell upon the earth and perverted him (Eze. 28: 12-20). Isaiah cried in a moment of vision, "How art thou fallen from heaven, O Lucifer, son of the morning! How art thou cut down to the ground, which didst weaken the nations! For thou hast said in thine heart, I will ascend into heaven, I will exalt my throne above the stars of God. . . I will be like the most High (Isaiah 14:12-14). . ." And Jesus Himself confirmed this statement, using the more common name for the adversary, when He said, "I beheld Satan as lightning fall from heaven (Luke 10:18)."

Quite simply and plainly the Bible teaches us that God created Satan with the hope of his being good, as He created Adam and Eve, with the hope of their being good (Gen. 1:26; John 12:31, 14:3). God, being good, made all, and quite truthfully made all good. But desiring that we should be His friends, adult and considering and understanding, God gave us free-will so that we could choose to follow the good He made for us, and in choosing, could become strong. God permitted this possibility of evil because He loved us. He loved us so much that He wanted us to love Him. He longed for a return of love from His loved ones, just as we long for a return of love from those we love. We cannot love Him if we do not know Him—if we do not grasp the reality of His being. We cannot grasp so great a thing unless our souls mature. Therefore, he gave us free-will, thus enabling us to choose and to create either good or evil, so that in learning and in struggling, in suffering and in joy, in battle and in triumph, our souls shall grow.

God Himself did not create evil. But in creating good, the possibility of dark became a reality. As Dorothy Sayer said in

her extraordinary book on the Trinity, *The Mind of the Maker,*
when Shakespeare created Hamlet he automatically created the
fact that all other heroes in all other plays were not Hamlet. This
static not-good would never have leaped into life and hurt anyone, she said, except that someone chose it and thus made it
active. And the Bible tells us that even before man chose it, one
among the angels chose it, rebelling against God, trying to be
equal with Him and so falling from His high places and becoming the prince of this little world (John 16:11).

This is most consoling. For when we know that we ourselves
are the children of light and that the shadows that fall upon our
souls are from an enemy without us, one whom we can fight
manfully under the banner of Christ, surely then we gain freedom and strength!

Above all, this belief is most consoling because when we
realize that there is an enemy, then we can believe that God is
a Father and that the tragedies of this world are not His doing.
His heart is grieved over them as our hearts are grieved over
them. And it is His will to end them. But the overcoming of
them shall be with our help and understanding, because He loves
us and trusts us and wants us to grow up to be His friends. A
mother yearns over a baby trying to walk and stumbling and
hurting his little nose. She will watch over him that he does not
fall downstairs or hurt himself past bearing. But even because
she loves him, she will not carry him for the rest of his life. A
babe in arms is entrancing. But a grown man carried is pitiable
and revolting.

So God is a loving father and He means to help us and He
will. He is so eager to help us that He came to us, long ago, in
a new way, entering this world through gates of birth, and in-
carnating His love in the Son of Man, Jesus Christ. On the plane
of our human suffering and need, He achieved the victory over
that old serpent the devil (Rev. 12:9), and to this day His name
is sufficient to rout the power of darkness. But we must *live* in
His name, that is in His personality, thinking His thoughts and
feeling His love, or else our commands, given in His name, may
not be obeyed (Acts 19:13-17). In order to hold and keep His
power, we must keep His commandments. We must follow those
rules of right living and of constructive thinking that He made
clear to us.

If we had fully understood the words that Jesus told us and if
we had effectively used the power that He released to us, our

heavenly Father would long ago have protected and healed His children as surely as a human father would have done, and far more victoriously. If we had for all these centuries learned to live in Jesus, and if His words had been written in our hearts, so that from the very depth of the subconscious we had known His will and had desired to do it, the spastic baby would have been well by this time. For the works that He did we would have done also (John 14:12) in His name and through His power. There would have been the springboard of a Spirit-filled church from which to work. There would have been those in the church so instinct with the gift of healing that the touch of their hands would have healing power (Acts 14:3). Some church would have prayed for that baby with the complete unity of Christian love that we find in the early church, without a shadow of jealousy or of bickering, of doubt or of wondering concerning the love of God. Someone would have gone to her and laid hands on her as Ananias did upon St. Paul (Acts 9:17-18) so that God would have had a completely whole and holy channel for His power. And she would have recovered.

Moreover, if we had not faltered or compromised in that battle against the forces of evil that Our Lord told us to undertake (Mark 16:15 and Luke 10:3), it is quite possible that we would have brought the day in which no child would remain or be afflicted (Rev. 21:4). To believe that such things are God's will is to deny that God is a Father. No father unless he is cruel and sadistic would will such a thing upon his child. It is blasphemy to attribute such a nature as that to God. The first step in any kind of effective prayer is to *know God*. For how can we have faith if we do not know whether God is a Father who feels toward us as a human father would feel, or whether He is a notional and tyrannical despot who refuses to explain His ways to us or to let us know what He is doing, but who loves to see us suffer? How can we pray at all if we do not believe the first thing that Jesus came to teach us: that God loves us as a father loves us?

The more we believe that God is a Father, the more He comes to us in light and peace and healing. The more definitely we expect Him to act as a good parent would act, the more he can do so.

So, first of all, let us try to revive our belief that God is a Father—a *good* Father who loves us, and that the cruelties of life are not His will.

How shall we revive our faith? Not by reason alone, for so much of us is below the level of reason. We must re-convince the subconscious mind as well as the conscious! Therefore, let us use the reiteration of praise as the Bible tells us to do, so that the whole being will accept His love! I wonder if there is any command given more often in the Bible than the command to praise the Lord, to let His praise be continually in our mouths. Surely the purpose of this command is not only to rejoice the heart of the Almighty, but also to make glad our own hearts and to release their power by filling the entire being, subconscious as well as conscious, with the love and the joy of the Lord. Therefore, let us remind ourselves a hundred times a day that He is our Father, and let us thank Him and praise Him for His love until the feeling of it revives in us.

And as this feeling revives in us, let us begin immediately to establish it by acting upon it. Let us assume that God is a Father and that He loves His people, and let us try to convey His love and His power to them, just as Our Lord did.

2. How to

Contact God

When we come to believe that God loves us and wishes to give us good gifts of health and peace, then another question confronts us. Is He almighty? Is He really able to do these good things for us?

"Why did God let Mrs. A. suffer so much," we are apt to ask, "when she was such a good woman and did so much for the church?"

One might answer, "She could have received much more help from God if she had known how to pray."

"But if God loves her, why does she have to pray? If God loves her like a father, why must she ask Him to make her well? Why doesn't He just do it?"

The answer is, of course, that in a thousand cases He does so, just as in a thousand cases we provide for our children's needs without their asking. But, in special cases and for special needs, He has ordained that we must draw near to Him and make our needs known unto Him.

Many people do not like God's insistence upon a free and personal relationship with His children. "I *don't* see why He doesn't just simply *do* whatever is best for us," they say. "I *don't* see why we need to pray for specific things."

Is that the way that a wise and loving human father would act toward his children? Would you forbid that your children come to you with their desires, their hopes and dreams? Would you say to them, "I don't want you to ask me for anything. I know what is good for you and I will give it to you as I please."

Surely not! Some things indeed we do give them without their asking—shelter, food, necessary clothing—just as God sends His rain on the just and on the unjust and clothes the world with beauty and provides our bodies with a healthy and recuperative power. But there are the special things—the desires of our hearts or the particular needs for a particular moment—and it is God's will that we come to Him and ask for those things just as it is our will that our children come to us. It comforts us—and them—to know that they can ask for their hearts' desires. Moreover, in so doing, they draw near to us and we help them to shape and mold their desires and so to grow to manhood or womanhood.

Jesus urged us to ask for our hearts' desires. "Hitherto have ye asked nothing in my name," He said. "Ask and ye shall receive, that your joy may be full (John 16:24)." He knew that the prayer of petition has a part in developing our relationship to God and in maturing our spirits. God is a loving Father and He desires our good, but for our own sakes, He does not automatically give us all that His Holy Spirit can give. He wants us to be His sons, not only His uncomprehending little babies. Therefore He has given us the power to choose and the right to ask.

Now in order to ask anything of any person we must draw near to him. And so we must first of all draw near to this Almighty God. In one sense, of course, we are already near to Him. In the beginning, remember, the earth was without form and void and there was nothing except God Himself. Therefore, He sent forth His word and life evolved from the Creator Himself. Thus in Him we live and move and have our being. He is in the world about us, so that those who see God in trees and stones and running brooks are glimpsing a bit of the truth. But God is not limited to the one aspect of His eternal glory that formed the inanimate creation. God is more than His creation.

However, the universal life of God around us can become a personal breath of God *within* us. At a certain stage in the process of creation—at the beginning of the sixth Day, so we are told—God chose the most highly developed of the life-forms that had evolved out of the dust of the earth, and into that one God breathed the breath of life (Gen. 2:7)—from that time forth man has been a living soul containing a bit of the creative nature of the Creator. "Let us make man in our own image, after our likeness . . . (Gen. 1:26)" Thus man became not only a higher animal but also a spiritual being, living in a body of flesh. The first spiritual beings were in such close communion with God that they could see His glory and hear His voice (Gen. 3:8). They were both clair-audient and clair-voyant. They could walk and talk with this God who existed, not only in earth and air, not only in their own spirits, but also apart from them, in His own divine Being, for this God did not cease to be, in giving them souls. He still IS, existing outside of them as well as inside of them!

This is a simple, obvious, primary. Yet some people today tend to minimize this tremendous fact from which all other facts evolve. "God is Divine Mind," they say, "and we have Divine Mind within us." "God is the creative principle, and we have and can use the creative principle." There is a shred of truth in this, of course. But this is only a small part of the whole great truth. God is not only in us or the sun or the rocks or the trees. God IS. Before all worlds, God IS. When all worlds shall be rolled up as a garment and shall disappear, still God IS. If there were no living being to know Him, still God IS. As the Presbyterian Shorter Catechism expresses it, "God is a Spirit, infinite, eternal and unchangeable, in His Being, Wisdom, Power, Holiness, Justice, Goodness and Truth." God is more than Divine Mind or Divine Wisdom. God is more than a current of power that heals. God is love, but God is more than love. God works according to truth, but God is more than merely a certain principle of thinking that one might call "Truth." GOD IS.

God is the Father Almighty, and man can make contact with Him and know Him. And in the prayer of faith it is absolutely necessary to make this contact in order to establish a channel through which the actual energy of God's healing power can flow.

Dr. Alexis Carrell wrote, "Prayer is not only worship, it is also the invisible emanation of man's worshipping spirit, the most perfect form of energy one can generate. The influence of prayer on the human mind and body is as demonstrable as that of secreting glands[1]."

Dr. Carrell used the word "generate". And I suppose that one may use that term as one may speak of a battery "generating" electricity. Yet the electricity originates in the air without the battery, and the energy of man's worshipping spirit originates in

---

[1] Quoted by Christopher Woodard in *A Doctor Heals by Faith*. Max Parrish, London.

the God whom he worships. Thus the first step necessary in releasing prayer-energy is connecting our spirits with God's Spirit.

We are prone to assume that we are in contact with God
when we are not.

For instance, I once talked on the telephone to a friend from
Los Angeles and he said this amazing thing: "You know, we are
not talking across the wires. We are talking directly across the air.
It is a new thing we are working out in Bell Telephone."

"But that's impossible," I cried.

"Oh no, it's not," he assured me, "not if you contact the
channel."

For me to stand on a street corner in Massachusetts and lift
my voice and expect to be heard in California would be ridiculous. But that very thing can be done if one contacts the channel.

Time and again people say to me, "But I prayed and prayed
and I know I have all the faith in the world, and nothing happened." Naturally. They were merely standing on a street corner
and lifting their voices. They were not "contacting the channel."

Our at-one-ment with God is through Jesus Christ. He opened
for us a channel that man had closed. All of our Christian living
in His name helps to bring us close to God—our baptism into
His church, our partaking of the sacraments in His church and,
indeed, all of our worshipping and serving God through our
Lord and Saviour Jesus Christ. If we did this with complete
faithfulness and with full understanding from the beginning, we
would need no further exposition of this matter, for we would be
so fully in Him that His power would shine forth from us to heal
and to save and to do His works. But our faith has wavered and
our understanding has dulled, and therefore we go to His church
Sunday after Sunday and yet remain dim in spirit and arid in heart,
not discerning the body of Christ (I Cor. 11:29). Thus while we
touch the hem of His garment from time to time, we do not
truly abide in Him. And only as we abide in Him, can we ask
what we will, that it shall be done unto us (John 15:7).

How then can we make a better contact, so that we may
actually feel his presence?

Can we hear His voice and see His light as did those first
creatures into whom He breathed the breath of life? Some day
perhaps we shall develop this amount of spiritual sensitivity, but
at the moment this is too big a leap for us to make. However, we
can perceive His life working in us, and that is a little step toward Him.

First of all, then, let us remind ourselves that there *is* a current of God's life that can be perceived both in our hearts and in our bodies. The Logos, the Word: the life-principle which became Light: still *is*.

There is an actual energy in the air about us, invisible, impalpable but nevertheless real, that can come into us and bring about results that are visible and palpable . . . "so that things which are seen were not made of things which do appear (Heb. 11:3)."

A hundred years ago, the ability to perceive this fact was called mysticism. But if we use that term today, we must broaden it to include scientific truth; for if this is mysticism, then science is mysticism.

Any child knows that a kind of light that cannot be seen comes into the aerial above his house and makes upon the screen of his television set a picture that can be seen. All praise be to those great mystics, the scientists, who dare to dream dreams and to see visions and to act upon their resultant theories and show us (perhaps unintentionally) that the words of Scripture are actually true! There is a power. There is a kind of light that cannot be seen but which has within it the principle of creativity. Perhaps it is the original creation—a moving, vibrating radiation that came into being when God said, "Let there be light," and there was light (Gen. 1:3)!

By the interposition of will *plus* faith, man can introduce into a situation an increased flow of God's creative energy. For there is in the universe a vibration like the vibration of light, and its tendency is to create life. It may well have been the first creation of all, and out of it all worlds may have evolved.

"There is a river," said another holy man of long ago, using another metaphor to explain what cannot be quite encompassed in human words, "the streams whereof shall make glad the city of God, the holy place of the tabernacles of the most High (Ps. 46:4)." There is a river, a stream, a flow of a life-giving element. And we can make contact wtih this Life that flows from God. In *The Healing Light* I have suggested simple ways of making this contact. I will now outline a more intense and advanced meditation toward contacting God's life.

First of all, subdue the energy of your body so that you can forget it. Make it comfortable—you owe it this courtesy. Stretch your arms and legs and then let them go in as easy a position as possible. Then advise your nerves and muscles to be still. They tend to become too taut in their ceaseless straining after that which cannot be received save through God's Spirit. Therefore, speak to them kindly and say, "Now you can just be peaceful . . . release all tension . . . just let go . . ." Say this to all your nerves, in silence, beginning with your head and carrying the same peaceful and comforting thought down to your feet. Imagine the peace of God creeping down over your head, stilling its stream of consciousness into a quiet flow of drifting thoughts, down over your arms and hands till even the hands are limp, down through your body so that your heart beats lightly and easily, so that your breathing is light and easy, down your legs and feet till even the feet are still and heavy as though they were asleep.

As you quiet the body thus, the mind tends to be more quiet So now, let go gently of all things that press upon your mind— all the things for which you would pray—set them aside and forget them. "But we want to pray about them!" you may think. No, you don't—not now. What's the use, when you have not as yet contacted the power? So drop them lightly, one by one.

"Be still and know that I am God," said the Almighty through His spirit to the psalmist of long ago (Psalm 46:10). So now that you are still, let your spirit enter into the spiritual king-dom. Imagine your spirit ascending through the heavens and into the presence of God.

Signs will come to you later on. Usually one becomes aware of His presence by seeing His works in the body and in life. Some people are also given to see visions or to have moments of cosmic awareness or of heavenly rapture or best of all, to per-ceive the form or hear the voice of Jesus Christ. If these signs come to us unsought, we may rejoice and praise God for them. But if we seek for signs or sensations or appearances, we distract our attention from our real objective—union of our spirits with God's Spirit—and we may stop short of our real goal, like Little Red Riding Hood, who was distracted by the flowers on the way and stopped in the woods and did not reach her grandmother's house in time. The little girl in the fable ran into danger from so doing, and we can also run into danger if we seek for signs instead of seeking for God. There are people who in their in-nocence ask for guidance or for signs through fortune-tellers or ouija boards or automatic writing. To most people this might be a childish but harmless amusement, but for the earnest seeker after God, it is not so. For one who would try to acquire spiritual power is a potential enemy of the old deceiver, Satan, and therefore Satan will enter any door that he leaves open. When one yields the mind to a fortune-teller or to a "guide" whose spirit merges with the spirits and works through the hands in automatic writing, he is leaving a door wide open to any current of thought or feeling that Satan might desire to put into them. The harmful results of so doing may vary from loss of our objective and a sense of depression all the way to a genuine disturbance of personality such as the Bible calls "possession." For further consideration of this point I will refer the reader to the work of a psychiatrist[1]. This book was written some years ago, true, but I have the word of four living psychiatrists who know that this is true, and furthermore, I know it to my sorrow from the actual experiences of some twenty people.

Therefore, keep the mind firmly and unwaveringly fixed on Jesus Christ. Jesus Himself is the express image of God (Heb. 1:1-4) and came to us in human form so that we may look upon Him with the eyes of the soul and may see God (John 14:9). So if we must needs see a picture in our minds for our comfort, let us hold before the eyes of the soul the picture of the risen and glorified Jesus. Meditate, then, upon the mysteries of God hidden in His holy birth, in His sacrificial life among men, in His redemptive passion and in His life-giving ascension. Most of all, strive to discern His presence in the profound mysteries of the Communion Service, which He gave that we might see Him face to face and that we might touch and handle things unseen[2].

Having thus meditated on Him, now imagine Him entering into you and quickening you with His own creative energy. Then give thanks that your spirit *is* in His presence. As you become adept at this kind of prayer, you will be able to sense the inner peace and joy that comes to you when you are indeed lifted into His light. In the beginning, you will need to take it by faith that this is so and to continue to meditate on Him even though it be without the support of any signs either of inner feelings or of outer perceptions.

Then in order to know Him by perceiving His working in your own being, turn your mind to those parts of you that you can know and see: your mind and your body. Imagine His light

---

[1] *Body, Mind & Soul*, Worcester & McComb.

---

[2] *The Hymnal*

shining into your body and quickening therein the flow of life, so that you will have more abundant life for doing His work. If any part of your body needs to be strengthened or healed, vision His light there, recreating in perfection that which He created in the beginning. Put your mind directly into that part of the body and see it burning with the fire of His creative energy. Then make an act of faith, and picture this part of your body well and strong. You need not over-strain your faith by telling yourself that it is accomplished, but at least having made this picture by faith, you can now say by the same faith, "Thank Thee, heavenly Father, because I believe that the life of Thy Spirit is now with me working toward health and strength."

"But I thought this was an exercise in contacting God," you may think. Certainly. But the simplest and humblest way of knowing God is to perceive His working in our own beings. And since we are simple and humble people, we may as well learn to contact the channel of God's power in the most simple and humble way.

So now turn this energy into the thinking of the conscious mind. Hold up before Him the work that you intend doing today with this mind that He has given you for a tool. Those of you who read, your work at this moment is the work of comprehension—of illumination—of a grasping by the mind of these truths which are centered in the spirit and are therefore not easy of understanding. So now vision the Spirit of God merging with your spirit and speaking to you, so that new understanding of His fatherly love will come to you, not only now as you read but during the whole of this day—perhaps flashing into consciousness as you do your work—perhaps leaping into life as you think on these things, perhaps even coming in a deeper way through dreams at night. And give thanks that He will illumine your minds yet more and more and lead you into the ways of understanding and the ways of power.

This beginning prayer will lead you on to intercession. You will find that having prayed for yourselves, others come into your minds and you desire to pray for them also. Or, perhaps, later on in your development, you will find that the Holy Spirit of God overshadows you, so that you enter into His glory and into His being and remain in a state of prayer without petition, merely beholding. Thus your prayer-time will expand naturally and without forcing. In the beginning, ten or fifteen minutes may be sufficient and any more may be a weariness to the flesh. Later on,

half an hour or even an hour may seem a natural amount of time
for this work of prayer. You cannot lose time by so giving time to
this work of prayer. You cannot lose time by so giving time to
Him—you gain time; for everything that you do with His added
power will be accomplished with more precision and ease.

When you have come to the end of your prayer-period, renew
your protection, at least with the statement that you go forth
walking in a circle of light and armed with God's power. And
then strive through the day so to live that the light and power
can remain about you. This will include a certain discipline of
your thoughts and words and deeds. For there are thoughts and
words and deeds that tend to open the mind to the old enemy.
Satan enters on the winds of anger and finds within a comfortable
dwelling-place. Hate and resentment open a door to him, and the
more one gives voice to this hate and resentment, the wider one
opens the door. We should by all means learn to control our
thoughts and our feelings and to live in the great charity of Christ
that is the only possible way for a Christian to live. And we shall
learn to do this more and more. It is easier to bridle the tongue
than to bridle the thoughts, and therefore, we take care that our
conversation shall be in Heaven (Phil. 3:20). "Every idle word
that men shall speak, they shall give account thereof in the day
of judgment (Matt. 12:36)."

This is quite contrary to a certain modern school of thought;
namely, that one should unbridle the tongue and give one's feelings release lest one get a complex. True, if we are stewing in
anger and hate, it may temporarily give us release to express
them. But first, we have no right as Christians to stew in anger
and hate (Matt. 5:21-27 & 38). Second, we are not only minds
and subconscious minds—we are also spirits. And we live not
only among men and women who may feel more kindly toward
us when we have punched them in the head (although this theory
seems somewhat doubtful to me) but we live also amid principalities and powers, the rulers of the darkness of this world,
spiritual wickedness in high places (Eph. 6:12). And words and
deeds of anger and hate draw toward us unwanted thought currents. Therefore, though we may temporarily feel a release because
of the satisfaction of telling someone exactly what we think of him,
in so doing we have opened ourselves to attack by the enemy
and he will usually enter and increase in us a tendency toward
bad humor and rage. And the more we unbridle the tongue and
express these feelings, the more they tend to grow within us. So

that while we may escape a "complex" by so unbridling our tongues, we will not escape the judgment. "Whosoever shall say, Thou fool, shall be in danger of hell fire (Matt. 5:22)."

Moreover let us consider this bugaboo, a complex. Let us put a Christian name upon it and call it simply a wrong thought-habit. Do we have to have a wrong thought-habit because we choose of our own free will to bridle our tongues—to put our-selves under the discipline of the cross for the sake of Jesus Christ? No one gets a complex from voluntarily undertaking a labor of love. A small unhappy child brought up in a home of cruelty and suppression may get a complex from the deep-eating bitterness and rage that he dares not express. But a mature Christian who determines for the sake of the Christ to give thought and expression only to those things that are loving and kind can-not thereby get any kind of an unhealthy state of mind. A con-vict forced to climb a high mountain and work on roads may increase his emotional unhealthiness by brooding with anger upon his unhappy lot. But a mountain-climber who through his own desire strives to conquer Everest, while enduring far more suffer-ing than the convict endures, will not get a complex out of it.

It all depends upon the desires of one's heart—upon the goals that one would attain. If one desires only to get something off his chest, well and good. But if one desires to develop spiritual powers, let him get something *into* his chest instead: namely, the love of Christ. Let him seek after forgiveness and love in all relationships. Let him bridle his tongue and *put on* a heart of compassion (Col: 3:6), expressing in words and deeds that Chris-tian love that he hopes to attain. And let him live in the purity and the honesty that are of God.

This, then, is the walk of the one who would attain God's power: first, to connect our spirits with His Spirit and second, to live before Him in charity and gentleness, in honesty and purity, that we may keep His life flowing through us during the day's work. If we find ourselves slipping into the temptations of irrita-tions or despair or dullness of spirit, let us say a prayer for for-giveness and renew our closeness to Him with a brief protection-prayer: let us put on the whole armour of God (Eph. 6:11) or let us place ourselves in heart beneath the shadow of the Cross, that our spirits may be cleansed by the light of the Cross, and then let us once more walk within the circle of His light.

3. The Nature of God and the Prayer of Faith

In the preceding chapter we studied a way of making contact with God, as we connect with a person when we dial a number on the telephone. Being connected, we then give and receive a clear message and speak toward a definite end, that the purpose of the call may be accomplished. In order to do this, we must know whom we are calling. We must have a concept of that person's nature and abilities, so that we can plan together to work out the purpose of the call. We do not call a window cleaning firm and ask them to put on a magic show for our Sunday School, nor do we call a sleight of hand artist and ask him to clean our windows.

Yet people are apt to do precisely this with God, because they do not understand His nature. They are apt to call on Him and ask Him to do magic tricks for them instead of asking Him to clean the windows of their souls so that His creative sunlight may shine through. Or they may refuse to call upon Him for help at all, fearing that so doing would be making a magician out of Him or "manipulating" Him.

We do not feel that we are manipulating God when we administer a Salk shot to prevent polio. We do not say, "We must not ask God to break His laws merely in order to secure our health." We understand that God is not breaking His laws, nor are we dealing with magic, when we administer an injection of a healing or preventive serum. We are simply making use of the healing and preventive agencies that God has built into this universe for our use and for His own glory, and thus we are doing

His will. We are not dealing with "magic"—that is, an unreasonable breaking of God's laws—when we conceive and construct airplanes, so that we cause something heavier than air to fly through the air. We could call this work of creation "manipulating God" if we chose to speak in such childish and anthropomorphic terms. But these terms would be scientifically inaccurate. What we are actually doing is learning God's laws of speed and weight and air and wind and working according to those laws, so that the concept that we have in our minds can be carried out. We are introducing a new interplay of laws into an old situation so as to produce new results.

A magician produces a rabbit out of a hat when there is no reason for the rabbit's being in the hat and no lawful and sensible way of materializing a rabbit. Or, at least, he seems to do so. If he is not really thus breaking the laws of nature, then he is deceiving us. God does not act in that manner. He does not break the laws of nature nor does He play tricks on us. He acts according to the laws of His own being and that being is creative. In other words, God is a Creator and *not* a magician.

How do we recognize Him as a creator? In the same way that we recognize any maker—by looking at the thing that he has made. We gaze upon a beautiful painting and say, "He is a painter." We listen to a symphony and recognize that its composer was a musician. So we look upon the creation—"the moon and the stars, which thou hast ordained (Psalms 8:3)."—and we recognize that God is a creator: "Maker of heaven and earth." God is a creator with a passion for beauty and perfection. We stand amazed at the intricacy and beauty of His creation. The miracle of the heavens and of this expanding universe, in which suns after suns and galaxies after galaxies are born and die in the vast stretches of the aeons—the miracle of the earth and of small growing things renewing themselves in beauty year after year—we contemplate these things and we know that God is a creator! To assume that the earth and the world just happened by blind chance would take more credulity than any one of us possesses!

There is an old apple tree in my front yard in the hills of New Hampshire. No one can remember when the ancient farmhouse was built and the trees were planted around it. Somehow during the years this old tree was bent, so that it leaned low over a bank and dropped its fruit upon the dirt road. But three years ago lumber trucks labored up that road, and every load

of lumber struck the limbs of that old tree and tossed and twisted them. The tree began to die. The horizontal limbs one after
the other stretched gnarled and black over the road without
a leaf upon them. But this morning I noticed that the tree is
putting out straight new shoots, high above the bank, so that
no lumber truck can reach them! It acts as though an innate
intelligence took account of the possibility of lumber trucks,
and adjusted its manner of growth accordingly. Who shall understand these things? Does a plant have a kind of mind that it
shall say "I will grow not this way but that way?" Does the
Creator brood over His creation in such an intimate fashion
that He takes note of apple trees and of the lilies of the field
and of the sparrows of the air? Does He even possibly have
small unseen helpers in the work of His creation? Who shall
say? His works are past finding out and the greatness of His
glory is beyond our ken!

But one thing we can see: His works are done by a definite
creative process and not by magic. The apple tree was not made
new by breaking the laws of nature, but by working according
to those laws.

I cannot shell kidney beans without praising the Creator for
His wonderful works. Why should He bother to make kidney
beans, for the one bright moment of shelling them, beautiful
beyond imagining with their tracings of rose and of cerise? These
tracings cannot be seen through the shell! They disappear as
soon as the bean is cooked! Why did the designer of the kidney
bean give it a pattern of beauty that cannot be duplicated anywhere in nature? Why, except that God our Father is the most
intense and passionate Creator imaginable, loving beauty and
bringing it to birth in ways too great for our visioning and too
small for our comprehension? The most high-powered telescope
cannot see the fullness of the raging beauty of His terrifying
galaxies of suns. The most powerful microscope cannot fully discern the beauty that He has hidden in the stamens and pistils
of tiny flowers.

But notice—He causes these things to evolve over centuries
and over milleniums and over aeons. So He works. He does
not come down with a paint-brush and personally paint the kidney bean.

How long it takes to evolve a kidney bean I do not know;
probably not so long as to evolve the earth upon which the
bean must grow— or the sun around which the earth rotates and

from which it receives its life. And if you were to ask me, "Can God grow a kidney bean in one second?" I would say, "Perhaps He can but He does not." And if you were to say, "Why? Don't you believe He is Almighty?" I would reply, "Yes, but I also believe He is a Maker. And so He chooses to work according to the laws of creative action which He Himself has ordained."

Let us consider these laws of creative action for a very practical purpose; namely, that we too may learn to create by His power.

God decided to make the earth and the world, as the first verse of the Bible and as the creation itself testifies. Having so decided, the plan—the blueprint—was in the mind of the Creator. But the earth was without form and void, and darkness was upon the face of the deep. So the Bible says and so science says: there existed the *possibility* of life, but no life; the *possibility* of light but no light, only darkness in that interstellar space that the Bible calls the deep or the waters (Gen. 1:2).

Having made the decision, having the plan of creation in His mind, God said "Let there be light" and there was light. The life that was potential flamed into life that was real. How could this be, when the sun and the moon and stars were not as yet created? This first light was the Word of God made manifest (John 1:1)—the light of God's creativity—the river of life proceeding from Him that maketh glad the city of the most High (Psalms 46:4)—the power that still flows in a vibration like that of light or of electricity, creating health and beauty!

Then this light, still invisible to human eyes, had there been any human eyes to see it, caught heavenly fire, as it were, and flamed into a light that is visible—the whirling gases of the nebulae out of which, according to astronomy, suns and earths evolve. Thus were created the suns and the earth. And through this flow of creative energy, in a reasonable, orderly and completely scientific fashion, the Creator caused life to evolve upon the earth.

On the second "Day", the waters above the firmament were divided from the waters below the firmament and the dry land appeared. So the Bible says and so science says. And on the third day, according to God's creative Word, the earth brought forth grass and herbs and trees, each kind having its seed within itself—having the principle of creativity built into it, so that having been made by God's decree, it continued working toward life by a certain inner plan and wisdom, even as our own bodies do to this day. So the Bible says and so science says. And in the fourth day, or epoch, when there were growing things upon the earth but when no living creature had as yet evolved upon it, the dense blanket of cloud thinned out so that the sun and the moon and the stars were made visible in the heavens, to give light upon the earth and to divide the light from the darkness; so the Bible says and so science says.

And on the fifth day (or aeon) living creatures were evolved, first of all in the water, water being a particularly sensitive medium for the working of the Logos, as we should know from the action of a physical power that we call electricity and from the action of a spiritual power in the rite of baptism.

Upon the sixth day these living creatures spread and multiplied upon the earth.

So the Bible says and so science says.

It is odd that we should be so concerned as to whether the word of God is scientific. It would be far more sensible if we were to concern ourselves as to whether science is used according to the word of God.

Now this is not a scientific study of creation, but merely a meditation upon the laws of creative action—a meditation in which I give to the words of this ancient document the same courtesy that I would give to any translation of any document, namely: the courtesy of my common sense. So we will leave with regret the infinite reaches of thought that the first chapter of Genesis opens to us concerning those ancient "Days of the Lord"—those days not bounded by earth and sun, for indeed the earth and the sun had not as yet flamed into being when God said "Let there be light" and light was, and the evening and the morning were the first day—those days not bounded by anything except the far visioning of God—those days NOT BOUNDED, for never do they end with the coming down of dark night but always with a new beginning: "And the evening *and the morning* were the first day (Gen. 1:5)—"

We will leave these fascinating matters that are so very much too great for us and come back to our brief study of the laws of creative action, for here they are: first, the decision to create, assumed, not told, for it would be unnecessary to state a thing so obvious; second, the pre-existing plan, seen in the world about us, not told, for we do not need the fact of it to be told nor could we comprehend the method of it if we were told; and finally the next step, told to us, that we may grasp it and use it; the speaking of the word of power.

God sent forth His Word in absolute and sure knowledge that it would not return unto Him void but that it would accomplish the thing to which He sent it (Isaiah 55:11). God sent forth His word in *faith*.

Now what does this mean to us? Everything. For as He created, so must we create. *We must*. It is written into our natures to so do. "Let us make man," said the Maker, "in our own image, after our likeness and let them have dominion . . .(Gen. 1:26)" We do not look like God, for God does not exist in any form that we can see. Terrifying as it is to us in our unworthiness and our inadequacy, in this one way, we *are* like God. As He is a Father, so we are fathers and mothers both of children and of His children and His world. As He is a Creator, so are we creators. To make and to create is the very breath of life to us, and when any man ceases to create, then life dwindles and turns toward death within him. We create with our hands and with our minds. We also create with the original creative Light that broods upon our spirits. We too, ourselves, can use this spiritual power that makes health out of illness and beauty out of ugliness. The Light that God set in motion when He said "Let there be light" can again in a smaller way be set in motion by us—or rather, through us, for we create nothing by ourselves, but only through the Father abiding in us and through the mercies of Jesus Christ who makes us one with Him that He may so abide.

Jesus called this creative action of the spirit doing His works. "The works that I do shall he do also (John 14:12)," He said. He also said that the principle through which we do these works is the principle of faith. "If ye have faith as a grain of mustard seed, ye shall say unto this mountain, Remove hence to yonder place; and it shall remove; and nothing shall be impossible unto you (Matt. 17:20)". He instructed and urged and trained His disciples to do this creative work of the spirit through His power (Luke 9:1, 2). St. James called this creative work of the spirit done through the power of Jesus Christ *"the prayer of faith* (Jas. 5:15) ".

Now what is the prayer of faith?

One reason for our confusion regarding this matter is that we have not distinguished between different kinds of prayer. But there are different kinds of prayer, just as there are different

kinds of English composition. The style and method of writing
blank verse is quite different from the style and method of writing
a book like this. The ground-plan of a novel is different from
that of a textbook. We approach God for different purposes and
in different ways. The first type of prayer, and that with which
we are most familiar, is the prayer of worship. We pray thus
whenever we come to church in order to give thanks to Him and
to glorify His name. This is the beginning of all prayer, but it
is not the end. Our Lord went into the synagogue on the sabbath
day "as his custom was (Luke 4:16)." But he did not stay
in the Synagogue. He went out again among the people.

There is also meditation and prayer such as we outlined in
the last chapter—prayer for the purpose of making contact with
God. Doubtlessly Our Lord prayed thus when He went into
the mountains to be alone with God. But He did not remain on
the mountain-top of contemplation, nor can we.

He came down again among the people. There the needs of
humanity forced Him to pray in different ways. One of these
was the prayer for guidance and for the strength to follow the
guidance. Thus He prayed in the Garden of Gethsemane: "Father,
if thou be willing, remove this cup from me: nevertheless, not
my will, but thine, be done (Luke 22:42)." This is the pattern
of prayer that He followed when faced with a task almost too
great for His strength. Thus we too should pray when faced with
difficult decisions and with laborious tasks. We should enter into
God's presence with the prayer of worship and should lift up
our problem before Him and ask Him to show us what to do.
We should then listen for an answer, and accept His will. This
is the prayer for guidance.

But the prayer for guidance never healed the sick. And when
our Lord prayed for the sick He never prayed the prayer for
guidance, but always the prayer of faith. We are not given all
the words of His prayer, but we can see from His actions that
He decided when and for whom to pray the prayer of faith,
checking on their own faith as He did so.

It is also obvious that He expected those for whom He prayed
to make a recovery. And the words that we are given are the
most significant words of His prayer of faith; namely, the words
of command, which are the words of power. He said, "Arise,
take up thy bed and walk." He did not say, "Either arise, take
up thy bed and walk or lie still upon thy bed and be sick."
He said, "Lazarus, come forth." He did not say, "Lazarus, come

forth if it be God's will, and if not, then stay in the tomb and remain dead." In other words, He did not combine the prayer for guidance with the prayer of faith, as we are apt to do in our hazy-thinking way, thus robbing the prayer of faith of its power. *He prayed the prayer for guidance first.* Naturally, He would not at any time have gone contrary to God's will. So He first made sure of God's guidance—possibly in the two days wherein He delayed going to the tomb (John 11:6). Of course He wanted to do God's will. He was persuaded, so He said, that God's will was always to give to His children all good gifts, just as we would like to give good things to our children (Matt. 7:11). But since God has made a partner out of man, it was necessary, if God's final will were to be done, that man should cooperate with a certain measure of faith (Matt. 17:20-21). If those for whom He would like to pray were not willing to provide sufficient cooperation, He did not feel that it was God's will for Him to stay and labor among them (Matt. 13:58). Moreover, He knew that a greater power of prayer and faith was needed for the healing of some ills than for the healing of other ills (Matt. 17:20-21). Therefore, He prayed no prayer of faith save with a clear decision and a certainty that His word would produce the result toward which He sent it. So He was always able to pray the prayer of faith, thus giving God the essential material out of which God's will could be done.

"Faith is the substance of things hoped for (Heb. 11.1)."

Webster's Dictionary defines "substance" as "That which underlies all outward manifestation; the reality itself; the real essence of a thing." Faith, then, is the real essence out of which healing is done. There is no use in asking God in an uncertain way to do something, because if we ask thus we are not giving Him the essential material out of which He can do His works. "The prayer of faith shall save the sick (James 5:15)."

Now we can learn this prayer of faith, just as we can learn anything else if we are willing to practice. And I will suggest, step by step, the very simple practice by which many people have learned faith.

First of all, choose the person for whom you want to pray. God does not ask you to pray for everyone, because there are too many people in the world who need help and your beginning faith is small. Choose then, according to the desires of your heart tempered by common sense and ruled by the law of love. Check on your choice of a prayer-objective by asking yourself

"Do I really believe that this person can get well?" If you dare not even try to believe it, then set aside that prayer-objective and try something nearer to your size.

Having chosen, then hold up your prayer-object before God and check on it again by praying the prayer of guidance, saying, "Lord, shall I pray for this person to get well?" At first it may be difficult to hear His answer and you may have to proceed on common sense and unselfish love alone. But after a while you will begin to recognize God's guidance. If you feel cheered and strengthened as you consider praying for someone, you will know that it is God's green light. If you feel dull and unhappy, God is probably saying "No, in this case the way is not open for healing." Why would God ever say "No"? Does God want people to remain ill? According to Jesus, He does not. If He did, Jesus would not have always made them well. Could it be that in some cases He is calling that one Home? Why, of course.

Healing of the body is not so important as healing of the spirit, and there come times when the healing of the spirit can best be accomplished in the larger life. At present, when the Holy City, the New Jerusalem, has not as yet come down from God out of heaven (Rev. 21:2), that time eventually comes to everyone. We should look forward to it with joy, as St. Paul did (Phil 1:21). However, in some cases our sense of dullness and heaviness in trying to pray for someone means not that the time has come for his soul's migration, but only that there are barriers in the way of his healing. God may be saying to us something like this: "My child, this is too difficult a task for you: your prayer-life is not yet deep enough to give Me a sufficient channel for this healing; let me put him in someone else's bundle of prayer, and you pray for someone else."

"But this is what I want the most," we may think.

Prayer is not a matter of getting what we want the most. Prayer is a matter of giving ourselves to God and learning His laws, so that He can do through us what He wants the most. And as we live in Him, we will more and more want what He wants.

"This is too difficult a task for you," I said above. In the experience of twenty-five years I cannot but have observed that certain healings require a greater measure of faith and holy living than others do. Some people cannot accept this. They feel that simply to say "With God all things are possible" and keep on saying it is the best way to hold their faith. If this way of thinking works for them, good. This book is written, however, for those who are not satisfied by this concept—those who are by nature skeptics, as I am. For them I say that if you and I had enough prayer-power to channel the full power of God's Holy Spirit, as that power was channeled on the day of Pentecost, then surely that power could always heal even a cancer instantaneously. But notice the "if"! "If" man has sufficient power to channel (or "generate," as Dr. Carrell more boldly says) a sufficient flow of God's healing energy . . . Do you have it, at this time? And is the church, the Body of Christ on earth, that transcendent, Spirit-filled group of people who lived in such breathless holiness that the first ones to cut across that white light of perfection fell dead before the feet of Peter? If we have not attained to this high estate, then we may rejoice at every miraculous and instantaneous healing (and thank God there are many of them) but we need not be disillusioned and perplexed when some do not take place.

It is not a matter of what God can do but of what the present measure of faith in you and me and in the church can do.

But why does God depend upon our faith for the perfecting of His will? That is His business. I do not know, though I might guess. Perhaps His very passion of love for us insists that we shall be His partners rather than merely His puppets. But this I do know: we are not merely spectators of the drama of creation — that is the trouble—or is it the glory of life? We are partners. From the time when God made man in His image, after His likeness, and brought to him the beasts of the field that he should name them—that he should have dominion over them—God has ordained that we shall be the heirs of His glory and the channels of His creative power. And when we pray the prayer of faith we are not merely asking Him to do something, we are actually taking part in His own work of creating and recreating—we are doing His works (John 14:12).

I once heard a lecturer say, "It is the electricity that makes the light. It does not matter how big or how small the light bulb may be."

But it does matter. A hundred watts of electricity cannot shine through a twenty-five watt bulb. A thousand-watt flood-light plugged into an ordinary outlet will blow out the fuse.

Therefore to the more timid and humble-minded like myself I would say, choose to pray the prayer of faith for those people whom you feel to be within the compass of your own circle of light.

And since no one of us knows enough of God and man to choose alone, let us ask God to guide our choosing. If we feel a door closed within us as we hold someone into the light of His love, if we feel a dimness of spirit, a shadow of depression, then let us leave the matter in His hands—release it, as some like to say. He is telling us to pray no more about it. Sometimes, as Catherine Marshall tells us in "A Man Called Peter," this is because we have prayed enough, and the matter only needs our release that it may come to pass. Sometimes, as in our Lord's own decision to do no prayer-work for the men of Nazareth, it is because God is saying to us, "No my child. It is blocked by men. Do not take that as a prayer-objective. Leave it in my hands until the way is open." Sometimes it is because God knows that the one for whom you would pray has lived his life upon the earth, and his spirit is ready to be born into the next world. But most often the hesitation of our spirits is just the voice of God telling us, "You are not yet big enough as a channel to bring forth so difficult a thing in prayer."

There is a story about Dr. George Washington Carver [1], who went into the woods every morning before dawn to talk to "Dear Mr. Creator."

"Dear Mr. Creator," he said one morning while night was dark among the trees, "Why did You make the world?"

And the voice of God said within him, "Little man, that is a question too big for you."

"Dear Mr. Creator," said the seeker, "Why did You make man?"

"That question is still too big for you," answered the inner voice. "Ask me a question nearer to your size, and I will answer you."

Whereupon the scientist said, "Dear Mr. Creator, why did You make the peanut?" And the answer came to him, and he invented more than a hundred uses for the peanut and revitalized the agriculture of the South.

The Christian name for the attitude of the scientist is humility, and I maintain, though it is a most unpopular thought, that humility is as great a virtue and as real a need as faith . . .

So then, if we check with God's Spirit and His answer is no,

---

[1] *The Man Who Talked With The Flowers,* Glenn Clark, Macalester Park Publishing Co., St. Paul, 1939.

what shall we do? *Change our prayer-objective.* Try something smaller in its scope.

Let us repeat: prayer is not a matter of trying to persuade God to give us what we want. Prayer is giving ourselves to God so that He can work through us what He wants. And the first step in all successful prayer is to find out what He wants.

For instance I was once requested over the telephone to pray for the healing of a serious and painful eye infection. "My brother does not know that I am asking you this," the sister told me. "If he did know, he would not believe it. He is a very bitter person. But he is suffering so terribly, and he has had to go back to work even though his eyes are swollen nearly shut, because he can't afford to stay in the hospital any longer."

I lifted him into the light of God's love, and felt joy at the thought of praying for this man. Joy is the earnest of God's presence and God's desire. It is God saying, "My child, I am so happy that this opportunity has come to you."

The next day the sister called again. "He called me up from across seven states," she said. "He said, 'What has happened to me? All of a sudden, my eyes are well. And I feel somehow that you will know why.' I told him and he cried! He shed tears, right over the phone, because his heart was so deeply touched! And he's always been such a bitter man!"

He was such a bitter man only because he was a lonely and unhappy man. The Spirit of God knew this, and let my own spirit know it upon the wings of joy. And the man was healed because his spirit was able to open itself to the healing and to find the truth of God, and therefore it was to the good of his eternal soul that he should be healed.

On the other hand I received lately a letter that ran something like this: "Will you please pray for Mr. A. He is very ill, and I think it is because he is so upset about Miss B. She is angry with the whole office and has turned Mrs. C. and Mrs. D. against him. So now will you please pray for Mr. A. and Miss B. and Mrs. C. and Mrs. D."

Certainly. So that Mr. A's life may be spared that he may live long to make trouble in his office. So that Miss B. may let him alone that he may be disagreeable in peace. So that Mrs. C. and Mrs. D may be foiled in their evil intentions and may go and pick on somebody else . . .

Why did not Jesus pray for the scribes and Pharisees, instead of challenging them to their faces and risking His own life to open their eyes that they might learn (Matt. 12:34, 39, and Matt. 23)?

I am sorry for Mr. A. and Miss B. and Mrs. C. and Mrs. D. But what they need is not that someone else should pray them out of the trouble they have made but that through that trouble they shall learn. As I inquired of God concerning the above letter, I felt that the one who wrote it should herself try to teach Mr. A the way of life, and should not merely dump the whole complicated problem on someone else. Mary Welch says from her long experience of prayer, "Thoughtful and earnest persons never glibly say, 'Pray for me.' They know that to request another's prayer is to demand the most costly thing possible—the most vital output of energy, the most precious expenditure of time, and the exercise of the highest skilled craftmanship under heaven in the hardest work known to man. People who know little of God or of His ways and who are self-centered are quick to demand the services of those who can pray. They often make of persons or of prayer-groups a dumping ground for their problems, instead of facing their own problems and learning how to solve them."

In other words, let us not ask for prayer too lightly nor too casually accept requests in prayer. Let us choose with discretion and guidance.

After choosing, then let us proceed to the second step and *create in our minds* the picture of that person well. Thus, we set in motion our powers of spiritual creativity. Those things that we see in our minds tend to become so. This is a law as certain as the law of gravity, and to this law we shall return again and again. Let us draw the image in our minds. Let us make the blueprint. Let us dwell at the time of prayer and at all other times, whenever the person comes to mind, on the picture of that one *well*.

At this point a horrible suspicion may arise in the minds of my readers; namely—am I talking about the power of positive thinking? Yes, I am—although Jesus, who did not know the term "positive thinking", called it "faith." This type of thinking, said He, had a positive actual power. It could move mountains.

"Verily I say unto you, that whosoever shall say unto this mountain, Be thou removed, and be thou cast into the sea; and shall not doubt in his heart, but shall believe that those things which he saith shall come to pass; he shall have whatsoever he saith. Therefore I say unto you, What things soever ye desire, when ye pray, *believe that ye receive them,* and ye shall have them (Mark 11:23, 24)!"

That was His comment on the power of positive thinking. I have never tried this on a mountain, because my faith is not great enough. It would be quite impossible at present, for me to believe in my heart (sub-conscious mind) nothing doubting, that the mountain would move. But I have tried it on mountains of illness and despair, and they have moved. And I know that there actually is within man the power to create by thought: "as he thinketh in his heart, so is he (Prov. 23:7)."

Man creates by negative thinking as well as by positive thinking. Our Lord states this very clearly: "For out of the heart proceed evil thought, murders, adulteries, fornications, thefts, false witness, blasphemies (Matt. 15:19)."

If negative thoughts of evil proceed out of the heart, they result in destructive actions and defile a man. If negative thoughts of fear proceed from the sub-conscious, they open the door to the power of the enemy, so that, as Job said, "The thing which I greatly feared is come upon me (Job 3:25)." If the inner being is clogged by negative thoughts of doubt, those thoughts make a barrier so that God's healing power cannot work through a man, as Jesus said to His disciples when they failed to heal the demoniac boy (Mark 9:19).

In other words, we create by thought whether we want to do so or not. By negative thinking we open the way to illness, frustration, failure and disharmony. By positive thinking, i.e., faith, we open the way to health, creativity, success and harmony.

When Jesus explained to men these ever-existing laws of life, the poor received Him gladly and the sick came to Him eagerly. But men in high religious places were quite upset about it and rejected Jesus because they feared that it would weaken the position of the church of that day.

Those in authority today tend to have the same fear. "But this isn't Christianity!" they say. "The Cross is the center of our faith!"

Of course it is. The Cross is in the center of the Creed. The Cross is in the center of the Bible. I shall have a great deal to say about the value and purpose of Our Lord's sacrifice for us and of the suffering that He endured for us—also of our sacrifice for Him and the suffering that we endure for Him. You will find the Cross in the center of this book. But right now, before we reach that great and thrilling sequence of the divine drama, let me say that our *first* step into His sacrificial life is to *follow Him* —to obey Him. The disciples followed Him first of all. Before

Gethsemane, before Calvary, before Pentecost, they looked upon Him and followed. And as they followed, they obeyed His Words. How shall we dare to attempt to comprehend and to act through the glory and the anguish of His cross if we do not first follow— obey? And this self-discipline—this training of our thoughts into patterns of faith or positive thinking if you like—is His express command to all of His servants[1].

It is strange indeed that His "followers" have rejected this great command—to go forth and do His works of prayer and heal-ing. This injunction is in the Scriptures and in the prayer book. In the service of ordination a minister is given by the authority of Holy Church all the gifts of the Holy Spirit, "For his use as a priest of the church." In First Corinthians you will find the gifts of the Spirit listed; among them the gift of faith, the gift of healing and (as though to cover all other challenges to faith) the gift of miracles (I Cor. 12:9). A Bishop when consecrated is specifi-cally commanded to heal the sick. Then how can we blandly ignore this great commission? This question first troubled me at the age of eleven while I studied the fourteenth chapter of St. John. Due to my careful Presbyterian training, for which I am most grateful, I was from infancy rooted and grounded in the Scriptures. (I cannot remember the time when we did not study one chapter of the Bible every day and when I did not in addition memorize certain verses of Scripture every day.) Thus I encountered the verse, "Verily, verily, I say unto you, He that believeth on me, the works that I do shall he do also (John 14:12)."

"Well, then, why don't we do them?" I asked someone in authority.

The answer given me was, "Because this is a new dispensation and the age of miracles is past."

The dear soul who so instructed me was only teaching what had been taught to God's people for several unhappy generations: the great heresy of the nineteenth century. It was not her fault, that of my missionary teacher, that this heresy came into being, nor was it the fault of her ministers or Sunday-school teachers. Away back in history it started, and for a study of that falling away from the direct commands of Jesus Christ I refer the reader to

---

[1] Matt. 21:21, 23:23; Mark 4:40, 11:22; Luke 18:8; Romans 3:3; Romans 4:5, 16:26; I Cor. 13:13; Gal. 5:22; Eph. 6:16; II Thess. 1:11.

Emily Gardiner Neal's book, "A Reporter Finds God Through Spiritual Healing."

I rejected this explanation, because it was not what the Bible said and it was not what Jesus said. Thus the whole foundation of my faith was shaken. From this time forth doubt and cynicism entered into a religious experience that had been very real since my conversion at the age of nine.

Yes, Jesus died for us on Calvary. He did so to take away our sins. He also told us, if we loved Him, to keep His commandments. And here among His commandments is this: to have faith in God (Mark 11:22, 23): to learn to believe without doubting and so, to do His works (John 14:12) so that men may see our good works (and He did not mean merely the envelope that we put in the collection plate) and glorify our Father which is in Heaven (Matt. 5:16). When we are baptised into the Christian Church we promise through our sponsors (later ratifying it ourselves) that we will fight manfully under His banner against sin, the world, and the devil. In other words, we are enlisting in His Holy Army, the Church. Now the first duty of a soldier is to obey. It is not the part of an enlisted man to say, "I must think this through, for I cannot accept anyone else's concepts except my own." While he is thinking through whether or not he shall report for drill, he will find himself in the guard-house. If he did not intend to obey, he should not have enlisted in the army. He made his choice then. Even if he is drafted and has no choice, it is still expedient to obey! Jesus Christ however, has no draftees. We must choose whether or not to enlist in His army.

But if we have chosen Christ, then we have no choice as to whether we will or will not follow His commands to learn faith. And the mere fact that some may call it positive thinking instead of calling it faith has nothing to do with this. Let us call it what we will, but let us do it.

"But it makes everything too easy," some people think. The one making such a statement has not tried this steep ascent to power. It does not make it easy. It makes it difficult. The mere training of thought is not in itself easy—the constant vigilance, the correcting of doubts and negative thinking until faith becomes an unshakable habit—even that is not easy. And along with that, as we shall consider abundantly in following chapters, goes the absolute necessity of living the Christian life at all costs. Because although God's grace may heal us while we are yet sinners, in order to maintain our wholeness, we must strive to sin no more

(John 5:14). Jesus coupled this with His words on faith that remove mountains; "And when you stand praying, forgive," He said (Mark 11:25-26). This can be arduous, it can be painful, it can be humiliating. A part of forgiveness is to establish love and charity with our fellow-men; therefore, forgiveness includes penance and seeking forgiveness when we realize our inadequacy. That is not easy! Also the keeping of our thoughts and the developing of our faith necessitates a holy and consecrated and sacrificial life, as we shall also consider in future chapters. Jesus wove this also into the incident of the demoniac boy and the failure of His disciples to heal him. "Because of your unbelief", he said, and gave them His thought on the moving of mountains. But then He added these words, "Howbeit this kind goeth not out but by prayer and fasting (Matt. 17:20, 21).

The ordinary church member makes a far easier thing of Christianity than does the seeker after faith. Christianity is so carelessly taught in many churches that one is considered a Christian merely if one has been admitted into the church, attends church services from time to time and pledges something for church support. One is considered a good Christian if one attends every service, supports the church well and takes part in all its organizational work. One may hate one's neighbors, refuse to speak to those whom one considers socially inferior, shade one's income taxes and dominate one's children and yet one is considered a good Christian. If anyone makes it too easy to be a Christian it is those who have a form of godliness and deny the power thereof.

Another objection is this: what right has a Christian to attain health and power and success and harmony, when Jesus died on the cross for us? No right whatsoever, if he attains these things just for himself; every right if he attains them in order to give them and himself to the service of Christ. To work oneself to death in the service of the sick and troubled is as good a way as any to enter into Life. To use one's power in prayer for the succour of those in despair and under the shadow of death is as good a way as any to use it. To offer one's success to God in His service is a worthy sacrifice. To achieve harmony in relationships is our bounden duty toward God and toward our neighbor and toward the Kingdom of Heaven.

Finally, the most comical objection that I have yet heard toward the learning of faith is the naive remark: "There is danger of religion becoming popular." Well, praise God. If religion should become popular, we would have love and charity among nations, we would have unselfishness and the willingness to die rather than to hurt another among all peoples, and we would have a Kingdom of Heaven on earth.

However, those who worry about the danger of too many people accepting Christ and doing what He said may, I think, rest from their over-concern. The danger is slight. Steep and narrow is the path nor is there any stopping-place upon it—not on this side of the River. Those who read might check on this by reviewing the eleventh chapter of Hebrews.

There is then a constructive power in positive thinking. It is not a substitute for religion. But it is one of God's laws and therefore unavoidable.

Many books have been written on faith, including my own. It seems to me unnecessary to repeat all that has been said in those books. Instead, I have indulged in the slight bit of apologetic writing above and to that I will add my summary: a simple way of learning faith is to make use of the visual imagination: to construct in the mind carefully the picture of the thing that one desires and to train the mind to dwell upon that picture.

Thus one might say that the first step in the prayer of faith is the choosing; the second step is the seeing—and the third step is the speaking.

For as God spoke and said, "Let there be light," so we must also speak the word of power, saying, "In the name of Jesus Christ, let this be so." "Speak the word only, and my servant shall be healed," said the centurion whose faith helped Our Lord to move mountains (Matt. 8:8). In every case where Our Lord healed He spoke the word that actually calls into being, or draws toward one, an essence of power: a living, moving energy that God sends forth to accomplish His will. This energy is as actual as the energy of electricity or of cosmic rays or of X-ray or of radium. It can often be felt as the disciples of Emmaus felt it (Luke 24:32) as a tingling or as a heat, or as a certain movement in the air described as a rushing, mighty wind (Acts 2:2). It can sometimes be seen as a fire or a light, as Moses saw it (Ex. 3:2) or as St. Paul saw it (Acts 9:3). In most cases today, however, our power is so slight and our spiritual perception so dim that it is neither seen nor heard nor felt—as the force of gravity operating through all nature is neither seen nor heard nor felt. But those of us who dare to try the prayer of faith know it is real because we see the result. No scientist, according to a recent article in the "Readers' Digest," has ever seen an atom. Yet he believes in atoms because he ascertains the results of their energy.

God's power is a real energy—a real force—a real living substance, built into this world to do His will. And it is set free first of all by a certain feeling in the heart and spirit of man: a feeling of certainty that the thing to which he sends his word is going to be done. And secondly, this energy is projected into action by the word of power. Jesus always spoke the word of power when healing, and He never qualified it by adding, "If it be Thy will." Any qualifying phrase decreases faith and thus narrows the channel of God's power. A prayer ending, "If this be Thy will" simply does not release the spiritual power of a prayer that ends, "Let it be so," or in other words, "Amen." Thirdly, a qualifying phrase suggests doubt both to the one who prays and to the one for whom the prayer is made, and that doubt weakens or negates the prayer.

For instance, in chapter one, I told of my own beginning of faith. At the time when my baby was healed, I was myself in great mental depression, and so I wondered whether the minister who had prayed for my baby could pray also for my healing. It was one whole year before I summoned courage to go to him, so great was my burden of depression. But at last I went and listened in a dimness and confusion of mind to some remarks, quite unintelligible to me, thinking, "If he would only stop talking and pray!" And when he did, I waited throughout his prayer for one phrase. "If he says 'if it be God's will,' " so I thought, "then I will not get well."

Thank God he did not use this qualifying phrase, even as Our Lord never used such a phrase when praying for healing. If he had done so, I would not now be on this earth.

Now I do not say that the mere uttering of those words will always be a matter of life and death, as it was to me. But we cannot tell when that phrase, for so long associated with resignation and failure, may crush the weak faith of the one for whom we pray.

"But what if it is not God's will?" we may think. That point has already been considered, but I repeat: if it is not God's will, *do not pray for it*. For instance, if one is praying for his own healing and feels that it is not God's will, then let him cease praying for healing of the body and pray instead for healing of the spirit. Also, to be perfectly consistent, I suppose he should cease taking medicine. For who is he to go contrary to God's will? One might say, "But I take medicine for any palliative effect it may have, whether or not it results in a healing." Very well, then let him also pray the prayer of faith for any palliative effect that it may have. He is doing the same thing that he does in taking medicine. He is taking God's medicine. He is making it possible for God's energy to enter the body, accomplishing whatever can be accomplished toward health or toward comfort. But let him not say, "If it be Thy will", for that is like spilling the medicine on the floor instead of taking it. He may say instead, "Let Thy life enter into me, working toward life in spirit, mind or body according to Thy perfect will." Or he may say, "Thy will be done in me on earth as it is in heaven." For while it is not expedient to say "If", it is a good thing to say "Thy will be done," provided we finish the sentence as Our Lord gave it to us: "Thy will be done *on earth as it is in heaven."* In heaven there is no more death, neither sorrow nor crying (Rev. 21-4). Therefore, when we pray as our Lord taught us to pray, "Thy will be done on earth as it is in heaven" we are praying for that heavenly state of freedom from pain and sorrow to be accomplished in us here on earth.

Let us close the prayer of faith therefore, by saying that tremendous affirmation, "Amen"; "Let this be so"; or, "So it is"; or, "So it shall be."

4. Hindrances to

Prayer Power

"These signs shall follow them that believe (Mark 16:17)."
We believe that God *is,* and that He is a rewarder of those who
earnestly seek Him (Heb. 11:6). We believe that He not only
wants to help us, but that He has the power to do so. We believe
that He is a Creator and so His works are done in an orderly
fashion and with our cooperation, and we try to learn His laws
so that we can cooperate with Him.

What then? Are we all healed? Many of us are. Indeed, many
are healed by the grace of God long before we even begin to
deserve it. But there are also many healings that we do not see attained. There must, then, be more to believe. There is! We must
believe not only that God is a Creator, but also that He is righteous, and that when we ask of Him wholeness of body He asks of
us wholeness of soul.

God is good. That does not mean that He is indulgent—
complacent—easy-going. Goodness includes severity, for only by
severity can real goodness be maintained (Rom. 11:22). God is
good, and since He has breathed the breath of life into us, there is
something in us that demands goodness. In most of us, this innate
longing for holiness is so stifled that it is almost extinct. Or
rather, we have it but we do not recognize it. We know not the
cause of our restlessness—of our constant yearning for something—of our inner discontent. But when our souls open to
God in prayer for His wholeness, then we become aware of our
longing for the goodness of God. Thus we find that part of prayer
for healing is a sincere and strenuous attempt to keep God's laws
of goodness.

42

Now let us consider from actual examples how this striving after goodness works toward healing.

I once prayed for the heart of a young woman in a Southern city. She had been brought to the church and laid on a sofa in the rector's study. As I was about to go and see her, a medical student said to me, referring to my lecture, "I would like to believe all that, but a lot of it, I must confess, sounds awfully silly to me."

"If you really would like to believe it," I replied, "perhaps you would care to be with me as I pray for a woman with heart trouble." I do not usually give such invitations, and I wondered why I had thus spoken on impulse. "That is, if you can do it without being a hindrance," I added, "and can keep your mind open and say to yourself, 'I'm not sure that I believe this but I'm not going to disbelieve it either. I'll give it a chance'. He assented so willingly that I added, "You may put your hands on her ankles if you like, and pray with me."

He did so. I laid my hands on the heart and prayed. As usual, I perceived the heat of the spiritual Presence, and the woman, whose legs had been without sensation, cried out, "I can feel my feet getting warm!"

The young man stood up and looked far away as though he saw Him who is invisible. "That is the first time that I ever felt the power of God," he said.

"What did it feel like?"

"Like electricity, a sort of tingling rush of life," he replied. And then he made a statement of the highest mysticism. "I have owed someone twenty-three dollars for a long time," he said. "I'm going home right now and write a check for it. I can manage, if I do without lunches for a while."

The woman made a recovery. But a year later she came to see me for further help.

"What's the matter with you, Anne?" I asked. "There must be something the matter, or your heart wouldn't act up again after it got well."

"Well, the real trouble with me is that I hate my mother-in-law," said Anne, stating a fact that a year ago she had not recognized. "My mother-in-law lives with me, and, honestly, she's the meanest woman I ever saw. I do everything for her and she has the best of everything in the house, but still . . . "

"Well, then, there's no use praying for you to get well, is there? We will have to pray for you to like your mother-in-law."

"I don't want to, but I guess I'll have to," said Anne with all honesty.

(That is the way with spiritual healing. We find that we simply have to be Christians whether we want to be or not.)

"But that will mean that I'll have to forgive her for all the things she's done and said," added Anne. "And that will be hard —much harder than just praying to get well."

"It will. But I believe it can be done."

We prayed again, this time for Anne to accomplish and maintain a real forgiveness toward her mother-in-law. As Anne had said, this prayer for forgiveness took much more faith and spiritual power than our former prayer for the healing of the heart. (One wonders, considering this matter, why "Christians" who have said for generations that they believe in forgiveness, are often unable to believe in healing because it is too difficult . . .)

Once again I visited that city, and a lovely young woman brought a sick baby to me. "You don't know me, do you?" she said, and on my admitting this charge, she gave me her name.

"Why, Anne, how could I know you?" I asked. "You look ten years younger and perfectly beautiful!"

"As a matter of fact, I am not the same woman," she laughed. "And, you know, now I just love my mother-in-law! Why, she's as young as I am, and we have the most fun together! I can't imagine why I ever felt that way about her! Honestly, she gets nicer all the time! And my husband is a different man. I never realized what it was doing to him—living in the house with two bickering women."

This story illustrates various points. First, God in His grace healed Anne's heart without waiting for Anne to become perfect, as Jesus healed the lepers and beggars who came to Him, not all of whom could have been leading saintly lives. But God's Holy Spirit entering Anne to give her wholeness, moved inevitably in her spirit as well as her body, and made her aware of her unworthiness. Becoming aware of her hatred toward her mother-in-law, her own spirit demanded that she must try to give forgiveness while she asked more of God's forgiving and healing love. So God's Spirit must have moved in many whom Jesus healed. He recognized this movement of the spirit and encouraged it when He said to them, "Sin no more."

Secondly, if instead of working for forgiveness we had simply decided that it was not God's will for Anne to make a complete recovery—if we had accepted a false "God's will" and had been resigned—she might have gone to her grave still hating her mother-in-law. There is a time for acceptance, yes. But most of us accept too soon; we accept what seems to be God's will before fulfilling the conditions that make it possible for Him to do what is really His will. We need sometimes a faith that rebels against illness so that it can accept *God*.

Thirdly, if Anne had tried to solve her problem by merely increasing the number of prayer groups that prayed for her, what then? She would have exhausted and disillusioned the prayer groups, lived a while longer on borrowed strength, and frustrated her own spirit by failing to make the needed correction in her life.

The procedure would have resembled that of a person whose standing lamp would not work and who tried fuse after fuse and outlet after outlet to send more electricity into it, instead of seeing that something was wrong with the bulb itself.

Now let us look once more at the mechanics of our beings and try to understand this matter. We are three in one: conscious mind, subconscious mind and an inner divine intelligence that we may call spirit.

Anne's conscious mind wanted to get well and she had prayed for years, "Oh Lord, please heal my heart." But her subconscious mind did not open itself to God's power because it did not believe.

When I prayed with her, with the laying on of hands, the inner being felt a great surge of power and life and suddenly felt, "Why, it can be done after all!" Therefore, the inner recuperative power released those energies God has built into the body and made a great new effort that for some time proceeded toward healing. The subconscious mind, being open to suggestion, received the powerful suggestion of life and health that we put into it in the name of Jesus Christ—received an injection, as it were, of a healing light—a blood transfusion, so to speak, of the life of Jesus Christ. "This can be done after all," said the subconscious mind.

But presently her awakened spirit began to say to her, "You are not worthy."

A psychiatrist would say that the subconscious mind had a sense of guilt, and therefore desired punishment for the person. But where does the subconscious get this sense of guilt? The subconscious does not make decisions for itself—it does not reason, nor is it subject to reason—how then can it conclude that she is not worthy and so bring punishment upon her?

The subconscious mind responds to suggestion. That is a law. The two most destructive suggestions are these: First, "I don't believe I can get well," and second, "I am not worthy."

The lack of faith comes from the oft-repeated suggestion of the conscious mind, burdened as it is by the unbelief of the world around us. The sense of unworthiness comes from the spirit. For just as God gave the body an ability to rebuild and heal, so too He gave the spirit an ability to know what is right and what is wrong.

But why did He give us this inbuilt sense of right and wrong that we sometimes call the conscience? So that we may correct what is wrong and do what is right. How perfectly amazing that some Christians feel that it is worthy to feel unworthy, and to go about congratulating themselves upon being miserable sinners! Jesus Christ did not die upon the cross that we should remain in our sins, but that by his grace we should correct our unworthiness and learn to live as new creatures in Him!

When we once see our faults and lacks and failures and repent of them and pray for forgiveness, then we can go back to our positive thinking and say, "I am God's perfect child and His power is working within me toward life and health." But if we do not see our faults, then the spirit whispers to us, "No, you are not God's perfect child. You hate your mother-in-law." We do not want to believe this and we try to close our ears to the voice of our spirits. "No, I don't either," we say. "I try my very best to love her with Christian love. I do everything for her and no one could be expected to do more. After all, I'm only human."

And as long as we continue in this self-deception the spirit says to the subconscious, "She is not worthy." And the subconscious weakens its efforts towards health.

Well, then, for heaven's sake, let us *get* worthy!

When Jesus healed people, He did not say, "Now if you have any further trouble, call up Peter or John and they will be glad to ask the group to pray for you again." He said, "Sin no more, lest a worse thing come unto thee (John 5:14)."

For here is the truth, and no evasion or denial of the truth can prevent it from being so: sin separates us from God and dims the power of our prayers. Therefore, inevitably the wages of sin is death (Romans 6:23). For when we are separated from God we begin to wither like a branch cut off from a tree.

If we observe and understand our own feeling, we see the working of this law even in the tiny incidents of life.

For instance, I once backed out of the drive and into a Bell Telephone truck. The horrid scrunch of metal on metal assaulted my ears and I got out with sinking heart to survey the damage. "Well," I told myself, getting back into my car, "it's not a very big dent in the fender. Probably no one will notice it. I'll just forget it."

But my spirit would not let me forget. I climbed out of the car again and looked up and down the street. "If God wanted me to do something about this," I said to myself, (or was it Satan whispering to me?) "He could see to it that the driver shows up. And I don't see the driver anywhere."

In due time I went home and tried to say my usual prayers. No use. I could feel them fall dead at my feet. "It's that telephone truck," I thought, with a justifiable annoyance that the truck should have been standing there anyway. Then the reason (or the enemy) made one final attempt. "I'm sure those trucks are insured," said I to myself, "and probably the insurance comes off the telephone bill. And I pay my telephone bills, so it's all right." But as the hours passed, I became more and more depressed and the power of prayer flowed away from me into thin air. I had promised to make a sick call that afternoon, but I cancelled it, saying that I was not in the right mood and so my prayers would do no good.

Finally, I called the Bell Telephone Company and confessed my sin against the fender. "Oh, I'm so glad you called," said the voice on the phone. "That would cost three dollars, and the driver would have had to pay the cost if you had not called."

I wrote a check for three dollars and with it brought such relief that I wondered whether the angels in heaven were singing with joy over one sinner who repented.

So you see there is something else that we need to do besides continuing with prayer. We need also from time to time, and especially if the spirit telegraphs to us a message of discomfort, to pray the prayer of guidance, saying, "Lord, what is wrong in me?"

There are times, in other words, when we should reverse our method of thinking. We should focus our attention not on those things that are good and beautiful but on the dust on the window-panes of our souls, so that we can wipe away that dust and increase our receptivity to the light of God's love.

In other words, there are times when we need, not the prayer of faith, but penitence, confession and life-changing. This is not contrary to the law of creative action. It is simply the second stage in the creative process: re-creation.

If you will look once more at that delightful story of God's creative processes in Genesis 1, you will find this illuminating sentence, "God saw that it was good (Gen. 1:12)."

God took an inventory from time to time. At regular intervals (Gen. 1:5, 8, 13, 19 & 23,) He ceased from that terrific work of the Heavenly Imagination—the Logos—The Concept Spoken Forth—that produced life, and entered into another stage in which He contemplated that life which had been created to see whether it was good.

The heaven and the heaven of heavens proceeded according to plan. The stars were born and flamed and changed and died and other stars evolved according to plan. The earth brought forth growing things according to plan, perfecting and evolving them toward beauty or storing them away beneath the earth for the future use of those who would live upon it. Only those living beings, when they were fully created, did not evolve according to plan. The Creator took a long chance when He made them—when He breathed the breath of life, His spirit, into creatures of flesh (Gen. 1:28) with the intention that they should conquer the flesh by the spirit and become a new order of being, spiritual beings clothed in flesh and subduing and controlling nature (Gen. 2:15 & 19), instead of spiritual beings like the angels, creatures of pure spirit like a flame of fire (Ps. 104:4). He took a long chance, because the only way for them to live in the full glory of the spirit—a glory that was not subject to death, neither under the law of decay (Gen. 3:3) was to obey the voice of spirit in all things. And it was necessary for them to obey *by their own free will*. They were not automatons. They were creatures to whom He had given the power of choice, so that they might be living souls.

Something happened. Something went wrong. A catastrophe took place upon this earth—a catastrophe that affected not only men but also animals. In the beginning there was no feud between man and those strong and beautiful and often humorous beasts among whom he lived. God introduced them to him in the beginning, we are told, that he might have dominion over them—the dominion of love for love. From time to time God's holy men have glimpsed this as the natural state, the state that will be fulfilled if there is sufficient faith among the Sons of God to bring the return of Our Lord and the establishment of the Kingdom. "The leopard shall lie down with the kid," Isaiah said, "And the suckling child shall play on the hole of the asp . . . They shall not hurt nor destroy in all my holy mountain," saith the Lord (Isa. 11:6-9).

What happened? The Bible tells us of this catastrophe in a quaint old story which may be literal or may be allegorical, but which, literal, allegorical or both, states the truth quite plainly and understandably.

Man heard another voice than the voice of God: the voice of the "serpent": a symbol or an incarnation of the devil (Rev. 12:9).

According to the Bible, then, man did not originate evil, nor did God. The enemy who led man astray was the devil. The old serpent tempted mankind to achieve knowledge by disobedience. Thus mankind ate (digested and absorbed into the being) the knowledge of both good and evil. And the evil took hold of the imagination of man's heart until he was completely under the law of sin and death (Gen. 3).

At a certain time, therefore, God looked upon man that He had made and it repented God that He had made man, for "the wickedness of man was great in the earth, and every imagination of the thoughts of his heart was only evil continually (Gen. 6:5, 6)."

The imagination—that was the real trouble. The subconscious mind—the inner being—the "heart" of man—dwelt only on evil. Therefore, since the imagination was evil, the created being had turned evil. And God said, "My spirit shall not always strive with man, *for he also is flesh* (Gen. 6:3)." What an amazing statement! Indeed and truly the Holy Spirit must have projected this truth into the mind of the ancient dreamer on God, for how else could man have conceived it? God said, looking on man, and tending to think of him as a spiritual being, "I made him to be spirit and breathed into him spirit which is the breath of life—but look, he also is a human being, a creature of flesh."

We could brood long upon this passage, asking the Father what it really means. Were we meant to be spirits only? Or were we intended from the beginning to be spirits templed in flesh and transmuting the flesh into the essence of immortality? And if we had from the very beginning accomplished this overcoming, would we really be free from the dominion of death, as the old story seems to hint? Door behind door opens as we think about this passage—vista beyond vista—truth behind truth.

Therefore, God did a work of destruction at that time instead of a work of creation. Through the flood, He did away with the terrible proportion of His created beings that had turned into flesh only, and made a new start with one family.

And this work of examination and of destruction was part of creation. *It is the second stage of all creative activity.*

For instance, in writing a book one first enters into a mood in which the book grows within one until the vision of it becomes clear, until the creative principle shapes and forms in the inner eye a picture of the final things: a thing of beauty, breathing life through a flow of creative ideas, through words of harmony and beauty.

In the beginning was the Word.

Secondly, the word was made flesh—the concept of the author takes form upon the typewriter—and all this time the author holds in mind the original concept or picture of perfection.

Or to make a simpler comparison, if one is making a dress, one first sees in mind the dress that one shall make; the style, the color, the pattern—and one sees it in perfection.

Secondly, the original concept "becomes flesh"—one cuts and bastes and sews and the dress takes form.

But this planning and making is the first stage in the work of creation, and if one is to become a good creator, one must in due time change one's point of view and see and destroy the evil, so that the good may remain. When an author has finished a book, he puts it away for a season, giving time for his mood to change, and he then looks at it in a critical frame of mind so that he can correct what is bad, destroy what is not up to his original ideal and so re-create that book, striving once more toward the perfection that was his original intention. Dorothy Sayer has expressed this thought far better than I could do in her wonderful book on creativity, "The Mind of the Maker."

When a dress is put together, one enters into another stage of creativity—one tries it on and stands in front of a mirror to see wherein it needs to be corrected. One may also ask help in this process of constructive criticism, saying to a friend, "Does this fit right across the back?" And the friend will not just casually "see it perfect", but will look for errors and mention them. She will judge righteous judgment (John 7:24).

Judging righteous judgment is an absolutely necessary part

of any creative activity, and the one who will not do it turns out a shoddy bit of work. Even if the original inspiration comes from God, His creative word filters through the dimness of our spirits into the confusion of our subconscious minds and thence bursts into the conscious and we need to correct, not God's sending of His word, but our reception of that word.

There was a time when religion made too much of judgment —when one went to church only to hear of hell fire and damnation. That is not the way of Jesus Christ. But to delete this matter of constructive criticism or of righteous judgment from our lives is also not the way of Jesus Christ, as we can well see when we read certain remarks of His to the scribes and Pharisees (Matt. 16:3, 23:13) and even to His friend Peter (Matt. 16:23). Here as always our need is balance. We can work out this balance if we understand that when He says, "Judge righteous judgment (John 7:24)," He refers to constructive criticism and when He says, "Judge not that ye be not judged (Matt. 7:1)," He means that we should not indulge in destructive criticism . . . criticism that is merely carping and fussing and accomplishes nothing.

The angels sang, "On earth peace," when He was born (Luke 2:14) yet He Himself said, "I came not to send peace, but a sword (Matt. 10:34)."

There is truth in both concepts, as in all the paradoxes of scripture, and to understand that truth one must balance one statement against the other.

As regards ourselves, our own lives and our creative activity, it is perfectly easy to understand this matter. We create by prayer, we look upon what we have created to see if it is good, and next we correct that which we have judged to be unworthy that we may bring it up to standard. Thus we go forward toward that perfection that Our Lord required of us (Matt. 5:48), by alternating steps of creative visioning and of creative judgment. This matter and also the church's teaching concerning it is treated at some length in "The Healing Light." There is a way, sound and churchly, of taking the one step and the other step, and we will learn it. But now at this point let us clear our objectives that we may take these steps. Where are we going? Toward what are we aiming? Toward health? That is good, but not good enough. Toward peace of mind? Certainly: the peace that passes understanding (Phil 4:7), because it exists in the midst of intense activity and great danger and hardship. Toward a life of joy and success in prayer? That is good. Jesus said that He came to give us His joy (John 15:11), and certainly He requires us to have success in prayer to do His works (John 14:12). But it still is not complete. He Himself stated the real goal in these words: "Be ye therefore perfect, even as your Father which is in heaven is perfect (Matt. 5:48)."

Too many of us have rejected this, making up our minds that we are "only human" or even that we are "sinners at all times."

He did not give His life for us to leave us "only human" but to set us free from the law of the flesh so that the righteousness of the law should be fulfilled in us (Rom. 8:4). He did not die so that we could be "sinners at all times," but so that we could become saints.

"But I am potentially a sinner at all times," a clergyman once said to me, apparently forgetting that on the previous Sunday he had asked the life of Christ to come into him and take away his sin.

"You are also potentially a saint at all times," I reminded him, "but it is hard for His Holy Spirit to make you a saint if you fasten your attention upon being a sinner."

"But we can't be perfect!" we may think. "We just don't have it in us to be saints!" No, of course we don't. But Jesus Christ does. And He undertook, coming into this world, first to give the life of His human body to cleanse the heart (subconscious mind) from sin, and secondly, to give us His Holy Spirit to fire our spirits with holiness. We have rejected the fullness of these gifts by just simply not believing Him.

The first step toward accepting them is to adjust our aims— to raise our sights—to become dissatisfied with ourselves as we are and long to become a higher order of being. In other words, as the Prayer Book says, to repent of our sins and intend to lead a new life.

In order to do so we must first look upon ourselves and judge whether or not we are worthy . . . not to condemn ourselves but that we may accept the redemption of Jesus Christ.

Now I said earlier in this chapter that the spirit of man knew what was right and what was wrong. I do believe in an instinctive sense of right and wrong — but in most of us this instinctive feeling has become warped and shrunken by the standards of today. We can hear the voice of spirit speaking through the subconscious (the voice of conscience) and refuse so often to listen to it that our minds become closed, or as the Bible would say, our hearts become hardened. And in certain areas of our life today the standards set forth by Moses on the Mount and ratified and fulfilled (filled more full of meaning) by Jesus Christ have been weakened or set aside.

Therefore, I suggest that we who have undertaken to follow Jesus Christ shall at this time look upon our lives and judge them that we may correct them. If we are in a state of feud with a neighbor, let us learn to forgive and to love, as Anne did. This first step, an increase in love toward our fellowmen, we all need to take, as there exists not a man perfect in love as compared to the perfection of Jesus Christ who forgave upon the cross the men who had placed Him there because they could not endure His righteous judgment of their works (Luke 23:34).

If our error is one of misguided love and if we are "having an affair" with someone, it is equally necessary that we cease from that affair. If our dealings with business or with the government are not honest, we should correct this matter and lift our standard of honesty to that perfection that Jesus required of us. If in order to do so we must make restitution, then let us make restitution.

"But this is difficult," the reader may think. Good!

If only we *see* that it is difficult—that there are steps to be taken in the steep ascent to heaven—then there is hope for us and joy ahead of us. There is only one type of person who is hopeless, and that is the one who thinks that he is already perfect.

A strange criticism has been brought to bear on the religious life of today—namely, that there is more spirituality and less morality than ever before. It is not the increase of spirituality that has decreased the morality! Those who really long for and "feel the power of God" as did the medical student mentioned above are the ones most likely to see their faults and to correct them.

No, the decrease of morality was a trend of modern life before the present upsurge of a spiritual desire began. The two trends are taking place at the same time. The tempo of both is increasing. The battle is on in the heavenlies. Satan hath great wrath, knowing his time is short . . . (Rev. 12:12) Since this is so, therefore, we cannot be content with the first stage of creativity, the stage of positive thinking, but must take the second step: the step of holy judging. If we do not go forward in a more intense striving after holiness, the very positive thinking that in the beginning was good, may deteriorate into complacency. A prayer group can become ingrown if the members are content merely to "pray harder" instead of striving after more holy living. Faith can become selfish, thinking more of what it can get than of what it can give.

(On the other hand, the penitent can become so absorbed with the care and nurture of his own soul that he forgets to pray the prayer of faith for others.)

In fact, selfishness or self-centeredness is Satan's constant weapon when dealing with the "saints." (We are not called to be sinners, we are called to be saints. St. Paul did not write, "To the sinners that are in Corinth, greetings." Judging from his epistles, the Corinthians were not at that time perfect. But he looked toward what they were called to be and what they would become through the indwelling of the Holy Spirit, and he dared to state that they were called to be "saints.") Even in prayer we can become selfish praying only for our concerns or asking others to do our spiritual work for us without returning kindness for kindness. Gratitude is a virtue and ingratitude is a sin—the sin that Shakespeare described as being, "Sharper than a serpent's tooth." In other words, it really hurts. If someone is learning to sew, she might go to a seamstress friend and say, "Please help me with this," but she would probably return kindness to the friend, inviting her to dinner or taking her for a drive in the country. She would not continually take her sewing and sit by and watch her do it and then say complacently, "How blessed you are that you can help people like this." If a farmer's fences were down and his horses got away, a kind neighbor might help him get them back into the pasture. But the farmer would not expect the neighbor to round up his horses for him every day and then say to the neighbor, "How blessed you are that you are strong and able to help me like this." After a while the farmer would mend his own fences. And some day he might bring the neighbor a load of top soil as a thank offering.

Jesus raised Mary's brother from the dead. But Mary did not seek Him out from time to time saying, "Oh, Lazarus has got a temperature again! Say a little prayer for him. You are so blessed that You can help us like that!" Instead, she gave Him the most precious thing she had (John 12:3). And we have our Lord's own seal of approval on this sign of gratitude. While he approved also of giving to the poor, as the scribes and Pharisees suggested, He seemed to feel that the spiritual benefit that He Himself received from her love offering was more valuable to God's kingdom than giving to the poor would have been. "The poor always ye have with you," He said (John 12:8). We can always give to world relief. But we do not always have the opportunity of doing a kindness for the particular one who has brought us God's healing, and we should seize that opportunity when it comes.

It is natural to be grateful when anyone helps us. Strange indeed would be the person who was set free from illness or mental darkness by prayer, as I once was, and who felt no impulse to return kindness to the one who prayed. That impulse should be given expression, as should every impulse toward kindness. As the psychologist, William James said, "Any emotion that is not expressed in action can become destructive instead of constructive[1]." Our own spirits are distressed or frustrated when the emotion is not expressed in action, and therefore time passes and the channel between us and the one who prayed may close, not because that one is hurt, but because our own spirits are saying to us, "You are not worthy. Do something for that person!"

Many people crush this impulse because they do not know what to do. To say, "May I pay you for this?" would certainly not be correct. The one who prays is not doing it for pay, and as a matter of fact rejoices at being able to give without money and without price—until he sees that he is being merely used. A young woman once said, "I used to go to a psychiatrist but he charged fifteen dollars so now I go to Mrs. A. because I don't have to pay her anything . . ." This point of view made it very hard for Mrs. A. was faced with the need of ceasing her work for others due to financial necessity. Indeed, three of my friends have been forced to cease from a most useful work of helping people in trouble and to work in offices. If these who were so helped had realized that even spiritually-minded people need their daily bread, they would not have lost these willing workers, or if realizing it, they had known how to approach the delicate matter of kindness for kindness.

To say, "May I do something for you?" is better, but still not correct. The one who prays is pretty sure to answer, "No, thank you." He does not want any gift that does not come so spontaneously, with such a surge of gratitude, that there is no need for asking. Moreover, he has probably discovered that those

---

[1] *Principles of Psychology*: William James. 2 Vols. Dover, N. Y.

who ask that question do not expect or desire an affirmative answer. No, if one feels grateful, let him not ask, "What may I do?" but simply do a kindness for the one who prays. When one is sufficiently powerful in prayer, then of course one can return prayer for prayer. But these just healed are not as yet able to do this. If they are in a position to do a neighborly favor for the one who has helped them, that is good. But this is not always feasible. Therefore, to send a gift of their means saying, "This is just an expression of gratitude—use it in any way you like," or saying, "Use this to further your work—", is perfectly proper and right. "The labourer is worthy of his hire (Luke 10:7)."

"But would that not make the one who prayed for me selfish?" some might think. That is the responsibility of the one who prays, not of the patient. Some of us who pray may have made a vow of accepting nothing or may have sufficient income or may prefer to earn their living in a commercial field and reduce the amount of their prayer-work accordingly. If that is the case, they may say so, and the thank offering may then be given elsewhere. Ministers would doubtless feel that their salary covered this type of work, in which case the thank-offering could be given to the church. But in many cases the one who prays has a very real need, the need of more household or secretarial help or even of the means to live, so that he may devote his whole time to the service of others. In this case he may graciously accept that which is graciously given and his acceptance is no more selfish than is a minister's or a missionary's acceptance of his salary.

This is only one aspect of the great law of love, but I mention it because it has not been elsewhere treated in my books. It is merely the carrying out toward the one who helps us of that same charity that in one way or another we owe to all for Christ's sake. And I suggest it not as a formal necessity but as a means of easing the heart and of comforting the spirit, both of the patient and of the one who prays, and thus of keeping the channel open for the flow of Christ's healing love. I need hardly say this means of returning thanks varies from person to person according to their means, according to their opportunity, and according to the development of their souls. To knit a scarf or bake a cake for someone may be more acceptable gifts than the gift of a check. To invite someone to dinner when he is alone may be a more pleasing courtesy than the offering of any concrete thing. Nor need any such gesture of grateful cooperation be the end of one's gratitude. These things are only a flicker of loving-kindness toward a person. The greatest and most abiding gift is the gift of ourselves to God, that in the name of Jesus Christ we may learn to help and to comfort others as we have been comforted and helped.

5. The Forgiveness

of Sin

We have outlined an arduous project, have we not? First of all we must believe, in spite of all the world's suffering, that God is a Father and loves us as a father loves his children. Secondly, we must believe that God is a Creator and, therefore, acts according to law and not contrary to law. This being so, we must strive to learn the laws of faith, which are the laws of spiritual creation. Third we must believe that God is good and requires of us righteousness. Is this enough? If we so believe and act accordingly will we attain the power to heal and to be healed: to do God's works?

Not completely. Because as we try to attain righteousness, we find it surprisingly difficult. Something other than God's holiness seems to have a hold upon the inner being, so that, strive as we may, we cannot do those things that we both know to do and want to do.

What then? Why did Jesus command us to be perfect (Matt. 5:48) if we cannot be perfect? He commanded because He Himself came not only to teach but also to *be* the door to perfection (John 10:1-19). He knew that we needed help, and He came to help us. And if we desire power in prayer, we need to believe not only in God the Father, righteous Creator, but also in Jesus Christ, the open door to God.

From the beginning, brooding over the fallen creation, which had been led astray by the enemy, the Creator considered a way of helping His people return to Him. In the third chapter of Genesis we are told in veiled and cryptic words of His intended plan. In the fullness of time, God would enter His creation in a new way and would replant the seed of immortality in His people. He Himself would come as the original Seed, bringing forth the fruit of an immortal life, and thus reestablishing the God-given image that the enemy had defaced. And He would thus enter in the most amazing and incredible and yet in the most simple and humble way, in the body of a man born of a virgin. He would make Himself so deeply a part of humanity that His love would reach not only the conscious but also the subconscious mind of man and redeem the imagination of man's heart. Thus mankind would become the first fruits of a new order of being, namely, the sons of God (John 1:12).

Now the more we try to fulfill the steps toward power—believing in God the Father, righteous Creator, praying according to His creative laws and straightening and purifying our lives, the more we see that we need this second manifestation of God to save us from our sins. For we find that we are blocked in ways past our understanding. Something within us fights this holy life. Something within us drags us down. We fall into black moods without knowing why we fall. We can pray ourselves into a complete faith and then lose it overnight, awaking dull and listless, cynical and discouraged, for reasons that we do not know. We can toss upon our beds and fume over matters known and unknown when there is no reason for our agitation. Or we can dream distressfully of dull, tangled things that somehow leave a load upon our souls as we awaken. Even our bodies seem to react to this vague inner discomfort. For no reason whatsoever we awaken often of a morning weary, dull, headachy, stiff up and down the spine and generally depleted of energy by something that seems to have gone on while we slept.

Whence this old unrest, this blind tendency toward darkness making us cross when we want to be sunny, mean when we want to be loving, fearful when we want to be faithful? Whence but "out of the heart," as Our Lord so truly said? Out of the diseased imagination of man's heart proceed all evil and destructive thoughts as well as all evil and destructive deeds, so that as St. Paul said, "The good that I would I do not: but the evil which I would not, that I do (Rom. 7:19)."

That we may understand this more fully, let us once more consider the "heart" or subconscious mind and how it acts. It does not respond to reason. It responds to suggestion. Therefore, if we suggest to it, "I am now going to live as a child of God, and

I am going to be well of this old trouble," it should act on that impulse. True, the spirit may not agree with the suggestion of the conscious mind. The spirit may say, "No. You are not worthy —not while you are cheating on your income tax report—not while you refuse to speak to your neighbor—not while you carry on an affair with this person or that person."

However, suppose you adjust your financial and personal affairs and make peace with your neighbor—then why does the subconscious mind not carry out immediately your order toward new life of spirit and body? Why is your progress toward life often wearily slow and uncertain? Because the subconscious, though it responds to suggestion, is very slow in changing its ways. It is a childlike mind, tending to be both obstinate and timid. And this tendency is aggravated by the fact that the subconscious mind exists not only in the present but also in the past. In other words, the subconscious remembers everything that you have ever experienced or thought or studied or felt. It is one of the functions of the subconscious thus to tend the memories. Everything that we have ever known or thought is stored away there, that it may be incorporated into our experience of life or recalled for our use. If only we understood this better, if only we loved the little mind within as much as we love our outer selves, if only we knew how to cooperate with it, how much happier our lives would be! It is amazing that our children in school are taught all kinds of facts, good and bad, crammed helter-skelter into the memories, but for the most part are not taught how to care for those memories and use them—how to study, how to think!

Many a time, as for instance in my book *Let's Believe,* I have taught young people how to take a test or examination. First of all, one sits quietly and gives thanks to God for His power, filling spirit and mind and heart. Then one reads the first question and if the answer to it comes readily to mind, one answers it. If one cannot think of an adequate answer he may say to the subconscious mind, "You have it somewhere down there in the files. Now look about for it, like the good friend that you are, while I go on to something else. And when you have found it, let me know. Thanks a lot!"

Then one answers the second question, the third perhaps, and comes back to the first. "Have you found it?" he says to his subconscious. And he waits for the answer, with a feeling of quiet expectancy. It is amazing how often that answer will float happily into the conscious mind as though the little one within were to say, "See, there it is! What fun!" But if it still does not come, then one says, "Well, take longer if you like. There's no hurry. I'll go on to something else and when I come back, I'm sure you will have it."

And one comes back, and very likely the answer will come to mind. That is, if one has ever put it into the subconscious. Of course if one has simply omitted to study that lesson, there is nothing the subconscious can do about it.

Now what does this mean to us who are not at the moment passing tests? It means as much as we want it to mean! If we care to do so, we can study ways of increasing and releasing our natural abilities until the dreams of our youth, long since given up, begin to come true. How tragic that we tend to think of the subconscious as an enemy when it is really our most faithful friend and servant! No wonder we frighten that inner caretaker! For the subconscious is like a child. It is easily upset and confused, and when it becomes terrified it can be very obstinate. "Oh, I'm going to fail," we think. "I can't pass this test! Oh, God, don't let me fail!" And the subconscious falls into dismay and loses all those precious memories that it was ready to give us.

Now let us come to the most important point concerning the action of the subconscious: that faithful servant stores away all the memories in neat files, permits the conscious mind to forget many of them, and produces them as needed . . . all of the memories except those of fear, anger, pain and guilt. The subconscious mind is like a careful housekeeper who will not put away dirty clothes or dishes, but insists on keeping them in plain sight until they are cleaned.

Sometimes we are aware of this, but more often we are not. Sometimes anger and hurt mill around in our minds and we brood upon them even though, if we are sensible, we know that it is doing us no good. We know that it upsets our digestion, confuses our thoughts, and stands in the way of our work, yet we seem unable to stop the troubled whirling. At other times, when the thing that frightens us or hurt us was in the long past, we push it down into the subconscious and refuse to think of it so that it torments us only in brief flashes of memory or in dreams.

We think that we are free of these forgotten torments, but we are not. In fact, psychiatrists tell us that submerged memories do us more harm than any others do. For the subconscious will not store them away in peace, as it stores away our pleasant memories. And since we have closed our minds to them so often that they can no longer enter the front door of consciousness, the subconscious tries to smuggle them in by another door. They are disguised as nervous tension, as fear, as obsessions and depressions and psychoses and neuroses and heaven knows what!

"It's like this," a doctor once told me. "When you bury anger and hate in the subconscious, it burrows under the ground and comes up somewhere else as nervous tension. It is as if I were to bury a rabbit under the ground and it were to pop up somewhere else as a gopher."

There is a theory among various counsellors that if we recognize the rabbit for a rabbit, it will cease to trouble us. Sometimes this is true, for seeing our fears for what they are, we know how to talk to the subconscious kindly and reasonably and help it to form new thought-habits. For instance, once when very young I was told that if I jumped off the dam into deep water, I would swim. I jumped but I did not swim and had to be hauled out by the hair of my head, spitting and spluttering and horribly embarrassed. Nevertheless, being adventurous and full of faith I tried it again, with the same result. A fright repeated makes a deep impression on the subconscious, like a groove in the gray matter of the brain. Therefore, from that time on I was afraid of dark, still water. This was not a reasonable fear, for the bright, moving waves of the ocean did not frighten me and I could wade far out into the breakers and leap through them, trusting them to take me back to shore. But I could not swim beyond my depth in still water, for panic would grip me by the throat and I would choke. This is not a great matter, and I consoled myself that being middle-aged I did not need to swim to the float if I did not want to do so. Nevertheless, until I understood this unreasonable fear it puzzled and frustrated me. So many other old fears had melted away in the light of God's love that I could not understand why this one did not go. And I was ashamed to think that I who taught others to believe could not believe in my own power to swim to the float! I knew the cause of the trouble well enough, but merely knowing did not help me. "Why can't I swim in deep water?" I would fume, "Just because I got scared when I was nine years old? This is ridiculous!" And I would tense my nerves and clench my teeth and try again. But each try made it worse.

When I realized, however, that it was not the woman that

I call "myself" who acted thus but the little child within her, then I saw a great light. And I went swimming and talked comfortably to that little one who had never grown out of this fear. "I know," I would say to her, "I scared you awfully. It was silly of me, wasn't it? But, you see, that really doesn't matter now. I'm sorry I frightened you so badly, and if you really don't want to swim to the float, I won't insist on it. But perhaps you'd like to swim just a little bit beyond our depth now that we understand each other. Shall we try, just for fun?"

I have not as yet reached the float. But the panic has gone away, and I no longer search for the bottom of the lake and stiffen with fear when I cannot touch it. There is an inner change, even though I have not made this tiny thing a matter of prayer but for the sake of the experiment have worked toward solving it by the understanding alone.

But what of the big things? What of the old darkness that for years hung black upon my mind so that for no known reason the joy of life departed from me? What of the unknown terrors that expressed themselves in fear of the telephone and of high windows and of knives? What of a dullness and a confusion and a weariness that did not have its beginning in the flesh and that no doctor could cure? What of nervous tensions and all their resulting ills of headache and indigestion and neuritis and bursitis and all the other "itises"? These things have roots. They come from old memories that are surrounded not only with fear but also with feelings of guilt. The subconscious will not assimilate these memories because the spirit will not permit it to do so. It will not store them away out of sight but continually forces them to our attention, and when we will not look at them directly, changes them into nervous manifestations of this kind and that.

Physicians and counsellors fortunately recognize this nowadays. But their methods of dealing with the matter are not always adequate. For instance, a girl on the West coast once came to me with the usual tale of woe: sleeplessness, nervous tension, headaches, fears, loss of appetite . . . .

"What are you worrying about?" I asked her.

"Nothing!" she replied. "I have no problems."

"Were you happy when you were a little girl?"

"Oh, yes. I had a marvellous childhood." She hesitated for a moment and then remarked brightly, "Of course I have had

several affairs, but I don't suppose that could have anything to do
with it."

"Well, no wonder you have these nervous troubles!" I cried.
"A guilty conscience will always give you fears and sleeplessness and all the rest of it."

"But I don't have a guilty conscience!" said this unfortunate
one with complete honesty. "My counsellor tells me the affairs
were good for me. They gave me release. And I have absolutely
no sense of guilt about it, so it can't be these affairs that are
bothering me."

But it was. Her counsellor had succeeded in persuading the
conscious mind that it was not sin, but only a natural impulse
and that her affairs would give her release. But he had forgotten,
or perhaps did not know, that she was not a two-fold but a three-
fold personality. He had forgotten the spirit. And her spirit,
which was born in the image and likeness of God and, therefore,
with His purity stamped upon it, knew perfectly well that her
affairs were wrong.

"But I've always been told that if you think a thing is all
right, it is!" she cried.

Not so did Moses inform the children of Israel when he came
down from the mount and found them dancing naked before the
golden calf and finding wonderful release (Exodus 32:21). Not
so did Jesus tell His disciples when He reiterated the words
of the law of Moses and added to them His own interpretation,
lifting them into an even higher standard of purity of thought
as well as purity of action (Matt. 5:27-33). How can we glibly
make up little mottoes for ourselves and dare to put them in
place of the laws of God? Are we great enough to make our
own laws of right and wrong, disregarding the thundering words
of Scripture that from first to last tell us that the wages of sin
is death (Romans 6:23)?

It is true that some churches teach that we should do one
thing and some teach that we should do another. To one person it is wrong to eat breakfast before going to the Communion
Service and to another person it is quite all right. Some people feel
that it is wrong to dance, while most find it a joyful recreation.
Some are total abstainers from liquor and others feel that it is
sufficient to be temperate and moderate in eating and drinking.

That much is true. And as St. Paul said in reference to eating meat that had been offered to idols, there is nothing really
wrong in these small matters unless to us it seems wrong (I Cor.

8:7). One might put it thus: some people make a decision of a fasting communion as a means of grace, and therefore to them it is wrong to break that fast. Some people make a vow of total abstinence from drink, and to them it is wrong to break that vow. Some may be unable to dance without uncomfortable and unclean thoughts, and to them it is wrong to dance.

In these small matters we may choose whatever discipline best suits our thinking and upbringing. But these are not the moral code as taught in the Bible. These are only personal observances that help us to keep that unbreakable and unshakable code. Concerning these we are allowed to choose, but concerning the code itself we are not allowed to choose. For those implacable standards of right and wrong are made by God Himself and are written into our natures and *our spirits know them.* First of all we are told in four commandments, the matter being reiterated and applied in different ways, that we are to worship the Lord our God in holiness and in purity and that we are to substitute no idol in His place: no idol of wood or stone, no idol of the Christ Spirit in us, no idol of a divine intelligence that is impersonal and controllable by man, no idol of another human being than the Son of God—Ghandi or the Great Masters of the East or some present day leader in whom we choose to see Christ. Secondly, we are told that we shall reverence this human life, taking care of our old people, saving life and not destroying it, sanctifying the sex impulse within the bounds of holy matrimony, living in honesty and without lying and envy.

Concerning these matters we are not free to decide. God has already decided what is sin. Or more accurately, these standards are inevitable and need no deciding, not even by God because they are of His nature, and we originally and by His intention are also of His nature (Gen. 1:26).

Those who live close to God and are not led astray by the Adversary know these things both with the spirit and the conscious mind. God's messengers of all times have told them to us, and have made known to us in no uncertain terms the dangers of disobeying these essential laws of our beings. They have done so not to make trouble for us, but to save us from trouble. For even if our conscious minds do not know them, and so like the unfortunate girl of the above story we have no sense of guilt, these things will destroy us just the same . . . not from without by a thunderbolt from the skies, but from within by the voice of our spirits that will not be stilled. For our spirits are created in holiness, and even through the dimness of the flesh they still behold the face of the Father. Our spirits know what is right and what is wrong, and no counsellor under heaven can stop that holy knowing. Our subconscious minds hear the voice of the spirit and respond to suggestion *not only from the conscious mind but also from the spirit*. And the spirit refuses to accept yesterday's unclean memories just as it refuses to accept today's unclean living.

All this I tried to tell the troubled girl who had had the three or four affairs.

"For heaven's sake go home and get on your knees and pray for a sense of guilt," I said. "For when one really is guilty, then there's nothing so healthy as a sense of guilt, because when we see our sin clearly we can begin to get rid of it."

Thus I tried to help her but failed. She did not want to keep the laws of God. She wanted to continue to break them and do so with impunity by means of getting me to say a little prayer for her nerves. She is not alone in this world.

"But after all, it was love," she said, "and all love is divine."

"Where on earth did you pick up that idea?" I asked her.

"Oh, everybody says so. The Bible and everybody."

In this she was gravely in error.

But what then should the girl have done? First of all, obviously she should have rethought her standard of life and ceased breaking the seventh commandment. But after that, what? Would she not be more depressed than ever, deprived of her "release," and forced to think of herself as a sinner instead of as a perfect child of God? Would she not brood more than ever on her shortcomings and sink even deeper into depression? Possibly she would, if she had no saviour except the power of her own thinking. If by affirmations only could she lift herself into peace, her last state might be as uncomfortable as her first one.

But there is another power besides the power of creative thinking. There is One who came into the world not only to show us the way but to *be* The Way. There is a second current of the life of God that can enter into the subconscious and heal those memories of grief and guilt and pain. *I believe in Jesus Christ Our Lord.*

Out of the timelessness into time He came to us. For He saw our need, and knew that while the conscious mind could learn and keep the laws of God, the subconscious mind, bound and hampered by unhappy memories, needed help in order to do so. If the girl mentioned above could have seen and grasped His power of transcending time for her, she could have been set completely free from those troubling memories and thought-habits and could have been made a new creature. I have known people to be so re-born by a single prayer.

For instance, there was a minister at a conference in the far West. His blue eyes were shadowed and his face downcast and as the days passed his shadows deepened and did not lift. On the last day of the conference I made bold to speak to him.

"Have you found what you need here?" I asked him.

With all honesty he answered that he had not. And in answer to my further questions he told me that he had come many miles to this conference, financing it, I gathered, from a very meager budget, in a last desperate search for peace of mind. He could no longer keep up with his small country churches. "I can't preach any more," he told me. "I am so terrified that I am stiff all over and my words stumble and falter and I just can't do it. I can't even make calls. It's getting so that I am so scared of people that the sweat drips off me even at the thought of making calls. And of course I worry all the time and can't sleep. I hoped I'd learn how to help myself. That's why I came, but—"

"Do you know of any special problem that worries you?"

"No, I don't. I have a good wife and four lovely children and wonderful congregations. The trouble must be *in me.*"

"Were you happy when you were a little boy?"

"No."

A few more questions and the picture was made clear to me—a tragically common picture. His parents were divorced and he had been sent to live with distant relatives. Their ways were not the ways of God. He was forced to hear words that hurt a sensitive conscience and to work among people who led him away from those paths of goodness that he desired. Therefore, the sub-conscious mind was filled with grief and loneliness, and that deep-laid pattern of thinking tended to draw toward him grief and loneliness. Also these feelings were surrounded with a sense of guilt, so that the spirit could not reach them with the comfort of God. And finally to this there was added an old and bitter resentment at the life that could treat him thus, at the parents who had deserted him for their own pleasure, at the men whose rough language and whose loose ways had led him into paths that revolted him.

Hurt, guilt and resentment had drawn toward him the very

things that he did not want—distress at his own inadequacy, fear of the punishment of his congregation's disapproval, and bitterness toward life.

"So you see," I said, "the trouble isn't in you—the man you are now. You're a good man, living a good life. You are of sane and sound mind. You aren't crazy! The trouble is in that little boy who lived some thirty years ago. Isn't that so?"

"Well, yes," he admitted.

"Then all I need to do is to ask Jesus Christ to go back through time—to go back thirty years and find that little boy still living within you, and heal and comfort him. Isn't that so?"

"Yes, but—how can that be?"

I tried to explain to him this great and elusive truth: *there is no time in the spiritual kingdom.* We live under the veil of what we call time. But in the spiritual kingdom, there is no time. As a matter of fact, even science tells us that time is relative. Time on this earth is measured by the rotation of earth and sun and moon, but if man in a rocket ship ascended into interstellar space, time would be no more. Certainly God is not bounded by time.

With Him a thousand years are as one day. And when He entered the world, incarnated as Jesus Christ, He entered from timelessness into "time," bringing into time His timeless power. "Before Abraham was, I am," He said (John 8:58). Thus he can transcend time. He can go back into what we call the past or forward into what we call the future, and therein can *act.*

H. G. Wells once write a novel about a time-traveller who in the fantastic way of novels managed to get himself re-born back in the dark ages. He tried to tell them about the marvels of the modern world from whence he came, but they would not listen. He tried to explain electricity to them so that they need not crawl about in the darkness any more, but they only laughed at him. He told them of the power of steam, but they rejected his words and continued to go where they would go upon slow horses or upon slower feet . . .

Jesus is our time-traveler. Out of eternity into time He came to us. "He was in the world and the world was made by Him and the world knew Him not (John 1:10)." But unto those who do receive Him, He does much more than the hero of the fantasy mentioned. He not only tells of the grace and the truth of the eternal kingdom whence He comes, but He also projects that grace and truth into them.

"Yes, but—I can't *do* it," said the minister.

"Let me try it for you in prayer," I replied. "It's hard for anyone to grasp it for themselves."

So I began imagining. I told myself a story about the Jesus who walked in Galilee. I imagined this Jesus finding a little lonely boy and healing that child, still living within the big blonde man, of all his sadness and loneliness and hate. Then I visioned Him actually entering into the subconscious mind, cleaning the old memories as a careful housekeeper might clean her furniture, wiping away the dust of old sorrow, the corroding rust of resentment, the stain and shadow of grief, and restoring the heart in joy and hopefulness.

"The memories will not be lost," I said, "but the emotional tone that surrounds them will be changed. Memories of old grief will no longer cause you grief. They will bring joy, for you will think, 'How thankful I am that that is all gone away!' Memories of guilt will bring exceeding joy, for you will think, 'Oh, how wonderful to be entirely free of that, so that it has nothing to do with me anymore!' Memories of resentment will be changed to tenderness, because the love of Christ will so fill and flood the heart that there will no longer be any cause of resentment, for even old bitter things have been changed to joy." I said much more along this line, repeating and repeating, so that the submerged consciousness would be sure to receive the impact of my own sureness that this was to be.

How could I be so sure? Because I know that Jesus Christ came to us, out of timelessness into our time, on purpose to transcend time in each of us, entering the subconscious and finding His way through past years to every buried memory in order to touch it with His healing power and set us free.

There was a new light in the eyes of this faithful servant of God as he went away. And two months later he wrote me that he was free. "I am not afraid of anything any more," he wrote. "I have never been so happy in my life and people tell me that I preach better than I have ever preached."

Certainly. This thing that he could not do for himself had been done for him by the second person of the Trinity, Jesus Christ, who came into this world on purpose to remove our transgressions as far away from us as the east is from the west (Psalms 103:12).

6. Our Lord Jesus Christ

Our Need of Him

& His Power

"I am the door."

A tourist in the holy land met a shepherd and saw his sheep-fold—a circle of rocks with one opening.

"Where is the gate—the door?" she asked.

The shepherd replied, "I am the door. When the sheep are returning to the fold at night, I lie down across the entrance. My own sheep know me and step over me into the sheep-fold. Those who are not my own run away from me."

Jesus was forthright and explicit in stating that no man came to the Father but by Him (Matt. 22:34-40). And the essence of Christianity is a belief in Jesus Christ—not merely in His teachings, but in Himself as the open door to God. Both the Apostles' Creed and the Nicene creed, summing up the beliefs of the church, state this unequivocally. They do not say, "I believe in the teachings of Jesus Christ," but, "I believe in Jesus Christ our Lord." Moreover, they summarize the holy events of His life and say that they believe in every one of them. It is strange, this being so, that many fuzzy-minded people think of Christianity as merely a belief in the teachings of Christ. His teachings were of course perfect, but He was not the only one to teach the laws of life. History is full of prophets and masters who taught truth. Even the great law of love was not His invention. As He Himself said, this is the law and the prophets. He summed up in the first and great commandment (Deut. 6:5) the essence of pure Judaism, which is also the essence of all righteousness. But Christianity is not founded on this law but on Jesus Himself who alone can help us keep this law.

A Jewish Rabbi once gave an interdenominational group an excellent summing up of Jewish beliefs. At the end of it a lady said in a puzzled way, "Tell me, aren't Jews Christians?"

This remark in its naivete illustrates well a common concept of Christianity: namely, that a Christian is anyone who tries to be good.

A Christian is not one who tries to be good, nor even one who tries to find power through prayer to God. We know that there is a power in any kind of prayer to any kind of deity. It is common knowledge that witch doctors and medicine men can actually move events toward either life or death through faith or fear. But this is not Christianity. And these healings are not the final healing: the healing of the soul.

"The Great Masters, by extreme discipline, can mount almost every step of the ladder toward perfection," a friend of mine remarked. "But the final step, union with God and the transformation of the personality, they cannot make. So the Christian way is more sensible—merely sit down on the bottom step and howl for help through Jesus Christ."

True, in the above chapters I have outlined some principles of faith. But as we try to practice them, we come to a block in our own unredeemed natures, and without Jesus we can go no farther. Who then, is this Jesus, and in what way do the holy mysteries of His life help us toward wholeness? Whence is He, and what value is there in believing the Bible account of His origin?

St. Matthew and St. Luke studied the matter of His holy birth, a subject which He, in His delicacy and out of His consideration for His mother did not mention. These two historians wrote down for us in the beginning of their Gospels, mysteries of a divine conception and of a holy birth. The Apostles' Creed which many of us repeat Sunday after Sunday states that He was "conceived by the Holy Ghost, born of the Virgin Mary."

What can we gain by believing this article of Christian faith? Could not the Christ Spirit have entered into Jesus at the time of His baptism in the same manner that the Christ Spirit enters into us, only in greater measure?

There was a time when I tried to believe thus: that He was

one of the Great Masters, not a unique Being divinely conceived and miraculously born. But a sadness would come upon me
as I thought thus, and at times I would feel like Mary at the
tomb: "They have taken away the Lord and we know not where
they have laid Him (John 20:2)." And though I told myself
that I must grow up in understanding and must not cling to
a childish and medieval concept, nevertheless this sense of loss
remained and dimmed the power of my healing prayers.

Not every seeker after truth feels this loss, I know. Those
who have never known Him as Lord may be content to think
of the Christ Spirit shining in them as in Him. But as the years
pass, they often feel the need of something, they know not what.
"My affirmations don't seem to help me as they used to do,"
they sigh. "And I even wonder whether I am demonstrating as
well as I did—"

The trouble is that they are believing only one-third of those
Christian mysteries that they need to believe in order that the
signs may follow (Mark 16:17-18). In order to receive the fullness of God's power we need not only God the Father but we
also need the second person of the Trinity, Jesus Christ and the
third person of the Trinity, the Holy Ghost.

What then is the actual meaning of the holy birth? Is it a
matter of "Silent Night" and colored lights strung from the telegraph poles—of toy babies in toy mangers and Santa Claus coming down the chimney—a matter of tinsel and turkeys and Christmas trees?

Let us look past these things, and consider *Him*. Jesus Christ, a
divine Being, existing before all worlds together with God the
Father Creator of this world (John 1:1-3)—He who being of
the very essence of the Godhead thought it no robbery to be equal
with God (Phil. 2:6), that He of His infinite mercy should accomplish this miracle of laying aside His glory and entering in
the hushed midnight beneath the veil of time!

Even for us it may be harder to be born than to die. Since
the spirit is breathed into us from God, who knows how and in
what manner that spirit may have lived before drawing near to this
earth? Since there is no time with God (Psalms 90:4) and
since we are heirs of immortality (Rom. 8:29), who shall say
when our spirits evolved from the Godhead, speeded forth at
His word—who shall say where they may have lived and in what
manner they may have served Him before they were sent upon
this desperate journey of life on earth? Who can tell with what

dismay they may have looked on this dark earth—this small lost planet—this bit of creation taken over by the enemy?

Even for us. How much more—how infinitely more difficult for Him, the Son of God, to accomplish a miracle of compression and to be born of the Virgin Mary!

No wonder that the angels, watching with terrible excitement the culmination of this miracle of divine action, sang with such joy that the faithful shepherds heard their voices from the skies! Do I believe this? Yes, for it is not unknown in mystical history (Luke 2:13). Yes, for I know two people alive who in a time of high spiritual perceptivity heard a singing that did not come from this earth.

Yes, for I myself once heard a singing that did not come from this earth.

No wonder that the stars told of His coming, and astrologers from the East travelled over desert and mountain to search for Him (Matt. 2:1-11). Do I believe this? Yes, for I have come to know the universe as a place of great mystery, no longer the small simple planet that we thought we knew so well. Day by day science adds new wonder to our concept of life, showing us the very air, that seems still and empty save for wind and cloud and flying birds, to be full of invisible currents of energy—light that cannot be seen until our television sets collect it, sounds that cannot be heard unless we tune in to them by radio—thoughts carrying from mind to subconscious mind! Indeed, since there is no time with God, why may not the thoughts of those long departed also exist in the air of this earth? Some mystics feel that they do, and that even these "Akashic records" may be tapped and read by those with spiritual vision. There are those who speak of the "mass subconscious" and feel that the inner being of man has a certain attunement to the race past as well as present. Why not? For thoughts of past generations still exist among the intricate thought-patterns of the air. Somewhere the song of the angels still is, small and fine amid the thunderous clamor of this frantic earth. Somewhere the wonder in the hearts of the shepherds still is a living thing. Somewhere the Holy Babe is still being born into the hearts of men, and in times of highest adoration and purest praise our spirits feel the joy and the wonder of His coming.

We are interwoven, all of us, with the warp and woof of the universe. And through the universe God breathes His life, creating, recreating and sustaining. His life eddies and whirls in patterns of spiritual creativity. And the same eddying and flowing of His life that affects the stars in their courses may also affect the lives of men. I do not say that this is so, I merely say that this is possible: that the being of a man may be mysteriously indicated by the lines in his hands—as though a man's life could be repeated in a great pattern above his head and in a small pattern within his hand—No wonder then that the wise men whose minds were open to the message of God through His stars, saw the coming of the Saviour there written and went to Him offering gifts! (There in the very beginning we see the holy pattern: adoration, thank-offering; spiritual benefits not left alone in the realm of the spiritual but turned immediately into the consecration and the sacrifice of material things, by a divine, instinctive understanding that all things come from God and therefore as He gave Himself to us, of our own we give to Him.)

Yes, I believe these things. And most readily of all, I believe that He was conceived by the Holy Ghost and born of the Virgin Mary. And I can believe this great thing for the simplest of reasons, namely, that I have seen His power working in small things and therefore I know that His power can work in great things.

I once taught the prayer of faith to a Jewish boy in an army hospital. He grasped the idea and used it well, so that in six weeks a leg that for two years had been full of shrapnel and osteomyelitis and from which two inches of bone was missing, became perfectly whole. However, I taught him only the teachings of Jesus Christ, lending him Dr. Emmet Fox's "Sermon on the Mount," still a standard for this purpose, and I did not venture to outline for him the plan of redemption.

He was finally released from the hospital, only to reappear after three months.

"I broke my leg again," he explained. "And I was quite discouraged for about three days. Then I figured it out like this: *there's something else you haven't told me and that's why I'm back here.* Now what is it?"

"That's why I'm back here." Would that mean that God ordained the breaking of the leg? Hardly. The boy meant simply that the bone while healed was still weak and that he needed more understanding that he might have more spiritual power for its healing and therefore, his return to the hospital could be used for this good purpose.

"Yes, there is something else," I admitted. "I have not dared to tell you, because when I try to tell Jewish people they usually get upset, and I can understand why. It is embarrassing to me to say, 'I am a Christian' to a Jew, for a Christian means someone filled with the love of Christ and we have not acted toward Jews as though we were filled with the love of Christ. So I didn't tell you. But you are quite right. Being a Christian means more than following His teachings. I still don't know how to tell you the rest so I will give you the story of His life and maybe you will see it for yourself."

I gave him the New Testament and told him to read the gospel of St. John. "At least we will skip the Virgin Birth for a while," I told myself. "At least we will evade that difficulty." For I knew that this young man with his keen, analytical mind and his fresh approach, would not be able to so smother that shattering truth with tinsel and carols that it would be made "sacred" by a certain pleasing emotion and be shielded from the sword of thought.

What would he make of this Gospel, I wondered? What would the mystic, St. John, say to a mind as free from preconceived notions as new-fallen snow is free from footprints?

"What do you think of Jesus Christ?" I asked him the next week.

And he replied, most amazingly, "I wonder if that's who the other one is?"

"What do you mean?"

"When I am doing my prayers, I often feel that I am not alone. So I just wonder if that's who the other one is."

"I am quite sure that that is who the other one is," I replied. And filled with curiosity, I added, "But what do you think of Him?"

"Well, I had to read this book three times before I got the idea," he said. "And then I read another book about Him. It was by a man named Matthew."

"Do you believe the things that Matthew said about Him?" I asked. "Do you believe that He was conceived by the Holy Ghost and born of the Virgin Mary? Do you believe He raised His body from the dead?"

"Of course I do!" said the young man, looking at me in surprise. "If even I, who am nothing and know nothing, can build in two inches of my bone with God's help, why shouldn't He have been conceived by the Holy Ghost and born of the Virgin Mary? And why shouldn't He have raised His body from the dead?"

That, it seems to me, is a perfect answer for us small crawling

creatures who cannot even explain the miracle of our own births—
how the cells know to shape themselves into the intricate patterns
of flesh and bone that make our bodies—how those beings of
flesh become sentient creatures—how the spirit enters into them—

Why not? God the Father, God the Son and God the Holy
Ghost are one God, manifesting Himself in three different ways,
each of those manifestations able to assume what we for want of
a better name call personality. Why not? We admit that God
moved upon formlessness and the unimaginable darkness that we
call interstellar space and called into being suns and moons and
earths and all the living things upon the earths. Then, if we admit
that the Creator could evolve men and women, trees and birds,
out of nothing at all except His own Being, why should we balk
at the thought that He can so invade and pervade one of His own
creatures as to cause Life to begin in her physical being? Why
could not the word of the Spirit implant in her so tremendous an
infusion of the Fatherhood of God that she should conceive a
child without human implementation?

I am glad that I can believe this, quite simply, as it is taught
in the Bible! I rejoice that I need not tell myself that this was an
idea handed over from the pagan religions—that such legends
were common to those who sought God! Thank God they were
common! The need of a Savior is a basic need and therefore even
before the thing happened there were legends concerning it! I do
thank God that I need not reason with myself and say that the
Holy Birth of the Savior is only a symbol, meaning that the
Spirit is born in all of us! How it would grieve me to spend the
holy season of Christmas celebrating a lie! How it would sully
my reverence for God the Father to think that He who "Stretcheth
out the north over the empty place and hangeth the earth upon
nothing, who bindeth up the waters in His thick clouds and
. . . divideth the sea with His power," should have
built His church upon an ordinary human man born out of
wedlock and upon the myths that were told to defend His unholy birth—or even upon an ordinary man and lies invented to
propound a false theory of His divinity. God forbid that I should
for a moment dare to believe that Jesus Christ was not con-
conceived by the Holy Ghost, born of the Virgin Mary.

I am not saying that this is essential to salvation. But this I
know: it is essential to me. Without it I waste any energy in an
effort to deny or explain away the words of the Bible, and so my
faith is injured with doubt and my healing prayers are blocked.

Without it I am helpless, struggling by my own strength to incarnate the Christ spirit, even as He incarnated it. Without it I have no Savior but only one of the great masters and teachers. I need more than that. I need a redeemer of the subconscious as well as a teacher of the conscious.

Thanks be to God, therefore, that in spite of all the jibes and taunts of the unbelieving, the Church has never faltered from its uncompromising stand and that we say together every Sunday, lest we forget, "I believe in Jesus Christ our Lord, who was conceived by the Holy Ghost, born of the Virgin Mary.

For as I believe that He did in a literal sense precipitate the full being of God into a human woman, I can then believe that He can precipitate His personal healing power into my own human being—into my heart. He can enter below the level of consciousness. He can project His life back through time in me and heal my oldest and most hidden memories, so that as His power works in the submerged mind, my outer reactions and my conscious thoughts more and more conform to the image of His joy and light.

For when He came upon this earth upon that starry night so long ago, He entered into humanity and He entered below the veil of time. He actually projects into those who receive Him that very Life and Light itself, so that He gives them what they must have in order to do the things that they were made to do: He gives them the "power to become the sons of God (John 1:7-12)."

Then how can we receive this power and in what way can we incorporate this holy act in our lives? The way is clearly taught us in the Bible, but some of us have rejected it as too simple. We receive this power by believing that He can give it to us and by asking for it (Heb. 11:6). Is this a denial of the ways of creative thinking? Not at all. It is acting in accordance with them. The first step in receiving any power is believing that there is such a power. When we ask for God's light to shine in the conscious mind we must first of all know that there *is* a God, an outside Life of some sort. As we do this, the principle that we call faith is set in motion. So when we need God's light to shine in the subconscious mind, we must also recognize that there is a Savior: that God through His second person or channel of power is able to heal our memories, or in more exact words to forgive our sins. And *according to our faith* it is done unto us. For an essential to our receiving any of the currents of God's power is that we ourselves by faith shall open the door to His action. He is divinely courteous. He never forces Himself on anyone, but waits with patience to be invited in.

There are many old, neglected words for this inviting of a Savior to enter and heal our sinful natures. Our churches are strewn with them. "Accepting Christ" . . . "making a complete surrender to Christ" . . . There is truth in all of them. But we do not like to think of that truth. The first step toward heaven pleases us—opening the windows of our conscious minds to God and asking for the sunlight of His love to fill us, then giving thanks that He is with us and that we are walking in His light—we enjoy that. But to look at ourselves with the eye of inspired criticism, to see that in spite of all of God's light shining in us we have fallen short of our heavenly heritage—that we do not like. It wounds our pride to see thought-patterns of unholiness within our inner beings, causing us to act and think in ways that we would not. Therefore, we try in every way to persuade ourselves that these dubious habits acting or thinking are really justifiable impulses. Or we love to think that even if we are not yet completely children of God, we are well on the way to it and certainly will be so after we have affirmed it often enough.

As we justify ourselves, forcing the conscious mind to believe that our one-sided goodness is complete goodness, we can batten down the hatches of the subconscious so tightly that the inner voice is stilled and the conscience ceases to report to us our own deviations from the path of holiness.

But do we not already have the Christ spirit, being made in the image and likeness of God?

We already have a spark of divine light, true, born into our spirits, speaking to us in the voice of conscience and striving to break through the density of our minds and fill us with the Holy Ghost. We may desire to call this the Christ Spirit and indeed the name has a certain significance, as this bit of eternal light submerged within us is surely a reflection of the very being of God. But if we use the word carelessly with the false assumption that our tiny candle of immortality is potentially the same as the Light that lighteth every man that cometh into the world, namely, the Being of Our Lord Jesus Christ, then we make a tragic mistake.

"He was in the world, and the world was made by Him, and the world knew Him not. The same was in the beginning with God. All things were made by Him; and without Him was not anything made that was made. In Him was life; and the life was the light of

men. And the light shineth in darkness, and the darkness compre-
hended it not (John 1:2-6)." Those words were spoken of Jesus
Christ, the son of Mary and of the Holy Ghost, the foster-son of
Joseph. Those words were spoken of Him who in the fullness of
time crashed through the sinful darkness of our world with the
very Light of God . . . God acting upon our humanity in a new
way to answer the cries of our hearts and to set us free from our
old captivity . . . God accomplishing the second great act of
creativity and releasing in this world a second current of power
. . . God the Son, the second person of the Trinity.

Those words were not spoken of you and me. And if we in our
pathetic and fervid straining for power assume that our "Christ
spirit" is identical with the Christ Spirit that was in Jesus of
Nazareth, then we miss the whole value of His marvelous self-
giving to us.

Then what is this value and how can we receive it? This
value is no less than the *complete healing of the memories of the
past* so that we can be released to become the persons that we
would be if there were no dark shadows in our submerged minds
at all—nothing to seep into our consciousness so that we wake in
depression and weariness, nothing to stiffen us with terrors and
unreasonable timidities, nothing to dim at any time the shining of
our joyful spirits. This is His joy, that He came into the world to
give us (John 15:11). It is so great a joy that it can even with-
stand the persecution of this world and still rise triumphant into
joy (Acts 16:22-26).

How then can we receive this most glorious current of the
eternal life of God, this Light that shineth even in the darkness of
our deep minds, so that the whole subconscious is redeemed into
joy—so that from the heart there will come welling up continually
the water of life and we will never again thirst for freedom and
for joy (John 4:14)?

First of all, we can receive this redeeming life of God by asking Jesus Christ to come into us.

For in some extraordinary manner, by His holy birth and
by His life and death for us, He has found a pathway through
the conflicting currents of time into the farthest reaches of our
memories—into the darkest corners of our hidden minds. We will
consider this at more length in the following chapters. But even
if we think of it no more—and indeed it is so far beyond our
imagining that some of us prefer to think no farther along the
line of understanding God's mysteries—even if we understand it

no better than we do now, we can still ask Him to come into us.

We cannot remember all of the fear and resentment of our childhood. He can. We cannot recall the agony of being born, the shock of leaving the warm darkness of the womb and entering into this beclouded planet. He can. Abiding as He does within all life, a current of His healing love can reach and touch the very dimmest and darkest of the memories of our past, if we will ask Him to do so.

Moreover, He can heal and redeem the grievous things that we *do* remember and would like to forget. He can remove the scar of them as though they had never been—if we invite Him to do so.

For instance, a Christian counsellor whose work was far across the waters in another land once gave me this story so that I might use it. He said that a young woman suffering from recurrent digestive trouble had been sent to him by her doctors. They could find no cause for the violent cramps and pains that assailed her about once a month, and therefore rightly concluded that the trouble was psychosomatic. In the course of his treatment, the counsellor found that she had previously suffered from nervous symptoms of fear and anxiety. She had asked the advice of a psychiatrist, who discovered that she had recently had an affair and decided that she was suffering from a sense of guilt like the counsellor quoted in a previous chapter, and thought to set her free from worry by removing the sense of guilt. He therefore persuaded her that there was nothing wrong in her affair. If man were mind and subconscious alone, he might have been right. But man is also spirit. In spite of her acceptance of his words, her spirit nevertheless knew that she had broken the seventh commandment and that therefore she deserved punishment. Her spirit had telegraphed this order to the subconscious and since the doors of the conscious mind were barricaded from the voice of conscience, her subconscious mind had brought punishment upon her through the body.

In the wise way of a good counsellor, my friend caused her to see this, and she said to him one day, "I believe that affair of mine was wrong after all. But what can I do about it now?"

The counsellor suggested that she go to her minister, make a confession and ask him to pray for her forgiveness.

She returned the next day in a worse state than before. "I went to him," she said, "but he *didn't do it! He didn't do it!*"

"What did he do?"

"He said what the psychiatrist said—he said, 'Oh well, we

all make mistakes and I wouldn't worry about it if I were you.' "

Probably the minister had had an idea that God was kind and good and understanding, and therefore would not be too harsh with her, but her subconscious mind was not convinced of this. It takes a sledge-hammer impression to change the feeling of that subconscious. The concept of God as understanding and tolerant did not do it.

"Well, then," said the counsellor, "you and I will do it together. Kneel here and tell Jesus Christ what you have done and say that you are sorry. And I will kneel beside you and ask Him to come into your subconscious mind and comfort it. I know that He will do so, for that is why He came into this world—so that He could heal the subconscious minds of men with His redeeming love. All that is needed is for someone to ask Him to come into his heart and someone to believe that He is coming in and doing His healing work there. You ask. I will believe—and nothing can stop it."

Thus the counsellor prayed the prayer of faith for the forgiveness of his patient. And the woman arose and went her way and she was well.

The doctor opened a door for Jesus Christ to be born anew in the subconscious mind so that His light took away all the shadows, His purity swept out all the dirt, His joy comforted all the sorrow. Potentially this woman, like all of us, had a bit of God's light in her. She had a spirit or a soul, or what some like to call "The Christ within". But this potential spiritual consciousness was like one small, dim light bulb shining in a neglected attic. And the trouble in her life was like stagnant water backed up into her cellar, the septic tank of foul memories draining into it. The bit of light in her attic could not probe this murky depth. Even when she opened the door of her spirit-attic with the counsellor's help and saw by its light what was wrong in her cellar, she needed more than that bit of attic-light to make it right. She needed a strong hand and a mighty heavenly Being to enter and purify the cellar of her being and make it once more wholesome.

Jesus Christ was the strong Savior and mighty Heavenly Plumber who could do in her this work of healing and cleansing. But out of His heavenly courtesy and because He has given us free-will, he does not come into the depths of our beings and cleanse them unless He is asked to do so. Since she was of weak body and of disturbed nerves, the counsellor helped her in this work of asking and of believing that He would come. But when we are of sound mind and of stout body, we ourselves can thus open the doors.

Therefore, let us ask Him to abide in us and there do His perfect work of healing and of cleansing. We can imagine Him opening windows in the subconscious to the sunlight of God's love so that all the shadows flee away from within us, so that we wake of a morning with expectancy of joy and of happy accomplishment, so that our spontaneous response to all stimuli are the responses of one triumphant and free in the eternal power of God. We can imagine Him working within us as a careful housekeeper might work to cleanse and freshen a house that has been long closed. We can picture Him dusting off our memories and redeeming them so that if they come to mind they will come with the joyful thought, "Oh thank God, that is all taken away and it cannot trouble me any more!" We can fancy Him storing away out of sight the pictures of evil that we picked up during the years. We can think of Him as bringing forth from the memories beautiful pictures, happy memories, and hanging them up on the walls of those cleaned rooms of the subconscious, so that the things that we see and the sounds that we hear will connect us with happy pictures from the past—and so will suggest to us spontaneous feelings of happiness. Jesus Christ can accomplish within our memories more than all the psychiatrists of all the years can do. He cannot merely reveal to us unhappy and faulty thought-habits for our correction, but He can correct them Himself! The great flood of His love will accomplish a divine miracle of redemption and of healing our personalities as He redeemed and healed Saul of Tarsus on the road from Jerusalem to Damascus (Act 9:1-7).

Yes, I am talking about receiving Jesus. But we have done this long ago, we think, or our parents have done it for us in baptism! That is true, and the act of faith accomplished by the parents does open a door to power. I know this, because I have seen that power enter through baptism into a baby supposedly dying and release a healing and even a resurrecting current of life. And I am glad that before memory I was baptised into the faith of Christ, for I know that has bound me to Him with an unbreakable chain.

But there is one trouble with being born and brought up in the church, and that is that we may not know whether we ever *of our own volition* accepted Christ or not. And if we do not really with the whole heart long for His indwelling, then, even though baptised, there are still closed doors within our subconscious minds. For though He may love us as His own when we have been baptised into Him, and He may hold us with His love and brood over us as a mother hen over her chickens (Matt. 23:37), still in His divine courtesy He does not open closed doors in us unless we ask Him to do so.

So then, you who read, I ask you—if you have never personally accepted Jesus Christ as your Lord and Savior and given yourself to Him, body and soul, conscious and subconscious, will you think of this matter with all honesty? And if you really want Him and His second current of the life of God for the forgiveness of your sins, that is, for the healing of your memories, will you with humility and deep gratitude ask Him for it? And if you feel a desire but a certain helplessness in accepting Jesus, will you go to your minister and ask him to help you in prayer that you may find this great salvation?

And to you who have accepted Him, I further say: will you go to Him again with your deepened and matured understanding and renew this acceptance and surrender, and restore to Him those bits of your personality that you have unconsciously taken back to yourselves, so that He may more completely abide in you and you in Him?

For the sake of your own joy and of the Great Joy-giver I ask you this.

7. Redemptive Suffering

that Sets Us Free

We have seen that the acceptance of Jesus Christ as Lord and Savior can work toward healing. The knowledge that He is within us, working his righteousness and wholeness, tends to relieve us of the burden of sinful and unhappy memories. The feeling of His companionship gives us hope and help, like a strong hand stretched forth to save us. And if we can have such a real vivid sense of His salvation as to forget ourselves—to lose ourselves in Him—then His life can spontaneously rush into us to heal us. There are many stories of healings coincidental with conversions: alcoholics who, after conversion had no desire to drink, invalids who releasing themselves in His love spontaneously recovered.

But there are more stories of alcoholics who had certainly been converted yet who were not healed, and of saints of God continually suffering in illness. And as a matter of fact, I myself, while converted at the age of nine and never for a moment doubting that Jesus Christ was my Lord and Savior, was yet not healed.

By my baptism and conversion I was His, and I know now, looking back, that He held me in life and sanity until one of His servants came to pray the prayer of faith for me and to teach me faith.

But the very fact of learning the laws of faith made the holy mysteries of our Lord's life something of a stumbling block to faith. His incarnation and His holy birth—that I could accept. But in view of my new-found understanding of the power of joy and hope, I could not grasp the meaning of His sufferings. In my old concept of Christianity, suffering was no problem. This earth was a vale of tears, I was a pilgrim here, it was God's will that I suffer until I died, and the sooner the better. This made the suffering of Jesus plain and clear—He wanted to share our sufferings, so He suffered too. Thus we could hug our sufferings to our bosoms and while enduring migraine headaches as a result of old hates and new fears, could tell ourselves that we were bearing our cross.

But learning faith robbed me of the old comfort of this inadequate concept of His sufferings.

When all the glory of the heavens was His, when He knew the laws of creating joy and peace, being Himself a Creator, why should He have suffered? Why did He not merely remind Himself that in the ultimate reality there is no suffering? Why did He not insulate Himself from the flesh, living so high upon a spiritual plane that no sorrow could touch Him? Why did He not abide forever in the serenity of the Buddha, smiling as He contemplated eternity? What is this Christianity that calls itself a religion yet speaks boldly of the value of suffering, which most religions tend to repudiate? How could He promise to give us peace (John 14: 27) and joy (John 15:11) and good things (Matt. 7:11) and then say, "And whosoever doth not bear his cross, and come after me, cannot be my disciple (Luke 14:27)"?

No subject has been more completely misunderstood through the centuries than this one of the sufferings of Christ. Yet the answer to it is stated in the passages to which we have just referred: we are to *bear His cross, to suffer as He suffered.* The answer to my own confusion came to me as I faced the question: what were the sufferings of Christ?

In a former chapter we told the story of a young woman who suffered heart trouble because for years she had kept herself under the tension of hate. Was this the suffering of Christ? No, and that young woman was honest enough to know it. She did not say, "This is my cross and I must bear it." She said, "This is because I hate my mother-in-law," and set herself to overcome that state of mind. Not everyone is so sensible. There is the woman who goes about with her mouth pulled down, whining and complaining and fussing and nagging until her subconscious mind, faithfully obeying her orders toward destructions, cripples her with arthritis—and who then says, "I must learn to bear my cross," thus identifying her earthly suffering with the divine suffering of the Redeemer. Surely there can be no greater blasphemy against the name of Christ than to assume that those aches and pains that result from our own unholy thinking are on a par with His holy sufferings!

Our mistake is that we do not distinguish between the two kinds of suffering, earthly and heavenly. For there are two kinds of suffering and both have value.

The suffering with which we are most familiar is the pain of illness and the grief of disharmony and failure that we have brought upon ourselves and that can be resolved by prayer and by a changed life. The value of this kind of suffering is remedial. Our own spirits cause us to suffer, so that we can see how to overcome and correct the suffering. But this is not the way that Jesus suffered. If Jesus Christ our Lord had at any time suffered from illness, which He Himself described as the binding of Satan, surely the Bible would have told us this significant fact. I cannot assume that Jesus endured illness as we do when the Bible tells us no such thing. Instead of that He Himself stated that the Prince of this world had nothing in Him (John 14:30)—no loophole for entrance that he might implant destructive thoughts within His heart—no tiniest crack in His armor of righteousness (Eph. 6:11).

The suffering of illness was not His cross! Then what was the cross of Christ? *It was an affliction visited upon Him from without and voluntarily accepted for the purpose of redemption* (John 10:15). And our greatest honor and privilege is that we are allowed to help Him in this redemptive work (I Pet. 4:13).

But in order to do so, we must first learn from that remedial suffering that the Bible calls chastisement, and which the Bible attributes to the working of God (Job 5:17). "As a man chasteneth his son, so the Lord chasteneth thee (Deut. 8:5, Ps. 94:12 & Heb. 12:6)." Certainly. How does a good father chasten his son? Continually and unreasonably, simply because He loves to see him suffer? No! He chastens his son so that his son may learn what is right and correct himself accordingly. The whole purpose of chastening is to awaken the person to repentance so that the chastening may cease, to arouse the person to a new appreciation of the power of prayer so that he may be set free from the bondage of sin.

God does not chasten us for His own pleasure (Lam. 3:33), but has so made us that *our own inner beings* bring destruction upon us if we are filled with hate and resentment, with fear and discouragement. Thus His Spirit working in our own souls chastens us, and the value of the suffering of chastisement is that we cease from the sin that brought it upon us and learn the faith and spiritual power that can set us free from it. To cling to it with a feeling that we are great saints because we are sufferers is to defeat that purpose.

But there are some illnesses, as stated in a former chapter, that are not the result of our own sins. There are the little children taken with polio or born into deformity or mental deficiency. Even these are not the sufferings of Christ. According to the literal and exact words of the Bible, He grew "in wisdom and stature and in favour with God and man (Luke 2:52)." Then if these are not the sufferings of Christ and if they are not the result of the individual's sin, where do they come from and what shall we do with them? He Himself gave us the answer to these questions. There was a certain woman who was ill, not apparently because of her own sins, but because Satan had bound her for eighteeen years (Luke 13:16). To this woman He did not say, "Thy sins be forgiven." He merely said, "Thou art loosed from thine infirmity (Luke 13:11)." Some people say of the miracles of Jesus that He began always with the forgiveness of sins. According to the Bible record, this is not true. Apparently He was able to distinguish between those diseases that were psychosomatic and those that were not. There were times when He refused to let Himself be trapped into any discussion of sin as connected with the illness, feeling the matter irrelevant. "Master, who did sin, this man or his parents, that he was born blind?" His disciples asked Him. And He replied explicitly, "Neither hath this man sinned nor his parents but that the works of God should be made manifest in him (John 9:2-3)." His general meaning is quite clear: the congenital blindness was not in this case a chastisement for sin. One may gather that He considered it part of the empire of Satan that He came to destroy, setting the blind man free as He set the infirm woman free from Satan's bonds. And the value of this to the disciples was not that they should cast carping eyes at the possible sinners but that with Him they should do the works of God in overcoming the results of Satan's hold upon this world.

From the beginning of time even until now, the agonies of this world are the will of the destroyer, not the holy will of God. "An enemy hath done this . . . (Matt. 13:28)" And from first to last, the work of Our Lord on earth, which work He commanded us to continue (John 14:12), was to bruise the serpent's head, to overcome the evil one until with the prayer of

His saints and the power of the holy angels that old serpent, the devil, should be cast out (Gen. 3:15 & Rev. 12:9).

Therefore, if we are to be His followers and to carry out His commands and to fight under His banner against the devil, the world and flesh (Service of Baptism), we must array the power of our faith against these afflictions also, even though they do not stem from our individual sins, and must do all that we can to overcome them, and in the meantime, while we travail together waiting for the manifestation of the sons of God (Rom. 8:19-23) who shall have the full power of the Spirit, we must endure them with the courage of knowing that one day they shall be no more (Rev. 21:4). And we may learn from them whatever we can learn while enduring them.

Then what are the sufferings of Christ? What are these holy sufferings that we are invited not to resist but to share and endure with Him? He undertook of His own free will a work of suffering that in some mysterious way had power to redeem us from our sins (Isaiah 53:5). C. S. Lewis has written a strange and beautiful fantasy for children, *The Lion, The Witch and the Wardrobe*. There is no word of religion written in this book, yet the plan of salvation shines forth in it. And for the childish mind he entitled his chapter on the sacrifice of the Lion "Deep Magic from the Dawn of Time". St. Paul used the word "mystery"— (I Cor. 2:7-8). The suffering endured in this great mystery was voluntary and it was redemptive.

And only those sufferings of ours that are first voluntary and secondly redemptive can we compare in any way to His cross.

He found in His sojourning among mankind that joy is not enough, that even the power of God that heals and resurrects is not enough to redeem the lower depths of man's nature. For years He walked the roads of Galilee and irradiated them with His joy and poured out His love upon the troubled and sick on every side of Him. But it was not enough. The multitude turned away from Him expecting signs and more signs, and were annoyed that He did not forever feed them with miracle bread and do their holy living for them (John 6:30-31). He trained His disciples to do missionary work among the villagers and sent them out two by two (Luke 10). But it was not enough. The very men whom He had trained retained their human faults of weakness and selfishness. James and John quarreled over the honors they expected in heavenly places (Luke 22:24-28). Peter denied Him (Luke 22:54-62). The disciples loved

Him with the conscious minds, and they did the best they could with those parts of their personalities that were open to the light, but there remained the hidden depth of the subconscious, and the channel to this hidden depth was clogged. From this submerged part of the personality, from the "heart", came weakening thought-suggestions, and the irritable sinfulness of pride and self-seeking. How could He reach the sub-conscious minds of these His friends? How could He open a door and find a way not only to their ears and their eyes but also into their inner beings?

He must have thought long upon these questions. He must have asked for guidance concerning them. And at some time in his walk upon the earth He must have remembered the greatest purpose for which He came: the purpose of releasing a flow of God's love especially ordained for the unconscious mind: or in other words, the purpose of forgiving our sins and redeeming us to everlasting life. For He not only taught the way of life but He *became* the way of life as He said that He would do (John 14:6).

Therefore when the fullness of time had come, He went into the Garden of Gethsemane and there began that great work that we call the Redemption. What did He do in that still place beneath the olive trees? What unthinkable burden did He take upon Himself so that His sweat was as it were great drops of blood falling down to the ground (Luke 22:44)? What was that cup of agony so great that even His victorious spirit shrank before it and He who had just said, "A little while, and ye shall not see me . . . but your sorrow shall be turned into joy (John 16:19-20)," now cried aloud into the shivering darkness, "O, my Father, if it be possible, let this cup pass from me (Matt. 26:39)"? What was He doing there alone in the dark?

Surely we cannot be so blind as to imagine that it was merely the fear of death that tormented Him! He had for years looked serenely upon the prospect of death. In His last discourse, knowing that He was going to die, He had spoken in radiant words about His joy (John 15:11) and of His peace (John 14:27). And so very true was this joy and peace that to this day we use these words of His as joy-giving words, binding them upon our hearts in time of trouble, that through the centuries we may feel the heavenly radiance that shone always upon Him.

Then what did He do in the Garden of Gethsemane?

He did the thing that was spoken of by the prophets of old

and that to this day we fail to believe: He made His soul an offering for sin. He bore our griefs and carried our sorrows. Yet as Isaiah said, we did esteem Him stricken, smitten of God and afflicted . . . (Isaiah 53:4)

How did He take into Himself our griefs and our sorrows, beginning His passion in the Garden of Gethsemane and there changing suddenly from a Son of God triumphant over death and serenely contemplating the coming cross, to a Son of Man suffering as no man has ever suffered before?

This holy mystery is too great for us to completely understand while we are here under the veil. But with all humility we will try to state those bits of truth that our spirits have grasped in contemplation. Some of the words that we shall use will be the old, familiar words, but since their familiarity sometimes blinds our eyes to their meaning, we will also try some new metaphors, using the words of our present day, to open the doors to a larger understanding.

In the Garden of Gethsemane, then, He broke down the partition between God and Man.

Man is spirit (or soul), conscious mind and subconscious mind. The spirit of man was in the beginning an offshoot of God's spirit—God breathed His own life into man when He distinguished him from the beasts of the field and caused him to become a living soul (II Cor. 5:17). This breath of life that God breathed into man was not the same as God Himself, as the sunlight shining into your window is not the same thing as the great sun in the heavens. Yet in another sense it is a tiny part of that same whole, being of the same essence and substance, as the sunlight is part of the sun. In that breath of life was the seed of immortality, capable of lifting man's whole being into the eternal kingdom. All who live in His joy and in His love are so abiding to a small and flickering extent. But the culmination of this heavenly abiding was intended to be such a transformation of man's mortal nature that man would be set free not only from the death of the soul but also from the death of the body. Even the body was to be transformed cell by cell into a new order of being (II Cor. 5:17), one not subject to death and no longer bound to this earth. The original intention was that man should not see death—that his body should be resurrected cell by cell from a mortal to an immortal body (John 11:25).

But the Enemy gained such victory over man that this

seed of immortality died within him, as a seed can die on hard ground when not fed and watered. Even the virtuous and good among men were no longer heirs of immortality. That was what Jesus meant when He said that even the least in the Kingdom of Heaven—the company of resurrected ones—would be greater than John the Baptist, the last prophet of the old order (Matt. 11:11).

For He came upon earth to create a new order—to change the species (Eph. 4:24)—to give to those who received Him the power to become the Sons of God (John 1:12). In order to do this, He had to reach the subconscious mind, or the heart, of every human being. For the barrier between God and man was in the heart. The imaginaton of man's heart had over the slow centuries again become incrusted with evil thinking, as in the days of Noah . . . covered with the darkness of pain and with the continual death of creatures not made to die. Man had become too densely veiled in flesh. The body and the brain had enmeshed and smothered him so that the spirit, wherein only he could know God, was well-nigh extinct.

There is a pathway between spirit and heart or subconscious. But this pathway was twisted and tortured and warped by long denial of God's words and long blindness to God's light. The channel from spirit to subconscious was like a canal choked by gathered sand and silt. Only a miracle could cleanse and open these channels. Thus Jesus Christ went into the Garden of Gethsemane and there began to accomplish this miracle that was completed on Calvary. He made a way for the forgiveness of sins of all people *in all times* for they were all visible and perceptible to Him, from the first man, naked and innocent in his garden, to the last man who shall be snatched out of the hand of the enemy.

He could not do this from outside of man. True, He had made Himself part of the human race by His birth upon this planet. But in order to redeem the human race it was necessary to sink deeper into humanity: to become part of the subconscious mind of every man. We cannot fully comprehend how He could do this, although a tiny bit of the way should be known to us, for in a smaller sense we become a part of those we love. Even we, by love, tune our minds and open our hearts to the griefs and sorrows, the sin and pain and death of those we love.

This Jesus Christ did with every one of us in the Garden of Gethsemane. Hitherto He had turned His heart always toward

God. He had gone to the mountain-top to forget man and be alone with God. He had worshipped in the synagogue to be with man and yet lift His heart into God's light. He had lived in the Father and the Father in Him at all times (John 14:10). In the Garden of Gethsemane He reversed this process. He tuned His heart to the feelings of the heart of mankind. He turned away from God's light and let his spirit sink into man's darkness. Thus He lived, not in God, but for the first time, in man . . . completely in man . . . submerged in man, so that He too seemed for the time being shut off from God. All the griefs and the sorrows of mankind rolled in upon Him, and He permitted that they should do so. No wonder that the sweat of His body was as great drops of blood falling to the ground (Luke 22:44). Surely the death that ended on Calvary began in Him now. Surely He let it come to Him voluntarily by this way that He opened, this blocked channel that He unblocked. Thus He died so that men would not have to die. Simple souls have grasped this fact. "Ain't goin' to die no mo' ", His black people sing in a spiritual that is most truly of the Spirit. But the simple souls have not been able to explain it. And some of us unfortunates who must reason have not believed it, but have weakened it down to mean only that He suffered so that we should also suffer; that He died and went to heaven so that we could go to heaven when we die. And this is a most inadequate expression of a small part of a great mystery.

Jesus Christ opened the channel between the subconscious and the spirit. He forged into that clogged channel like a dredger, drawing out the dirt from the channel, taking it into itself, then casting it away upon the shore. Thus He cleansed, beating His way into man with the force of a terrible love, taking the dirt from the mass subconscious of the race into Himself, then throwing it away upon the shore of God's Being, where the fire of God's Spirit devoured it.

But as no ship is forced to enter a channel just because the channel is cleansed, so no human being is forced to enter into this redemption of Jesus Christ. Jesus Christ, the second Person of the Trinity, gave Himself to man that He might draw man into Himself—but He waits that man shall give himself to Him—He does not force him.

How shall man receive this great redemption? Jesus Christ Himself has ordained a way—a way plain and simple. This way need not require the full comprehension of the reasoning mind. Indeed, these things are both beneath and above the under-standing. They are beneath, working a hidden alchemy in the heart like yeast in a loaf of bread—working a strange trans-formation even in the cells of the body, increasing in them the impulse of life which shall eventually resurrect them into the type of cell containing the seeds of immortality. They are also above the conscious mind, working in the spirit, to restore sight to the spiritual eye, to lift the wings of the spirit into the height of contemplation, so that the inner being shall once more behold the glory of the Father. Therefore, the way of abiding in Him so that He may abide in us requires more than a mental grasp of these transcending truths. It requires smaller and yet greater things: sacrifice—a giving of ourselves to Him as He gave Himself to us—a complete willingness to do His will and an earnest desire to be cleansed by His redeeming love. Secondly, it requires also that we state our need of His forgiveness and cleansing (Lev. 5:5, 26:40 & Num. 5:7). And that we may do this with complete surrender, we are advised to confess our sins in the presence of a human being (Jas. 5:16). This ensures the reality of our confession, it guards us against self-deception and it gives us a spiritual helper to speak for us the word of faith which is the word of power: "Go in peace. God has forgiven all your sins."

I do not say that every living person must have an inter-mediary. There may be those who have no need of anyone to help them in this great work of being forgiven. But there are also those who do have such a need, and do not recognize it. By their fruits we shall know them (Matt. 7:20). If a man does not attain health through prayer and refuses help through the laying on of hands, we conclude that he has not used all the resources available to him. Similarly if a man refuses to open his heart to anyone and to ask any to pray for his forgiveness, and continues to live in frustration and sorrow, in unrest and sickness, then he probably needs a confessor. And it is quite possible that the humbling of himself to accept the ministrations of a human chan-nel might set him free.

The old enemy is pride. It is very hard for us to see our-selves as Jesus Christ sees us when He enters into the heart. It is also hard for us to see ourselves as He sees us when He enters into our spirits and looks ahead through time to the glory that can be revealed in us.

Through what we call time . . . let us bend our minds once

more upon this great mystery: He lives in all of what we call time. Jesus Christ, the same yesterday, today and forever (Heb. 13:8). He lives in what we call two thousand years. That which is past to us is not past to Him. Somewhere in those dark ages HE LIVES. Therefore somewhere in what we call time, the redemptive act of Gethsemane *is still going on.* True, His present living consciousness exists in His glorified body at the right hand of the Father where He pours out His life to us through His Holy Spirit (John 14:16-21). But also, somewhere in time the act of Gethsemane is still going on. When we come to Him in sorrow and in contrition, when we let our hearts brood upon His redemption and ask for the cleansing power of His love, we once more touch that particular flow of His love that went forth to us from Gethsemane. But when we go to His altar too carelessly, we fail to discern the body of Christ (I Cor. 11:29) and our connection with Him is faulty. A faulty connection with electricity can be dangerous. Broken connections and loose wiring can cause disaster. The flow of His life to us is a high-powered energy. A careless gesture of receiving that life may wound both our hearts and His. Not only in Gethsemane was the heart of His human being broken for us. Not only in Gethsemane did He bear our sins and carry our sorrows.

We cannot comprehend His living both in time and in eternity at once. But so He lives . . . both in time and beyond time. Before Abraham was, HE IS. In that eternal living, beyond time, the glory of the Father floods His spirit and His joy is full. There is another living, within time, which He took upon Himself in two gardens: in the Garden of Eden wherein He first contemplated wounding the serpent's head and in the Garden of Gethsemane where He delivered that fatal wound by becoming part of evil that He might destroy evil. In that human living, His heart is ever open to our sorrows, ever hurt by our neglect and ingratitude, ever laboring under our sins. When will we set Him free so that His kingdom may be established and His glory may cover the earth as the waters cover the sea?

We can set Him free not only by coming to Him ourselves that He may fulfill in us His perfect will of holiness and wholeness, but also by helping to convey His forgiveness to others. *This is helping Him carry His cross.* He took the cross of His own will, knowing that He would do this labor of love, knowing it before coming into this world (Luke 11:50 & Rev. 13:8). It was a voluntary sacrifice for the purpose of conveying the love of God to mankind. *And every voluntary sacrifice that we make for the purpose of conveying God's love to mankind is helping Him to carry His cross.* Involuntary suffering that we endure as a result of our own sins, our own mishandling of His laws of soul and body, these things have a remedial value for us, but no redemptive value for others. There is no redemptive value in our catching a cold because we have carelessly got ourselves chilled or because we have made our bodies sluggish with too much artificial food or because we have put ourselves under nervous tension by irritability or worry. There is not even any redemptive value in our picking up a symptom from someone for whom we have prayed. This is merely an involuntary over-identification with the patient and an under-identification with Him. If this happens let us not dare to think, "I am suffering as Jesus did on the cross." We are suffering from our weakness, our inadequate protection, our insufficient faith. Only He is great enough and good enough to die on the cross for mankind—we are not. He did not ask us to do so, nor did He suggest that we try to drink of the cup that He drank of in Gethsemane (Matt. 20:22). He asked us only to help lead others to Gethsemane. To think that we can actually take part in the redemptive act ourselves is presumptuous. We can, by "prayer and fasting" connect others with the flow of His redemptive love, but we cannot ourselves be redeemers. Moreover, if we could do so, it would negate the value of His self-offering for us. Why should He suffer for us except to set us free from the suffering that our sins would otherwise demand of us? He set us free that we might work in His service, true, but not that we might turn back to death when He has given us life.

His heart must be broken still when He hears us say, "Why should I pray to be set free from sickness and pain when Jesus died on the cross for me." We should pray to be set free from sickness and pain *because* Jesus died on the cross for us. Sickness and pain are part of the kingdom of Satan that He came to overthrow. They are brought into this world by sin, and they are the wages of sin, whether our own sins or the sins of the race. If we give up the fight against sickness and pain, we are disarming ourselves for the battle against the world, the flesh and the devil which we have promised to carry on under His banner. The more we attain wholeness the more we can be used as His helpers in redeeming others—and there is room in that service for as much suffering as we are willing to endure. This is holy suffering: sacrifice, the offering of ourselves, as Albert Schweitzer did when he gave up the life of fame and glory that might have been his and went to Africa, as St. Paul did when he relinquished family wealth and endured for Our Lord stripes and imprisonment and stoning and finally death. Thus St. Paul knew the fellowship of His sufferings (Phil 3:10) and thus we can know this joyous fellowship—for there is a strange joy in thus suffering with Him. There is no fellowship with Him in having a virus, for He never had a virus. The Holy Book is devastatingly honest and we may be sure that it gives us a fair picture of Him. Can we imagine His saying, "Oh rejoice in me, my child, for so I suffered—I was weak and fearful and careless and mean and irritable and so I got sick too—" St. Paul glorified in the very weakness that persecution had brought upon his body (II Cor. 11:23-30), for if the thorn in his flesh was a physical weakness, it certainly stemmed from the wounds and injuries that he had sustained in Christ's service and not from the reasons that give us a virus!

There are no St. Pauls today—true. But there is Bishop Gordon, flying his own plane over the frozen wastes of the far north to take the word of the freedom of Christ to the Eskimos. There is Corrie Ten Boom, turning her persecution in a prison camp into a work of forgiveness for her persecutors. And there are smaller people who train themselves to make the difficult choice of service instead of pleasure, of sacrifice instead of indulgence. As a friend wrote me on expressing thanks for a recovery, "I rejoice that I am set free from the suffering of illness so that I can suffer more constructively for His sake."

The more we overcome the flesh and offer ourselves as channels for His spirit, the more effectively we can be used as His helpers in redeeming others.

"But do you not believe that perhaps we can best serve Him in illness?" some people ask me.

No, I do not. Jesus did not. St. Paul did not. Whatever his thorn may have been (and life had wounded him with many thorns) he certainly was not an invalid (II Cor. 11:23-28). Job did not. He is the Bible's one and only example of a sick man, but he sat among the ashes (Job. 2:8 & Job 42:12-17) as a worthless outcast until he was healed, whereupon he became a holy well man. I cannot find a single example in the Bible of one to whom God said or to whom Jesus Christ said, "No, you can serve me best in sickness." Nor can I find in present-day life a single case in which the sick person could not have done an even more effective and victorious work by overcoming the sickness than by enduring it. In some cases, true, the trouble is so severe that we do not overcome it in this life. If those cases lead to overcoming it in another life, well and good. If they lead to remaining in this world and doing the best we can under our limitations that is a good second-best, but it is still not the completeness of power that Jesus came to give us.

Not only can we do more physical work when well, but also we can pray with more power the prayer of redemptive love. Ancient rules of sacrifice typify this fact. Even an animal offered for sacrifice was required to be without spot or blemish (Ex. 12:5). A diseased creature was not worthy to be offered on His altar. Redemptive prayer requires tremendous stamina of body as well as of spirit, and a weak or sickly person should not try to undertake it.

What is redemptive prayer? It is the final step in carrying the cross of Christ. His sacrifice of leaving the glory of the Father to be born into this world was His first step in redemption. His relinquishment of easy ways to power and His enduring of hardship and weariness in the service of others was his second step. The carrying of the cross up that dark hill was His last step toward the actual work of redemption. And after we have offered our time and our energy and our money toward the carrying of His gospel into dark lands and the carrying of His healing and forgiving power into dark souls, we can, if spiritually strong enough, undertake also a redemptive work of prayer. He called that type of prayer "prayer and fasting (Matt. 17:21)." The church calls it reparation. We will consider that prayer-work in the next chapter. But before we venture to consider it, let us get quite clear in our minds this distinction between remedial and redemptive suffering.

Any sacrifice that we voluntarily make for His name's sake has a bit of redemptive value. That value is increased if we undertake this service with joy. Even going to church to worship Him whether one feels like it or not, has prayer-value if offered to Him with joyful heart. To be sick and die in the service of humanity as did those doctors who permitted themselves to be bitten by mosquitoes carrying yellow fever so that they could save others from having yellow fever—that has redemptive value. To lose a leg in saving a comrade from a bomb explosion

—that has redemptive value, if it is offered to Him with a joyous heart and not endured grudgingly and with complaint. To live triumphantly above an accident of birth, as Helen Keller has done—that has redemptive value.

But to suffer from migraine headaches and say, "I am a great sufferer, but of course Jesus carried His cross and so must I" (with a sigh and fluttering eyelashes as though to say "What a saint I am!") this is offering Him, in reality, our failure to carry His cross. Migraine headaches result from unwise living or from unhealed memories or from worry or from disharmony in the home. It is our bounden duty to find out the cause of this failure, to walk in wholeness and to be transformed by the renewing of our minds (Rom. 12:2). A migraine headache is not divine, redemptive suffering and is not in any way comparable to the holy passion of Christ. It is human, earthly suffering. It has a value, true, but its value is remedial. It is the chastening of the Lord, or, in more modern words, it is the striving of our own inner spirits to tell us that something in our lives or in our bodies or in our circumstances should be healed or forgiven. The way in which we receive its remedial value is to *accept the remedy* . . . to correct the original mistakes and then to grow in grace and in faith until we no longer have migraine headaches.

Jesus went to Gethsemane for us and bore our sufferings in His own body on the tree. Shall we make His most loving sacrifice an excuse for spiritual laziness and a supine surrender to the enemy? God forbid! Rather let us work to overcome the small, earthly sufferings that come from Satan that we may undertake with Him the joyful sacrifice of a wholesome life given to others in His service.

8. The Current of God's
Love on Calvary

A comprehension of the values and purposes of suffering, both remedial and redemptive, helped me to receive an increase of healing power. But yet another stumbling block stood between me and the abundant life that Jesus came to give: my own inadequate concept of the reason for the crucifixion. Granted that there is redemptive suffering, would a loving Father wish that suffering upon His Son because He was angry with someone else? "In His mercy He gave His only begotten Son—" even now I have to make a quick leap of the understanding to grasp the meaning of those words, so that they may give to me faith instead of doubt! Even now I must remind myself that God is one and indivisible, doing His work of creation and redemption in three different manifestations of His own being. God, then, incarnated one manifestation of *His Own Being* to die on the cross for us. If I may be forgiven for using childish words to answer my own childish misconceptions: God Himself in human form died for us—He did not send someone else to do it for Him. And God Himself, incarnated in Jesus Christ, went on from the Garden of Gethsemane and accomplished the giving of His life upon the cross for definite reasons over and above the purpose of death. Death might have come to Him from strain and suffering even if He had remained in the garden.

An average man could live about twenty-four hours on a cross. Jesus was stronger by far than the average man. If the cross alone had killed Him, surely He would have hung there for forty-eight hours rather than for twenty-four. On the contrary, we find from the Bible records that He was on the cross only six hours (Mark 15:25) (Matt. 27:45-51). Moreover, we are told that when the centurion pierced His side with the sword there came forth blood and water (John 19:34) which to the centurion meant that He was already dead . . . the heart was already broken. He was slain not only *for* our iniquities, but *by* our iniquities.

If this was so, why did He not stay in the garden among His disciples instead of being made a public spectacle? The first reason is obvious: if He had stayed in the garden, no one would have believed that He had really died. They would have said from that first Easter day even through the history of this fading planet that He had merely been unconscious and had aroused again to life. It was, therefore, necessary for His death to be known so that His resurrection from the dead might be believed.

But surely this was not the only reason for a deed so black that the heavens dared not to look upon it and darkness covered the earth from the sixth to the ninth hour! Surely God could have found some other way to teach us, so that this cup might have passed from Him! Of course there were other reasons. But these reasons go so deep into the unplumbed depths of our fallen natures and so high into the spiritual realm that we cannot conceive of them. We have sung of these reasons for years— "There is plentiful redemption in the blood that has been shed, there is joy for all the members in the sorrows of the Head . . ." ". . . We take our sins to Jesus, the spotless Lamb of God, He bears them all and frees us from the accursed load . . ."[1] But have we the least idea what we are talking about, or are we thinking vaguely of some heavenly bookkeeping in which our debts are automatically transferred by St. Peter into the Book of Life? Whatever Jesus did, it is not a matter of transfer taking place in some other sphere of life and at some vague time in the future. It takes place here and now in us, in both our souls and our bodies. This transfer of His life into us extends beyond death, as all of our present spiritual growth extends beyond death. But the beginning of this inner healing is now (Eph. 5:8 & I Thess. 3:8 & I Tim. 4:8 & I John 3:2). And the change in us can be felt and known by joy (Acts 16:34 - 13:52 - 8:8 & Rom. 15:13 & Gal. 5:22 & I Pet. 1:8).

There is another aspect of the mysterious interplay of spiritual cause and effect that took Him to Calvary. The sins of mankind

---

[1] *The Hymnal*

had become His. Being His, His own spirit was grieved and horrified by them, and this spiritual condemnation of evil carried to the subconscious the command toward death. "The wages of sin is death (Rom. 6:23)." The three-fold mechanism of man is so made that when sin enters and fouls the inner personality, the spirit cannot endure to abide therein and cries aloud to be set free. Therefore, the subconscious loses its grip on life, obeying the order of the spirit toward the dissolution of the body, so that the spirit can escape to its own place. Inherent in this cry of the spirit is the unshakable principle of justice, as much a part of God's nature as is the principle of mercy. The spirit, being made in the holiness of God, demands that wickedness shall be destroyed so that His holiness may remain unsullied. Thus on the spirit of the Son of Man who at that time made Himself not only completely man but also mankind, there was an urge toward a death justly deserved by the sins of mankind.

So complete was His immersion in the sins of mankind that He actually felt that God had forsaken Him. He cried out, "My God, my God, why hast thou forsaken me (Matt. 27:46)," quoting indeed from the Psalms (Ps. 22:1) but identifying his own feeling with that of the psalmist. At that moment the crisis passed. The at-one-ment had been made with the very last soul who lived or who had lived or who was to live. The spirit of Jesus Christ was satisfied. And the spirit of the Father abiding in Jesus Christ looked upon these things and was satisfied (Isa. 53:11).

Thus the cloud departed from his spiritual eyes and once more He saw and knew the Father. He was free to return to the Father and to begin with joy and gladness the culminating act of His work for mankind—the resurrection and the sharing of His resurrected life with those whom He had redeemed. Therefore, He directed His spirit to return into the hands of God— "Father, into thy hands I commend my spirit (Luke 23:46)."

With what joy He must have returned to His heavenly home! The joy of His coming into life at Christmas time had brought heaven so near to earth that man could hear the angels singing. But when He returned, having won the final victory over the power of the enemy, the excitement in the heavens wrought such a burst of glory that the eyes of men could not look upon it, and darkness covered the earth (Matt. 27:45). The gathered thought currents of humanity from the beginning to the end of time were shaken and changed, as His redemptive love entered into them.

The mass-mind of humanity was pierced to the very depths. No wonder there was a great earthquake and the veil of the temple was rent (Matt. 27:51). One can imagine His angels rending it! No wonder the graves were opened and the bodies of the saints wandered about the city and appeared to many (Matt. 27:52). The principle of resurrection took tremendous hold on men at that time, for although the resurrection had not yet taken place, the seed of immortality had been replanted in humanity. This was true although the fact and the method of resurrection were yet to appear. So overwhelming was this urge toward the achieving of a resurrected body that among the souls of the departed was a great unrest—a feverish activity—a heave of life toward Life—toward the culminating event of man's progress through the seven heavens to the Great White Throne. Did those who arose from the tomb succeed at that time in achieving the kind of body in which Jesus Christ later appeared to His beloved ones? We do not know. If any of those attaining to the first resurrection (Rev. 20:6) were among us now, would we perceive them? Would love draw them toward us or would fear keep them away from us? Only to those who loved Him could He appear when his own resurrected body was set free from the tomb . . .

These are strange things and hard to believe. Yet why should they not have taken place, when all the long night through His spirit and soul and heart and body were deeply involved in this work of redemption?

"It is enough," He said to His disciples as they slept in the garden after He had asked them to watch with Him one hour (Mark 14:41). What was enough? He had asked them to watch with Him—to watch in prayer—to pray with Him; as we might say, to hold Him up in prayer for one hour. (How it touches our hearts to know that He wanted His friends to help Him in this dark hour!) But they could not hold their intense spiritual concentration for one hour. They did not know what He was doing, but they sensed His straining spirit and felt as much of the world's sorrow as they were able to feel. The power of evil was too much for them and they slept for sorrow (Luke 22:45). But they had helped Him as much as they could help Him, and in His divine courtesy He did not upbraid them for failing to watch the hour through, but said, "It is enough."

From that time forth He carried the load Himself. But all night long as His captors dragged Him here and there, His spirit was struggling with the souls of men, and in His deep involvement with this work He had no mind to answer Pilate when he asked, "What is truth (John 18:38)?" Pilate was a well-meaning man, only weak, and so he washed his hands of Jesus (Matt. 27:24), unable to stand against the pressure of the crowd. He conformed to the pattern of this world. How many others, well-meaning but weak, have washed their hands of Him! And how many even of those who have accepted Him through the water of baptism, have failed to discern His body and to receive the fullness of the inner healing that He gave to them on that dark night!

How can we receive the fullness of His redemption? Let us turn our minds away from Him now, back to ourselves, and consider this.

Let us cease contemplating the heavenly results of what Jesus did for us on Calvary and consider the immediate and present benefit to us in His sacrifice. Let us try to express His salvation in the words of modern psychology instead of the old Biblical words and so bring the matter into sharp focus. My words may not be precisely the words that the Holy Spirit would use to you, so as you read, pray that the Spirit will retranslate this for you in whatever words you best understand. My words are merely my own attempt to comprehend the crucifixion as a present and immediate necessity and not as a matter of heavenly bookkeeping . . . as a transfer that is real and takes place now, not a judicial transfer of guilt at the gate of heaven.

First of all, what does the Bible tell us about the practical and immediate value of the crucifixion? "But now in Christ Jesus ye who sometimes were far off are made nigh by the blood of Christ (Eph. 2:13)." "For if the blood of bulls and of goats, and the ashes of an heifer sprinkling the unclean, sanctifieth to the purifying of the flesh, how much more shall the blood of Christ, who through the eternal Spirit offered himself without spot to God, purge your conscience from dead works to serve the living God (Heb. 9:13-14)?" "Forasmuch as ye know that ye were not redeemed with corruptible things, as silver and gold from your vain conversation received by tradition from your fathers, but with the precious blood of Christ, as of a lamb without blemish and without spot, who verily was foreordained before the foundation of the world (I Pet. 1:18-20)."

Is it medieval, savage, primitive, unscientific and at best out of date to talk of the blood of Christ? Or do we dare to bend our minds to this matter and see whether it makes any sense in the light of our modern science?

The blood of Christ: the life of His body, made perfect through suffering (Heb. 2:10); the literal essence of His Being, instinct with His own love and energy. We read books about the robe that was His and the feeling of His love and life that emanated from it: about the silver chalice from which He drank, still radiating His life. We may think of these books as fantasies, but there is something in us that recognizes and loves them. We read in the history of the church of holy objects that seem to convey a spiritual power. The more simple among us believe that a cross that has been blessed upon the altar gives us a feeling of the peace of God, or even that a certain shrine or holy place is filled with His presence (I Kings 8:10-11). In this, as in many other matters, the child-like in heart are shown in the end to be more scientifically accurate than are the more sophisticated. Science, in its present understanding of the reality of thoughts and of the actual presence of a power of thought, is coming nearer to the truth that the Bible states quite boldly: that there is an *actual power* in the blood of Jesus Christ.

Why not? If we toy with the idea of a power emanating from His robe, if we look with tolerance upon the thought of His chalice as somehow being filled with His presence, then why should not His blood be filled with a life-energy?

Again, science tells us that matter is indestructible . . . also, that matter is energy, itself being vibrant with an invisible motion.

Then what is the blood of Christ? It is His life, the very essence of His being, nearer to Him than His robe or His chalice, and instinct with His power and His love. It is indestructible. This moving energy was at first encompassed in the visible flow of blood and water. Very soon the water evaporated and became an invisible vapor, as water becomes, but an invisible vapor vibrant with His life. Very soon the clotted blood dried into dust, and was disseminated by the wind and mingled with all life so that it could be no longer seen. But the life in that blood is indestructible and still remains, an invisible current of an heavenly energy, and ACTUAL energy, a PERCEPTIBLE energy, and EFFECTIVE energy. Why not? We cannot see the wind, but we know when it blows for we perceive its effects—we see the things that it does. We cannot see electricity but not one of us would doubt that it is real, for we see and know the things that it does. We cannot see the force of gravity, but we could not walk a step without its energy. God sends His love to us through wind and electricity, through sunshine and rain, through the love of friends and family. But since none of these can enter the closed rooms of the subconscious, God came nearer to us in the person of His Son, who lived our human life for us, took all of our sins and sorrows into Himself and gave back to us our own human life purified by His holy thinking, sanctified by His holy feeling. He gave it back on Calvary in a direct and effective current of redemptive power that emanated from His very Being and was won at the cost of His life: the Blood of Christ.

That heavenly energy still remains in the air that we breathe, a direct and particular current of the love of God, a love within a love, a life within a life. It does not supplant the universal love of God that witnesses always to Him, filling our hearts with food and gladness (Acts 14:17). It exists within that love and acts in harmony with that love, supplying to our needs what that universal love of the Father is too diffuse and too impersonal to supply: the healing of the memories—the freeing of the sub-conscious mind—the integrating of the personality—the bringing forth of the creative energies—all those things that we madly seek, running up and down the earth to psychiatrists and hospitals and rest homes. In the words of the Bible, the direct current of the love of God that is in the life of Christ given for us ac-complishes for us the *forgiveness of sins.*

Therefore He was crucified, dead and buried.

Now this being so, why do we still walk in frustration and in the chains of fear?

Because, strange and pathetic creatures that we are, the miracle of the forgiveness of sins is so overwhelming that we still cannot accept it. When the price of a redeemed life becomes too great, we evade the issue by ignoring the present results of forgiveness, considering only the effects of it in the next life and debasing the whole matter to a bargain between man and God. This bargain, we vaguely feel, is made on earth between man and the Church, by certain acts and rituals and then is ratified at the gates of heaven, presumably by St. Peter. So a man can buy or win on earth a contract for eternal life and then can live comfortably in his sins, or shall we say, in his straightened personality.

But Jesus promised much more than this! He said that His heavenly alchemy would so transform the inner being that we should be born again (John 3:3).

He said that the refreshing and life-giving energy that He would give to man would be a well of water springing up into everlasting life, so that he who drank of this living water would never thirst again (John 4:10-15).

And what would be the signs of this transforming of the personality that He came into the world to give us? We would be filled with His joy (John 16:22). We would outgrow even the tendency to sin as the Holy Spirit, the Comforter, filled our spirits more and more with His light (John 3:6). And we would have the power to overcome Satan himself, to speak with heavenly inspiration, to have dominion over any dangerous enemy, to throw off sickness and poison, and to lay hands on the sick that they should recover (Mark 16:17-18).

We are, however, just beginning to believe this. With faltering footsteps we come a few steps closer to the great Redeemer of our souls and then back away again. And Sunday after Sunday His matchless offering of Himself is given us for the complete transformation of any hampering tendency that may be in us, for the complete healing of the hidden causes of all our fears and nervous tensions, yet we fail to accept it fully. We simply do not believe that it will do for us the things that Jesus promised. For He said that His life incarnated invisibly in the bread and the wine as it was incarnated visibly in the flesh, would make us part of His very personality (John 6:56-57). His stream of life given to us on Calvary would penetrate the subconscious mind and there accomplish a heavenly transfer, giving us actually the personality tendencies that are His. His life so entering would free us from any inherited weaknesses and tendencies to failure, from all the trauma inflicted on us by life, from all the obsessions and the nervous tensions and the fears and neuroses and psychoses fastened upon us by a sense of guilt. And as this glory of His joy filled the deep mind, the eternal light of the Father (I John 1:5) would so invade our hearts that we would walk as children of light and there would be in us no darkness at all (Eph. 5:8). We would be born again (John 3:3).

But we do not believe this. We do not expect any such transformation when we come to Him at the Communion Service, and so we go away still carrying the burden of our sins, or at least the earthly part of it. Perhaps we expect the final result of this transformation which is eternal life (John 4:14). But the immediate and present result we certainly do not expect, and therefore, we do not receive.

How can we receive more of this forgiveness for which He was crucified, dead and buried?

By enlarging our expectancy. And by being definite, precise and exact about what we expect. If we have already asked Christ to come into our hearts and to be born there and have already given ourselves to Him in His service, then the door to the subconscious is open to His redeeming power. Our next step is to hold up into the light of His love the exact things that need to be changed in us, to ask Him to make that change that He called a rebirth, and to expect Him to do so. In the words of the Bible, we *confess our sins.* And as we do so, He is faithful and just to forgive us our sins and to *cleanse us from all unrighteousness* (I John 1:9). He can break every unrighteous thought-habit in the subconscious mind, as one might break the links of a chain. He can wipe away every unclean or unhealthy emotional tendency as one might wipe away the writing on a blackboard. He can make the memories of our lifetime wholesome, so that the subconscious can store them away in peace and leave us free. Thus our expectancy of trouble will be changed to an expectancy of good, our inferiority complexes will melt into a knowledge of our power through Him, our bad tempers will mellow and change to kindness. And as this shift takes place in the subconscious mind, the bodily forces will work more freely toward health.

But though this great work of His is the free gift of God through Jesus Christ, He will not give it to us unless we ask for it. Therefore we are commanded to confess—to bring to His attention as accurately as we can, those things that are wrong in us. One way to do this is to go back through our lives and remember as far as possible those things that we have done and thought and said that have stored trouble and confusion in the subconscious mind—or as the Bible would say, our sins. And as we remember each one, we ask Him to take away from us all its ramifications in the personality, all its thought-habits and emotional connections and leave us free. And finally we *accept* this tremendous thing: we build in our minds a concept of ourselves as we will be when it is accomplished and we give thanks for it.

It will simplify our efforts toward doing this spiritual psychoanalysis if we will take it step by step, perhaps considering one sinful tendency each Sunday or perhaps going back one year in our lives each Sunday and making that the subject of our prayers and of our Communion preparation. And as mentioned in a previous chapter, it will strengthen our acceptance if we can find a priest or counsellor who has the faith to act as a true confessor to us. We read in our Prayer Book, in the warning and exhortation that the priest is commanded to read to his people from time to time, the following words: "If there be any among you who . . . cannot quiet his own conscience . . . let him come to me or to some other minister of God's word and open his grief . . ."

Tragically enough, there are some ministers too busy raising money and holding committee meetings to pay much attention to a person if he does come. Even more tragically, there are some ministers who do not understand their power and authority to forgive sins in the name of Jesus Christ and who fall back on weak platitudes that are empty consolation, merely stating that the troubled one is not a sinner when that one's own subconscious mind feels that one is a sinner.

However, if we do not have a minister or a friend who can help us and therefore must go directly to Jesus Himself, making the tremendous effort of not only seeing our sins, but also seeing ourselves walking in the light of His forgiveness, we may be stronger in the long run because of the intensity of our effort.

This concept of forgiveness does not in any way contradict our former concepts of the redemption. It only complements them. Surely and certainly God does not impute to us iniquity when we call upon the name of Christ in faith, but imputes that faith to us for righteousness (Rom. 4:23-24). But why? Because He makes us *righteous!* He does not deny Himself and say that we are good when we are bad! The redeeming love of Christ *makes* us good! The doors of Heaven do not stand open day and night that everybody, good, bad and indifferent, may troop into them! "For without are dogs, and sorcerers, and whoremongers, and murderers (Rev. 22:15)." According to that unequivocal statement, He does not impute righteousness to those who persist in lying and stealing and murdering and living in sexual immorality. Time would fail me to enumerate the Bible passages that tell us that the wages of sin is death but the gift of God is eternal life through Jesus Christ our Lord (Rom. 6:23). But does that mean that He says to us, "Go on sinning, little children, it is all right for I will see that you get to heaven just the same."? On the contrary, He has given us a most strict and rigorous way of life that we must live in order to attain eternity, and it ends with the tremendous words "Be ye therefore perfect, even as your Father which is in heaven is perfect (Matt. 5:48)." This is so high an ideal that St. Paul himself said that he did not know whether he had as yet attained it, but he was struggling toward the high calling of God in Jesus Christ (Phil. 3:10-15).

How can we reconcile these two things? God wants us to be good, but He forgives us through His Son if we are not.

If we remember our first premise, that we believe in God as a Creator, then it is not at all difficult. Suppose you were a poet and you said to one poem, "You are not good. Your meter is terrible, your rhyme is inaccurate, your rhythm is out of kilter. But I am indulgent to you, therefore I will put you in my book just the same." What a careless artist you would be!

If you really loved the poem, as God really loves us, seeing in it infinite possibilities, you would make every effort to correct it—and *then* you would put it in your book, but not before.

God is not a careless artist. His creation cries aloud to us of His passion for perfection, His irresistible urge toward beauty.

Suppose you were a business man and you said to your account book, "You are not a well-kept book at all. Things that belong here are omitted and sums that do not belong here are added in. Everything is incorrect. But I am merciful and therefore I will hand you in to the Boss just the same."

God is not a careless Workman. He is a good workman: one who produces good works, one who is satisfied with nothing less than perfection.

Then how can we placidly assume that forgiveness means the denying of the very character of God? How can we claim that God changes to a careless Creator without integrity or intelligence because Jesus died on the cross? How can we smugly tell ourselves that since Jesus took our sins upon Himself, therefore God now tolerates evil and permits it to come into His heaven? Shall we crucify Him again by failing to apprehend the great thing for which He was crucified, dead and buried? For He died to make us good, as we sing in our hymns.[1] He died not to excuse us for being bad, not to soften the heart of God so that God would forget His delight in perfection and permit small shoddy souls to enter eternity and confuse and confound it as this world is confused and confounded, but He died that we might be healed of the very things that hold us to sin—that we might be changed into the image of His glory—that we might become the sons of God (Rom. 8:14).

The full meaning of forgiveness then is not extenuating or

---

[1] "There is a Green Hill Far Away,"—The Hymnal.

condoning, ignoring or tolerating sin but *removing* it and transplanting the holiness of God in the place where it had been.

Narrow is the way which leadeth to life (Matt. 7:14). It took the very life of Jesus Christ to provide for us a current of God's love deep and human and powerful enough to enter the subconscious and there wipe away the results of wrong thinking. And it often takes our efforts one for another to receive this deep current of the love of God. We need not only to accept it for ourselves and to incorporate it into our own lives, but we need also to try in every way we can to pass it on to others, that we may help Our Lord in this work of redemption, that we may help to carry His cross.

This is a tremendous subject, and we have touched on it in the chapter on the forgiveness of sins. But that we may again at this time turn our thoughts toward it, I will try to pass on to you the way in which the matter first began to come clear to me in my own prayer life.

As so often happens, understanding came to me through praying for someone else. I have learned ten times as much from praying for others as I have ever learned from praying for myself or for my own. Perhaps one of the reasons why some people learn so little is that they blind their eyes by holding themselves up in front of them so closely.

I was praying for a dear lady who had been driven out of Germany because of her Jewish ancestry, and who had suffered a great deal in the years before her escape. She had overcome these sufferings in a most wonderful way. She had forgiven her persecutors and her tormenters and had gained stature thereby. She had learned the laws of prayer and had healed or helped many through her intercessions. But in spite of this, there was a sorrow in her mind that no prayers could lift. She would fall into unaccountable depressions and the thought of suicide would sit upon the doorstep of her mind and look at her with baleful eyes. More alarming than this to one who was essentially kind and loving, she would become possessed by a deep and brooding anger, and when in those moods she would have strange impulses to hurt the very ones she loved. We prayed together about this inner trouble in every way that I then knew, and none of these prayers availed.

Jesus said that when we ask and do not receive, we should not continue forever blindly asking, but we *seek* (Matt. 7:7). I began to seek a way of prayer that would be triumphant for this woman.

And a way of prayer was revealed to me. At first I rejected it, it seemed so contrary to the ways that I had known. But finally I tried in thinking, "I will never know until I try it whether there is any truth in this or not."

This was the concept that came to me: there was nothing wrong with this great-hearted woman of today. Her conscious personality was beyond reproach and needed no forgiveness. The trouble came from the subconscious. In simple words I thought, "It is the little girl inside of her, still not comforted, who acts like that. That little girl could not throw stones at those who threw stones at her. She was only one, and they were so many. She could only crush deep in her heart the awful feelings of helpless resentment and of fear that she felt at that time, when her father and mother were in concentration camps and she did not know whether she would ever see them again. How can I reach that little girl still living and still uncomforted inside of her, and bring the love of Christ back over the years to her?"

And again I thought, "There is no time in heaven. In the sight of God, time is relative—time is rolled out like a carpet before Him—He can see all time at once and He can live in all time at once—therefore He must be able to go back over the years and find that little girl and heal the wounds in her mind."

But how to open a way for Jesus Christ back over the years? The door to the subconscious is opened by an act of confession and repentance, as we have seen. That little girl who lived so many years ago—how could she see her own tormented and confused thoughts that she might ask for their forgiveness? We had tried to bring them to her mind, and had failed. They were buried so deep that she was completely unaware of their existence. A psychiatrist might know a way to draw them out of her. But I was no psychiatrist, only a simple Christian.

So I thought, "I will repent of them in her name. I will say to Jesus Christ, 'Let the grown woman go free, for I will take the responsibility for her sins of fear and hate. Since she cannot see them to repent of them herself, I will repent of them in her name, and so open the door for the forgiveness of Jesus Christ.'"

I had planned to make her my "special intention" for the Communion Service, in the way outlined in my book *Lost Shepherd*. But it was not necessary to do so. Before Sunday came the miracle took place in her. "I don't know what has happened to me," she said three days later, "but all those old feelings have gone away and somehow I know that they will never come back again. And furthermore, I am happy! I am just absurdly happy all day long! I have never known before what it meant to be happy! The only thing that worries me is: now that I know what it is to be happy, how shall I stand it if the old feelings should ever come back?"

"They will never come back," I told her.

And they never have.

What had happened to her? Something like this: we will indicate the being of man by a chart such as one sees in books of psychology:

The small upper triangle indicates the conscious mind. The rest of the larger triangle indicates the subconscious, the part of us that is hidden from consciousness as nine-tenths of an iceberg is below the surface of the ocean, hidden from view. In the chart we show in the depths of the subconscious little arrows going in this direction and in that direction, but more or less in an even flow. These represent the unhappy and uncomfortable memories of a normal person—memories of guilt and frustration, fear and hate—kept down by the will, represented by three arrows pointed downwards. A moment's reflection shows us the truth of this. We all have memories that we do not want to remember. We refuse to think of them when they rise to the surface of consciousness, and after a while they rise no more. They are forgotten—by the conscious mind. But nevertheless they remain below the conscious and the effort of will to keep them there is an unconscious strain and drain upon our energies.

When the accumulation becomes too great a load for our energies or when our energies are depleted by weariness, illness or shock, sometimes the will weakens and the buried memories rise nearer to the consciousness and express themselves in feelings of depression, agitation, inexplicable rage, loss of control and so forth. Let us indicate this condition by another chart, showing the little arrows out of control by the will, zooming around in all directions.

This was the state of the Jewish lady when overtaken by sudden and uncontrollable fits of depression or anger.

If she could have remembered and recognized her old torments and we could have discussed them and prayed about them, she could have been relieved of the intolerable strain of keeping them down at all times. But to this day she has not been willing to speak of them and not being a psychiatrist, I did not know how to draw them out of her. But being a Christian I was able, *when I understood what Christ did for us in Gethsemane and on Calvary,* to find a way into her spirit through faith and to bring into her spirit a flow of the forgiving love of Christ which entered the depths of the subconscious and actually healed the stings of old memories as the body heals a wound on the hand. "Purge me with hyssop, and I shall be clean: wash me, and I shall be whiter than snow (Psalm 51:7)." Until I understood the redemption, I did not grasp the tremendous meaning of those ancient words. They are actually true! The marks—the wounds—the little pricky arrows of old guilty memories—can be washed away as though they had never been! "As far as the east is from the west, so far hath Thou hid my transgressions from me." It is really true! And when one understands it, then one has sufficient faith to comfort the broken-hearted and to release the imprisoned and to break off the chains of those held in old darkness! The chains were broken. The wounds of her past were healed. We will draw one more chart to indicate this reality:

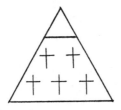

And since nature abhors a vacuum and without an abiding protection the old memory-habit might tend to return, we will fill the empty places of the subconscious with crosses, to indicate that from this time forth the life of Our Lord from the cross would keep in perfect peace she who was stayed on Him.

What then had happened to her? She was forgiven.

The blood of Christ, the current of the love of God made human and powerful and released for us through Jesus Christ on Calvary, had been made available to her by one person's understanding faith. Therefore, this healing flood had entered below the depths of consciousness and had healed her wounded memories. A real energy, as real as those invisible forces that we call electricity and gravity and light and sound, had penetrated all the thinking and had actually altered thought-impressions and emotional tendencies, wiping away the marks of sorrow and anger in the gray matter of the brain and filling the empty places with the love of Christ.

From that time forth, she was a new creature in Christ Jesus and an inheritor of immortal life. As she had borne the image of the earthly in her troubled thinking, so she now bore the image of the heavenly (I Cor. 15:49). She was reborn into the image and likeness of God which was her original being (Gen. 1:27) and all the chains that Satan through the awful sins of the nations had put upon her inner being were broken off.

9. The Resurrection and the Ever-Present Christ

We have seen how an *understanding* belief in the Redemption of Jesus Christ can increase our faith in healing and our healing power.

As I said before, Jesus Himself is the door to the life of power and the mysteries of His life open to us more and more vistas of spiritual light and increase our faith and our power of healing.

What then of the next act in the heavenly drama—what of His resurrection?

To His disciples, the resurrection was the final triumph of spiritual power (I Cor. 15:17). It was the complete miracle of healing: the healing of death itself, transforming it into newness of life (I Cor. 15:54).

The beginning of miracles that Jesus did in Cana of Galilee concerned the material creation (John 2:1-12). From this He went on to countless miracles of healing (Matt. 8:16). Next He raised Jairus' daughter from the dead, as she lay upon her sick bed (Matt. 9:24-25). Again he raised the widow's son, whose death was less open to doubt, since he was being carried through the city to his funeral (Luke 7:14). Thirdly, He raised Lazarus, whose death was unquestionable, since he had been in the tomb four days and decomposition had actually set in (John 11:11).

And finally, He raised His own body from the tomb and transformed it into the new order of being promised to all of us: the resurrection body.

First, this means to us that the same power that heals also resurrects: occasionally by renewing life within a corpse but usually by giving us in the heavenly kingdom a new body so that we become a new order of being, verily and triumphantly the Sons of God. This very spiritual power that we exercise, first in illnesses and troubles of this life as Jesus did, is the actual energy of resurrection—the very essence of immortality; thus it sweeps us from life to Life. Our interest shifts to an eternal interest—our longing for life of body changes to a longing for Life of the spiritual body—the values of spiritual power and discernment gained on the earth-plane carry us over to the heavens and are seen to be of everlasting value, transcending any value of physical healing with which they may have started.

Second, the resurrection and ascension of Jesus Christ mean to us that as He shared His human-divine being with us on Calvary for the remission of our sins (which entails the healing of the subconscious mind) so now He shares His spiritual body with us for the resurrection of our souls and the enlightenment of our spirits.

Let us, therefore, contemplate the resurrection with the reverent intent of gaining all that our circumscribed minds are able to comprehend, so that our power of faith may be increased.

"Destroy this temple," He said, meaning His body, "and I will raise it again in three days." He: His spirit: His living soul, returning on that third day from the land of the shadows, entering into the tomb wherein lay the holy corpse wounded with five wounds, would raise that body from the dead.

He must have gathered all His spiritual powers and focused them upon His lifeless and bloodless body, seeing it from without (as some of us have done when near death), that it might be transformed into the new order of being.

His lifeless and bloodless body . . . He had left the greater part of His blood on earth, to be for man an ever-increasing current of spiritual power for the healing of the heart: the forgiveness of sins (John 19:34). Therefore, the body of Christ in the tomb not only had to be resurrected cell by cell, as the body of Lazarus was resurrected, but also presumably the process of making blood had to be tremendously speeded up, so that as nature replenishes the blood for one who has given a blood transfusion, so nature should replenish His blood stream—after the blood transfusion that He gave to humanity.

Can we not see this? We sing about it in our hymns: "There is plentiful redemption in the blood that has been shed—." Why does the idea so appall us when presented in plain words? We bear it, when science tells us that energies that cannot be seen abide within matter that can be seen; we even believe that energies that cannot be seen (the sound-waves, for instance, that become audible in our radios) abide within an element that also cannot be seen: the air. Are we willing to give Our Lord the same respect that we would give a scientist, and bend our full attention to those truths about His redemption that the Bible teaches? Let us try!

The Bible teaches us that death could not hold Him—that He was triumphant over it. His blood was instinct with the life-principles of resurrection, as our bodies, through Him, shall become. Two physical processes take place at the same time in a man who believes in Jesus Christ: the process of losing energy in the body, and the process of renewing strength in the spirit. If appropriated by faith and understanding, this process of renewed life should also overflow into a transformation of the body. "The spirit of him that raised up Jesus from the dead shall also quicken your mortal bodies by his spirit that dwelleth in you (Rom. 8:11)." "They that wait upon the Lord shall renew their strength—they shall mount up with wings as eagles—they shall run and not be weary and they shall walk, and not faint (Isa. 40:31)." If life works fast enough in the spirit, it can overtake and transcend the death process in the body. Thus there exists the possibility, which one day shall be a probability, that the new order of being of which Christ was the first-fruits, can be achieved without the pain of death. "Whosoever liveth and believeth in me shall never die," He said (John 11:26). It is possible to translate this "Shall not die eternally," I know. But it is also possible to translate it as it is written: "Shall never die." And looking upon the testimony of the Scriptures, I prefer so to translate it. For the Bible tells me of those who have pre-figured this as yet unattained goal of man and have not died. Did not Enoch walk with God and disappear, because God took him (Gen. 5:24)? Did not Elijah depart to heaven in a chariot of fire before the eyes of his disciples (II Kings 2:11-12)?

Why did he depart? Why did he not stay on earth in his transformed and glorified body? Because that body, at the present point in the evolution of the race, cannot live comfortably on the earth, as a diver cannot remain long under water. As water is a foreign element to an earthman, so the air of this present earth is a foreign element to the resurrected man. He finds it hard to breathe this air, heavy with man's sorrow, dense with the pollution of man's sins. The resurrected body, while a real body, exists at a different rate of vibration: lives by a different kind of energy. Indeed, the way in which the body can attain resurrection on this earth, being not unclothed with the body but being, as St. Paul desired to be, clothed upon with the body which is from above, is to learn to live by spiritual energy. The vibration of the spirit can be so immensely speeded up that the whole body is lifted into it. Why does this seem so strange to us? It is much the same as the process which takes place in a healing. What happens when a man filled with the Holy Spirit lays his hand upon a goitre and it disappears?[1] What happens is that God's power entering the patient pervades the area of the throat and changes the rate of vibration of the cells therein, so that the spiritual energy in the combined spirits of the minister, the patient and the expectant congregation, overcomes the tendency toward death manifested in the form of a goitre.

This is the drama of creation: the eternal conflict of life— the principle of death introduced upon this earth by Satan, the principle of life inherent in the Creator—the two principles intermingling in man. Which shall win: death or life? In the day (epoch) wherein man chose to follow the enemy and turn away from God, he placed himself under the law of sin and death. Satan won the first round (Gen. 3).

Then Jesus Christ came into the world to bring man nearer to God. He gave His blood that man might be healed of the damage that the racial thought-habit of sin and death had done to him. He gave His life, in other words, for the forgiveness of man's sins. In so doing He gave the death-blow to the power of the Enemy (John 16:33).

Again, He shares with man His resurrected Being so that the principle of life can once more take precedence over the urge toward death in the creatures of this earth. If man accepts this transfusion of His life (for always and forever man has free-will, and the death of Jesus Christ does not automatically make anyone immortal), He can replant in man the seed of immortality that the serpent corrupted (Gen. 3). This seed of immortality is a cell of His body, born in holiness and made perfect through suffering (Heb. 2:10). This cell came from the blood of His body, which

---

[1] *A Reporter Finds God Through Spiritual Healing,* E. Gardner Neal.

fluid and mobile part of Him was left upon the earth when the rest of His body was placed in the tomb and thence burst forth victorious. His body has not decayed and mingled with the dust of the earth. But His blood has become a part of our common dust, and the cells within His blood-stream, instinct with the principle of life, expanding like leaven, or yeast, as He told us (Matt. 13:33), vibrate to the vibrations of immortality. Thus an ever-living cell of His body, transplanted into our bodies so that we are branches of His vine (John 15:1-8), can transform the body cell by cell as yeast can transform a loaf of bread.

Then why do we still die? Because sin has so great a hold upon us that we cannot believe this. Also because those who try to believe it do not exist alone. We are a part one of another. And in this present generation, the over-growth of the mind and the starvation of the spirit has so cut down the energy of the spirit that the possibility of attaining a resurrection while here in the flesh is practically zero. Nevertheless, the principle of immortality remains. And when Our Lord once more breaks through to be Our Judge, bringing His saints with Him (I Thess. 3:13), then we will round out and complete that victory over Satan that Jesus has potentially won in our names. Then the old enemy will be bound for a period of time (Rev. 20:2) and finally will no longer exist as an instrument of evil (Rev. 20:10). What God will do with his spirit we do not know, but certainly the enemy himself, existing as a negative and destructive force upon this planet, will be destroyed, so that the very impulse to hurt and destroy will be removed from man. "They shall not hurt nor destroy in all my holy mountain (Isa. 11:9)."

"For the law of the spirit of life in Christ Jesus hath made me free from the law of sin and death (Rom. 8:2)." When this freedom is carried out to its ultimate conclusion, then we will have on earth a Holy City, a New Jerusalem, whose spiritual climate will be such that the resurrected ones can live in it on this earth.

For there are already resurrected ones. There are those who have achieved in the spiritual kingdom that we call "heaven" the resurrection of the body. For Heaven is a place of growth. And though we are told that there will come a tremendous and cataclysmic change when at "the last trump" the dead shall rise (I Cor. 15:52), we are also told that there are certain ones in heaven who have washed their robes (the human bodies in which they are clothed) and made them white in the blood of

the Lamb (Rev. 7:14-17); there are the redeemed from among
men, being the first-fruits unto God and to the Lamb (Rev. 14:4);
there are those who have attained to the first resurrection (Rev.
20:5). First the ear of corn: Christ. Then the grain: those who
grew from His holy seed and contained within themselves the
seed of immortality (I Cor. 15:35-50): finally the redeemed
among the nations (Rev. 21:24).

Now let us bring our minds back from the far vistas of
eternity and consider the work that His own spirit did on returning from Hades to that tomb. *He* raised His body from the
dead. He with God the Father and with the Holy Spirit (Rom.
8:11) accomplished that act of re-creation, as He with God
and the Holy Spirit accomplished the first act of creation (Gen.
1:1-2 & John 1:1-3).

How did He do so? In the same way as He did all of His
mighty works, by the power of the Father abiding in Him and
by His own power, through the Father, taking control of every
cell in His body. He said, remember, speaking of the temple of
His body, that in three days He would raise it up (John 2:19-22).
Why three days?

Perhaps He knew that the body needed to rest for that length
of time before the blood in it could be renewed. Perhaps a
change was taking place in the body during all of those three
days, as a change takes place mysteriously in the pupa of a
caterpillar while in a cocoon.

His spirit, returning from Hades where He preached to the
spirits in prison (I Pet. 3:19), stood beside His own body that
was not only dead but almost bloodless, His blood having been
shed upon this earth for us. He Himself, by a miracle of spirit,
changed every cell in that body from a dead cell to a living cell,
making a real body that could be seen and touched (John 20:27 &
Luke 24:39). Yet those living cells were not of the same order
as are the cells of our present bodies, for they were completely
under the control of spirit, so that at His command His body
could become invisible (Luke 24:31), could transcend matter
and space (Acts 1:9).

He became a new order of being, that we too might become
new creatures in Christ Jesus. "Christ the first fruits; afterward they that are Christ's at his coming (I Cor. 15:23)."

In what way does it help us in our present problems, then,
to know that Jesus Christ rose from the dead? In what way does
it add power to our prayers? According to the Epistles, the

early Christians felt that the church was founded as much on the resurrection of Christ as on His crucifixion—in other words, that just as the sacrificial death of Christ released for us a current of power for the forgiveness of our sins, so also the resurrection of Christ made available for us a current of power for the transforming of soul and mind and body. "If Christ be not risen, then is our preaching vain, and your faith is also vain. (I Cor. 15:14)" "If Christ be not raised, your faith is vain; ye are yet in your sins (I Cor. 15:17)." But does not the crucifixion of Christ, His redeeming passion, complete and make perfect the way of the forgiveness of our sins? Apparently not. According to the plain teaching of the Bible and of the Creed, the passion of Our Lord is not complete without the resurrection of Our Lord: "And the third day He arose again from the dead (Apostles' Creed)."

What then did it mean to the disciples? Most simply it meant that they had not lost Him; that He was alive and was with them in their walk toward heaven. With great love He came and showed Himself to them that they might live in this joy. Mary Magdalene saw Him in the garden amid a veil of tears and with all His love for her, He nevertheless said, "Touch me not, for I am not yet ascended to my father (John 20:17)." He was in a body, a body that could be seen though possibly not clearly, since she thought that He was the gardener. But it was not a body that could be touched—not yet. For He had not yet taken that body into the direct light of God. He by His own spirit had transformed His lifeless clay into a new kind of body—but He had not finished that work. Possibly, as Dorothy Sayers points out in *The Mind of the Maker,* if Mary had touched that body she would have felt nothing and it would have frightened her.

Later on He came to His disciples, the doors being closed, for He was able to transcend matter—and He came to them in a finished body, a body that could be felt and touched and furthermore a body that still showed the wounds of His violent death.

He never showed Himself to those who did not love Him, Pontius Pilate or Herod or the Pharisees. In His humility He did not come to them and they never saw Him again save perhaps in troubled dreams at night. Yet one wonders . . . why did He not show Himself to the authorities who had put Him to death, thus completing the public testimony to the resurrection

that the open tomb began? Could He not have come to them
not in pride but in love, that all men might know that He had
risen from the dead? Perhaps he could not. Perhaps that resurrection body of His, being made of spiritual elements, needed
a spiritual atmosphere to breathe. Perhaps He could not appear
except when drawn and summoned by love . . .

Certainly as time passed He could not remain here among
men. The glory of the Father finally and inevitably drew Him
upward, as the sun draws moisture from the sea. And as He
ascended His body was changed from glory to glory until when
He appeared to St. Paul on the road to Damascus the light
of it was well-nigh unbearable. St. Paul fell to the ground as
that light shone upon him, and when He arose again, he was
blinded by more radiance than the human eye can stand (Acts
9:3). And the Lord had to come to him through the hands
and the faith of a humble human man in order to heal his eyes.
He could not remain among them in that glorified body.
It was not expedient for them that He try to do so.
And yet He said on departing, "Lo, I am with you alway, even
unto the end of the world (Matt. 28:20)."

And because they had seen Him and knew that He had in
very truth risen from the dead, they believed that He would
be with them alway. He would be with them to help them, as He
had always done. But now that all power in heaven and earth
had been given unto Him (Matt. 28:18) through His victory over
death, now that He held the keys of death and of hell (Rev. 1:18),
His help would be infinitely greater than it had ever been. And His
power working through them would accomplish the signs that He
told them would follow them that believe: would cast out Satan
and triumph over danger and over illness and heal the sick (Mark
16:17-18 & Acts 3:1-9 & 9:40).

So the resurrection from the dead meant to them first of
all that He Himself would be with them, in that glorified and
triumphant body that they had seen, filling them with His power
and doing His mighty works through them. Therefore they
gladly called upon His name, and through His power they healed the sick and resurrected the dead and raised such a furor
of triumphal gladness that the civilized world shook for fear
of them and the powers of evil tried in every way to destroy them
—and failed.

They had seen Him triumphant over death and so they believed. But He said, "Blessed are they that have not seen, and yet

have believed (John 20:29)." And we, who have not seen, are blessed if we dare to believe that Jesus rose from the dead and that He is with us now. But how strangely we forget this fact! We think of Him in the past, teaching and preaching in Galilee and in Judea. We think of Him upon the cross. But do we remember that He is no longer on the cross but is living now, not merely a spiritual energy but Himself, a BEING, a Personality, administering all power in heaven and earth and holding the keys of death and of hell? We look upon a cross and a crucifix that we may remember Him, and it is good that we do so, for it connects us by love and gratitude, by faith and by earnest desire, to that flow of His redemptive power that having been given for us on Calvary, still remains in this world.

But He is not on Calvary now! Where is He now? How can we forget that He is with us as none other in heaven and on earth can be with us—more actually than our friends in the flesh, for He is in a body more powerful and more real than a body of flesh; more actually than our loved ones who have passed on, for He is here not merely as a spirit but in a body that can transcend time and space and that can send the radiation of His love whither He will send it?

Therefore, there is nothing that we need to fear, on earth or in heaven or in hell! Therefore, we have hope not only in this life but also for all eternity (I Cor. 15:19-21)! With St. Paul we may cry, "Oh death, where is thy sting? O grave, where is thy victory (I Cor. 15:54-55)?"

But do we? No. Instead we turn these words of triumph into a funeral dirge. And generation after generation passes and death is victor still. We have forgotten that He is here in His risen and glorified body and so we do not use the power that is given to Him and that He can transfer to us. Forgetting this, we do not find the victory even over disease, much less over death. And so the grave consumes generation after generation those who are born to be the Sons of God (Rom. 8:14).

The church has never denied the resurrection. It is there in all our Creeds, calling aloud to us to believe in it. But we of the church while acknowledging the sacrifice of Christ, have somehow contrived to ignore the triumph of Christ that is our triumph too. We crawl upon our bellies into church and out again, being miserable sinners all the while. And we have so over-emphasized the regrettable fact of our sin that we have

failed to see the glorious fact of our going forth, when forgiven, as new creatures in Christ Jesus.

We have fixed our eyes too exclusively upon a dead body on
a cross. True, we should from time to time turn our minds
to Calvary for our inner cleansing, as has been abundantly set
forth on these pages. But we should not *remain* there in our
spiritual visioning any more than He remained there.

"The thing upon which we fasten our attention tends to become true"—remember.

Therefore He has given us the highest thing of all upon which
to fasten our attention: a risen and glorified Savior.

He alone raised His own body from the dead and holds
the keys of death and hell. It is a long way to eternity and a
dark way, our eyes being dimmed by the veil of Time. And only
He has trod it, eternity to time and time to eternity again, and
is able to lead us safely past the dangers on the road. He has
conquered death and lives in a body that although transformed
is yet the body of humanity. Therefore we can look upon His
glorified body and grow not toward death but toward the resurrected life.

Looking on Him, we can indeed do the things that He did
on earth, not because the Christ Spirit that was in Him is now
in us, not even entirely because He shows us the way to do
them, but because He Himself in His risen, glorified Being,
is here with us helping us to do them.

So when we would pray with power and try to overcome the
satanic kingdom of illness and death, we call upon His name.
What does that mean? Merely that we give His name as a testimonial, so that God will favor us, as we might give a friend's
name as a testimonial to a bank? Not at all! When we call upon
His name, we call upon *Him*. It is not a dead name that helps
us, but a living Person whom we call by name as we call any
living person. When I call my husband by name, I am calling
my husband. When I ask him to come and help me, I mean
precisely that I expect him to come and help me. I expect him
to lend his strength to me so that with him I can lift the bushel
basket of apples that alone I cannot lift. He helps me by stretching out his hand to work with mine, as Jesus Christ stretched
out His hand to the lame man at the gate of the temple. But
my husband's hand is visible and it exists outside of me. The
hand of Christ is invisible and it exists both outside and inside
of me. As He came through the doors, the doors being closed,

so He can come into my very being and fill me with a power that is more than the original light of God that shines upon the just and upon the unjust. It is the actual power of Jesus Christ the Son of God, working in my subconscious mind and in my conscious mind, in my spirit and in my body, in a way that only He can work . . . because only He in heaven and in earth has trod the path of humanity and entered into the depths of it and given His life for it and risen triumphant from the dead.

"Abide in Me and I in you," He said. "As the branch cannot bear fruit of itself, except it abide in the vine, no more can ye, except ye abide in me. I am the vine, ye are the branches; He that abideth in me and I in him, the same bringeth forth much fruit: for without me ye can do nothing. If a man abide not in me, he is cast forth as a branch and is withered; and men gather them and cast them into the fire, and they are burned. If ye abide in me and my words abide in you, ye shall ask what ye will, and it shall be done unto you (John 15:1-7)."

This is the end result of His rising from the dead; he is now living, a Presence, a Personality, yet a Being so infinite in power that He can go through the doors of our bodies and enter into us and abide in us—a Being so great that the light of His presence can shine like the sun on millions of people and yet not be diminished.

If we have given ourselves to Him, if we love Him, He can come into us as He came to His disciples, the doors being closed. Let us ask Him to abide in us more and more. If we would practice a continual prayer of repetition as some saints have done, we can think of no better phrase for our constant prayer than this: "Lord Jesus Christ, abide in me more and more, filling me with Thy own life."

As we become more and more filled with His life, it may come to us to change our prayer and to say, "Lord Jesus Christ, receive me into Thy own glorified Being that I may abide in Thee." Words are not great enough to describe that sense of walking about in a body of light that is not our own, but is His light. If only we could so walk all the time and every day, that His will might be done through us continually! This will be so as we come to know the risen Lord as our present Companion and Friend. We will be able as we pray to abide in Him more and more, so that even while we sleep our spirits are working in His service. The most powerful prayer that we can say just before sleep is this: "Lord Jesus Christ, receive my spirit, that all night long I may abide in Thee."

And He who is eternal will brood over us with His love and receive our faltering spirits into His risen and triumphant Being so that we may sleep in peace and awake with the joy of His presence.

10. The Holy Spirit
and His Power

When Jesus Christ ascended into the heavens, He told His disciples that they should go to Jesusalem and there wait till they were endued with power from on high (Luke 24:49). Subsequent events showed the nature of this power. It was the power to do miracles: works that He did (John 14:12). He had promised it to them before His death, intimating at that time that this new power would be released through His ascension. This power, including the real gift of healing not only by God's power acting through human faith, but also by a direct lightning-flash of a miraculous energy, is the power of the Holy Spirit given to the disciples on the day of Pentecost. And those of us who seek to heal by faith without being endued with the full power of the Spirit are like an author who does not use a typewriter or a seamstress who has no sewing machine.

What do we mean when we speak of the Holy Ghost or the Holy Spirit? Do we refer to the Christ spirit within us . . . the breath of God that fills the universe . . . or the voice of God guiding our thoughts and actions? These three phrases express quite different concepts. Let us try, therefore, to clarify our thinking concerning the Holy Spirit. In order to do so, let us once more think of the trinity of our own natures and endeavor to understand a little about our own spirits.

Let us consider the symbol of man's being:

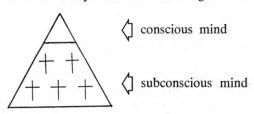

conscious mind

subconscious mind

Where is the spirit? It cannot be located in the brain as one locates the conscious mind. Nor can one connect it with bodily functions as one connects the subconscious with bodily functions. (The Bible words that most nearly approximate "subconscious mind" are "heart" (Prov. 28:26 & Eccl. 1:16), "belly" (John 7:38), or even "bowels" (Philem. 1:7) No one has ever succeeded in any examination or autopsy in finding the spirit within the body. Naturally. "That which is born of the flesh is flesh; and that which is born of the Spirit is spirit." (John 3:6)." Let us then indicate the spirit by a dotted triangle, similar in shape but larger, not within the body but adjacent to it. And let us indicate the connection of spirit with mind and subconscious mind by a canal or channel between the two.

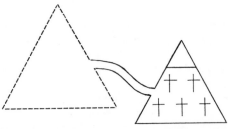

We connect this channel, in our sketch, with the subconscious rather than with the conscious, because the subconscious is more open to the voice of the spirit than is the conscious. If we will but observe our own reactions, we can clearly see that this is so. How often do we have unexplainable awareness of things about to happen . . . "hunches," as we call them! Sometimes we sense these premonitions in feelings of restlessness or unexplainable fear. At other times we act upon them not knowing why we veer from our courses upon what would seem to be irrational impulses. For instance, my daughter once travelled home from college on the Zephyr. She planned to detrain at Chicago and spend the night with a friend. As the train neared Chicago, she and her friend, who had been visiting other college friends in the train, started back to the first car to retrieve their baggage. The train stopped at a suburban station and on impulse my daughter said, "Let's get off here! It's nearer to your home than Chicago is!"

"But our baggage—and Mother is meeting us—"

"No, no, let's get off!" said my daughter.

And the two girls leaped from the train, hatless, coatless

and empty-handed, just as it gathered speed for its last three miles into Chicago. When they reached the friend's home they called the station and said, "Please hold our baggage. We left it on the Zephyr."

"The Zephyr!" answered the agent. "Lady! That train wrecked just out of Chicago."

The train had struck a tractor that had dropped from another train upon the track, had buckled and gone into the side of a tall brick building. The building had fallen on the first car, and every person on the side of that car where the two girls had seats, was either killed or seriously injured.

Now what is the explanation of this? My daughter's spirit, being spirit and not flesh, was not limited, as is the subconscious mind, by time and space. Her spirit therefore was able to see a bit ahead of her physical eyes and mind, and to perceive the wreck of the train. The spirit managed to telegraph this information into the subconscious mind. The subconscious, being unable to speak directly to the conscious mind, simply put into the mind the apparently irrational impulse to leap from the train. (Is it possible that others on the train had such an impulse but "rationalized" and did not heed it?)

Notice also in the chart that the canal or channel between spirit and subconscious is indicated by a wavy line rather than a straight one. This is meant to suggest an elastic tube loosely swung from one to the other. The spirit is apparently able to travel quite a distance from the body and still maintain a connection with our beings. Some call this ability of the spirit "astral travelling." It would seem that our spirits are able to respond to the call of prayer or to the need of some loved one to go and minister to them without the awareness of the conscious mind. It would seem also that the spirit can, by stretching the "silver cord" that links it to the body (Ec. 12:6), reach the heavenly kingdom while we sleep and return to us refreshed and inspired with new knowledge. These two abilities of the spirit of man explain a number of our extra-sensory gifts: prophecy or pre-cognition, the gift of the discernment of spirits, clairaudience, clairvoyance: all of these being natural results of the developing and expanding of spiritual powers. The Bible gives us hundreds of examples of these things: Philip and the eunuch (Acts 8:39-40)—astral travelling; Isaiah (Isa. Chaps. 2-36), Jeremiah (Jer. 21-27), St. John (Rev. 1-22) and countless others—prophecy, or looking forward into time; Elisha and the king (II Kings

6:12)—clairaudience; Daniel (Dan. Chap. 2), Ezekiel (Ezl.
8-12) and again countless others—clairaudience. Modern man
longs to explore these mysteries and searches after them on the
realm of the psychic, yet they are a natural and integral part of
the life of the spirit, and if the spirit of man is energized by
the Holy Spirit of God, these super-sensory gifts come to one
in a more usable fashion than can ever be attained by mere
psychic research. In most psychic research one concentrates one's
attention upon the bits of knowledge that filter into the mind
from without. Thus one increases the denseness of the human
by dwelling upon it; and while gaining information concerning
extra-sensory things, one is apt to lose the very source of the
information: God's Spirit breathing through our spirits.

Those who focus their attention upon the psychic plane are
like desert-dwellers seizing upon a trickle of water, studying it
and draining it away and analyzing it and never discovering or
developing the source from whence it flows. We cannot apprehend God by concentrating upon man; either man in the flesh
or man out of the flesh. But if we seek God and His Holy Spirit,
all these lesser things are added unto us. For the Holy Spirit is
by His very nature and being the giver of all super-sensory gifts.
The Holy Spirit is moreover that aspect of the God-head sent
into the world for the express purpose of giving life to our
spirits. As the love of God was incarnated in Jesus Christ for
the redemption of our subconscious minds, so the light and fire
and power of God is released through the Holy Spirit for the
redemption of our spirits.

There is in all of us an uncomprehended longing for a third
person of the Trinity. We ourselves are three, and as the mind
gropes after comprehension of God's laws and the subconscious
mind walks heavily burdened until released by the action of
God's Son, so also the spirit stagnates and dries up without
the refreshing and activating power of God's Spirit. Our subconscious substitutes demonstrate this fact. There are those, as
Dorothy Sayer points out, who would seem to worship the
Father, the Son and the Virgin Mary; those who believe in the
Father, the Son and the Holy Scriptures; and those who found
their faith on the Father, the Son and the Church; and there are
even those who seem to derive their spiritual power from the
Father, the Son and the minister[1].

---

[1] *The Mind of the Maker* by Dorothy Sayer, Harcourt, Brace, N. Y.

For many years I thought that if I were transformed by the renewing of my mind and redeemed by the forgiveness of my sins and the healing of the subconscious mind, that was enough: I was a re-born person. But I found as the years passed that it was not enough. As I learned faith, more and more demands were put upon that faith. As I became a better channel for the love of Christ, there came to me more and more demands for His redeeming love and a greater sensitivity to the sorrows of the world. The result was exhaustion, heaviness and grief. I needed an over-weight of joy to counteract this weight of sorrow.

Mankind has always sought for this heavenly ecstasy, and sometimes in strange ways indeed. As we study the Old Testament we find heathen idol worship filled with frantic attempts to arouse such feelings (Ex. 32:18-19). The technique was to arouse the sexual emotions and then sublimate these feelings into spiritual ecstacy. Somtimes they aroused these feelings indirectly through the sadistic or masochistic emotions connected with sex (Jer. 19:5 & I Kings 18:28). Sometimes they worked them up through rituals of nakedness and dancing (Ex. 32:19 & 25). Sometimes they actually introduced adultery and fornication into their worship . . . the "went-a-whoring after other gods (Judges 2:17)", serving Baal and Ashtoreth (Judges 2:13).

Baal has departed and Ashtoreth is no more and their temples have crumpled into the dust of centuries, as the Bible said that they would. But the ancient need of joy remains because of the sorrow of the world, which would break our hearts save for a heavenly elan, a lifting and shifting of man's emotional system so that we can walk above all sorrow and find joy (I Pet. 1:8).

There was a time, then, when I had great need of this joy. I was exhausted. Every time I prayed for others it drained me of power. Intercession tightened every nerve till I was like a violin keyed too high.

At this time the Lord guided two friends of mine to invite me to a prayer-retreat in a far-away city. "God told us that you were to do no lecturing while you are here," said my friend. "You are not to pray for anyone. No one is even to know you are in the city . . ."

I found that my two friends were also exhausted. "I asked God why we who help others all the time should be so tired ourselves," said my hostess. "And last night I had a dream. All three of us were climbing up a hill, toiling and puffing and hardly able to get up there because we were laden down with other people's burdens . . . "

So we prayed. And it came to us that what we needed was the power of the Holy Ghost. We had prayed through the Cross of Christ. We had prayed through the creativity of God. But we did not know how to pray through the joy of the Spirit. What would happen if we prayed through the Holy Ghost we did not know. But we knew that we needed a great awakening of some kind. And it came to us that possibly our real need was the "baptism of the Spirit."

We went into the prayer-room of my friend's house to pray for the Holy Ghost. I am glad that God gave us tremendous expectancy, but an expectancy that was entirely and completely free! We did not look for flames of fire or for a rushing mighty wind or for the gift of tongues or for any of those physical manifestations that were seen and heard when the Holy Spirit first burst upon the church on the Day of Pentecost (Acts 2: 1-7). We did not even think of these things. Neither did we ask the Holy Ghost for anything, not even for a renewing in strength. We simply told our Heavenly Father that we had come to the end—that if He did not do something about it we were through. "Whatever the next step is, we must take it," we said. "Whatever is the next spiral in the Christian life, we must enter upon it." Then we remembered that the Apostles had laid hands on people that they might receive the Holy Ghost (Acts 19:6). Therefore, we knelt before the home-made altar and laid hands two upon one till all had received this laying-on-of-hands. And we prayed for each one that she might receive the Holy Ghost.

And there is no question about it, the Holy Ghost fell upon all of us. There were no tongues of fire, but there was a deep burning in the middle of the head. That burning lasted for days and has returned from time to time, when we have stirred up the gift of God that is in us (II Tim. 1:6). It was a strange burning, yet not unpleasant; a burning combined with a drawing sensation as though we had brushed our hair the wrong way. There was no rushing mighty wind, but there was a sense of freedom and of joy in the air about us, so that all beauty was more beautiful, as though the light of heaven shone through it. There was no speaking in strange languages, but there was a bubbling, inner joy that found expression in a freer flow of speech and in merrier laughter. Furthermore, there were other changes, deep and profound, that took place in the three of us according to our need. Every one of us was healed of all physical weakness and weariness, and there is in all of us to this day a deeper well of the water of life, just as Jesus said there would be, so that we do not thirst for life as we used to thirst (John 4:14). We can do more work in less time. If we act according to the guidance of God, not according to the demands of men, we can pray for others without weariness. The actual feeling of life flowing like electricity through our hands when used in healing diminished abruptly almost to nothing. This would have frightened us, except that we saw that the results of our prayers were even more surely established. It came to us that the flow of life in the hands was the power of God working through the body and the subconscious mind, as the intangible yet faintly exhausting power of intercession was the power of God working through the conscious mind; but that now there was added to us another power working through the spirit without strain or exhaustion or any physical sign.

But the greatest of all the gifts of the Spirit is joy. It bubbled up within us like a well of unfailing water, refreshing and cheering us no matter what the sorrows of our days might be. It enabled us to look with serenity upon the burdens of life, enduring them unto the end as though seeing Him that is invisible (Heb 11.27). For what is that joy indeed but the inner spirit beholding the glory of the heavenly life and feeling its perfect bliss even through the darkness of this pale shadow that we call life?

I believe in the Holy Ghost, the Comforter!

What happens when the spirit of man is thus infused with the life of the Holy Spirit? Man's spirit is then given such life that, body and mind being yielded to it and put under its control, it can interpenetrate and illumine both conscious and subconscious minds. We could suggest something like this truth by erasing the dotted triangle we drew adjacent to the solid triangle representing conscious and subconscious, and redrawing it upon and around the solid one.

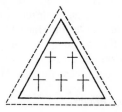

Notice that we drew little arrows within the subconscious, representing the pricking of old unforgiven memories. We also considered the manner in which the forgiveness of Jesus Christ washes away these little arrows and we indicated the reborn Christian by a chart showing the subconscious filled with crosses, the symbols of redemption, instead of with the prickings of our sins. But this is not the final state of the sons of God! Those who go farther in the Christian life make room for the Holy Spirit by the cleansing of the subconscious being and then fill that inner chamber with the light and holiness of the Spirit, so that the impulse of sin dies within one and the new creature in Christ Jesus is born (Rom. 8:1-11). "Whosoever abideth in him sinneth not (I John 3:6)." If a person repents and is forgiven and is not filled with the Spirit, the prickly arrows tend to return, for the subconscious is predisposed toward sin. Forgiveness then must be repeated day after day and Sunday after Sunday and when returning to the altar to seek this forgiveness one quite rightly proclaims oneself still a miserable sinner. But when the total being is filled with the Holy Spirit, then the Holy Spirit directs and rules the heart[1], the subconscious, and due to His purifying and sanctifying action, the impulse to sin dies out. One might change the crosses in one's symbol of the subconscious into stars, and come somewhere near the truth.

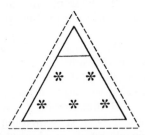

This symbol helps me to understand the fact that God is one God acting in three different ways through three different and personalized aspects of His Being. He acted first as Creator of all things. But the enemy entered into His creation and fouled those whom He made in His own image and likeness. Therefore He entered the world in another aspect of His Being, assuming the visible form of a man in order to do His cleansing and redeeming work. Yet even though He provides a way of

---

[1] *The Book of Common Prayer.*

salvation for us and continues to carry it on, we need still more of Him. We need His light to give us joy, His fire to burn away evil tendencies from our beings, His power to accomplish through us His will in the world. Therefore, the final action of the Savior in this world was to send us the Holy Spirit, the Spirit of God manifesting Himself as light and fire and power, and filling us with His joy.

This is a humble example but let us consider it: Three Persons in One God is a bit like three channels in one television set, using not three kinds of energy but one, the vibration of light as it comes in the aerial.

Anyone of any tribe or nation or language who in any sincere way turns to a Great Spirit, calling Him God or Allah or Life or whatever else he will, opens a door that God may enter his conscious mind and answer his prayers according to his faith. One may turn to Channel One only and the overflowing love of God will do for him whatever is possible through one channel alone. But this power cannot reach to the depths of the subconscious mind. If we want the cleansing power that frees the subconscious, which we call forgiveness, we need to tune in to Channel Two of this God, the channel adapted to that very purpose: Jesus Christ, the second Person of the Trinity. And finally, if we need still more light to dispel the darkness of the world and to guide us into the way of peace, we can turn to Channel Three, the Holy Spirit, the Comforter, the Light-giver, whom the Father sent to us in the Son's name (John 14:26) that we should have new light in our spirits.

To return to the story of three women in the desert—why had we not received this third current of God's power until that day? Because until that day we had *never really asked for the power with faith and understanding*. We had prayed a thousand times for the Holy Spirit to guide us and to do His healing work through us. But we had never before conceived of the Holy Spirit as a Person—a personalized aspect of God's Being—the third Person of the Trinity. So naturally we had never prayed for that Person to fill us with power as He filled the disciples at Pentecost. Therefore our concept of the Holy Spirit and our prayers for His help had opened only a small door in our spirits. Through that opening He worked for us *from without* as best He could, but He could not enter and invade and pervade the personality because we did not expect Him to do so.

Yes, there is a third Person of the Trinity: God, the One God, manifesting Himself through a third divine Personality. Even as Jesus always IS ("Before Abraham was, I AM") so also the Holy Spirit always IS. In the very beginning, the Spirit of God moved upon the face of the waters (Gen. 1:2). As the ever-existing Being of the Son leaped into time upon earth on the first Christmas Eve, so the ever-existing Holy Spirit was projected forth from God through Christ and leaped into time upon our earth on the day of Pentecost.

The Holy Spirit speaks always of Jesus (John 15:26), not of Himself, for Jesus is the mediator of this earth and its people —He is our agent at the right hand of the Father—He is the representative of humanity among the ranks and orders of spiritual beings that forever and ever stand before the Great White Throne (Rev. 20:11). Are we, children of flesh, His only children? How should we be, when all the heavens are aflame with His glory—when star after star bursts from the womb of His timeless creativity and over ages and aeons and the incredible span of interstellar space evolves and whirls and throws off planets who in their turn harden and cool and breed life?

If we could hear the voice of God, perhaps He would say to us something like this: "Children of earth, you are My lost sheep for whom I left My home—whom I went forth to rescue and to save out of the mouth of the lion. Children of earth, when you return it will be to a glorious company of your enfolded brethren— children of earth, how little you have known Me, how little you have known! I have had to veil My light in flesh that you might see Me. And again I have had to transmute My light into spirit through the spirit of this One, The God-man, Jesus Christ. Through His ascended spirit there emerged a new current of My life—or rather, an everlasting essence of My creativity made newly available to man—stepped down to a voltage suitable for man's spirit—choked down into a rhythm in which man's spirit could arise and function."

Perhaps. Something like this.

But let us come down to earth and consider: how is He received? He, the third Person of the Trinity, the Spirit of Truth? By invitation and by faith; an invitation to *Him,* not to a vague something that we call the Christ within or Divine Mind or even the Universal Spirit. That is good, but it is not good enough. It is a step *toward* Him, but a step not long enough to actually reach Him. We need to ask Him, the divine Personality perfected through Christ's work on earth and sent to us through the ascended spirit of Jesus Christ, to come into us and set on fire the spiritual parts of us. As we do this, our spirits will awaken and leap into a higher activity. Our potentialities will be stepped up into actualities. The gifts of the Holy Spirit will pour into us and become effective upon the earth plane.

Behold! We merge our spirits into *His* spirit—the spirit of Jesus. As He shared His body and His blood with us on earth for the forgiveness of sins (the healing of our subconscious minds), so He shares His spirit with us from heaven for the resurrection of our spirits. Thus as our spirits merge with the spirit of Jesus Christ, as He abides in us and we in Him (John 15:4), then the new adaptation of an everlasting divine essence, the Holy Spirit rushes over us and into us like a great breaker of the sea and we are baptized into a new life—we are risen with Christ (Col. 2:12).

With most Christians today the acceptance of Christ is not followed by this baptism of the Spirit, for we do not even know that there is such a thing possible. We are like those Christians who did not even know that there was any Holy Ghost (Acts 19:2). We are like someone who received many Christmas gifts from a wealthy friend and forgot one of them, leaving it wrapped up on the closet shelf. In one sense we have the gift—in another sense we do not, for we have never unwrapped it. We do not even know that there is anything inside the package. We think it is only bright colored paper and tinsel string. Too much of our religion today is the bright colored paper of church windows and candles and the tinsel string of ceremonial. *What is inside those wrappings?*

As Rufus Moseley once said, "Religion of today amounts to an inoculation against religion. We have just enough so that we can't catch the real thing, and neither can we pass it on to someone else." And again he said most profoundly, "If a man thinks he has gotten where he is going, he is not likely to get there."

We think we have gotten where we are going. We think that because we repent of our sins and are reborn to a new life through the forgiveness of Jesus Christ, we have accomplished that new life. We have not. We have begun but we have not finished. We have made a promise of allegiance to Him but the marriage has not taken place, and so the new creature in Christ Jesus is not brought forth in us.

There is no question about a new creature being brought forth by the union of man and woman: there it is, the baby. The baby is not the father nor is it the mother, but it is a new being brought forth by the union of the two. He that is born of flesh is flesh, and he that is born of spirit is spirit (John 3:6). It is possible for a new being to be brought forth in us, through the union of spirit and Spirit, and these new creatures are called the sons of God and the whole creation groaneth and travaileth together waiting for their appearance (Rom. 8:19-24). These new creatures—this new order of being—this changed species will have within it a potential of developing new gifts of spiritual power and of redeeming this fallen earth.

The original tendency to sin, suggested to man by the devil, deepened by race-inheritance and reinforced by the mass mind of a fallen humanity, this "sin of the flesh" shaken in its hold on man by baptism, shall be given its death blow. The law of life that is in Christ Jesus hath made me free from the law of sin and death (Rom. 8:2). The tendency toward holiness takes precedence over the tendency to sin.

The light-vibrations of the spirit shall be increased and stepped up to a higher current of spiritual energy by the infusion of the Holy Spirit, ministered by Jesus Christ from the heavens where He sits at the right hand of God. It is as though His Spirit were printed over a million times, as a negative can be printed many times, and these prints were super-imposed on the spirit of man, lifting his spirit into the spirit of Jesus and thus making available to him the final culmination of Jesus' work for him, the Holy Spirit of God, the highest vibration of the life of God that can be available to man, the third Person of the Trinity operating upon the being of man and changing the species into a new order of being, the sons of God (Rom. 8:14).

Even our own spirits can merge with the spirits of others on the wave-lengths of human love. As has been said, our spirits can travel to a distance. Sometimes we thus make contact with those we love, so that we sense their joy or sorrow or their need of prayer. Many of us are aware of this. Others do not recognize the reason for the sudden moods and the vague discomforts or inexplicable feelings of elation that seize us at times. *This is the reason.* Man does not live to himself alone. The spirit of man is corporate. The spirits of all who enter into the new life become one body, the body of Christ on earth. This body cannot be achieved by organization. It is achieved by an actual merging of our spirits into His Spirit, so that He abides in us and we in Him (John 15:4). Do we not say this is our churches? "That we may be very members incorporate in the mystical body of Thy Son."[1] This cannot mean that our bodies enter into His physical body, and it certainly does not mean merely that we join a body of people called a church. It means what it says as clearly as words can say them: that our real selves, our spirits, become actually a part of His spiritual body. Surely this deepening of the spiritual life is the purpose of the church's service of confirmation, and those who are confirmed receive as much as they are prepared by understanding and by faith to receive of the power of the Holy Spirit. If congregation, candidates and clergy prayed together with the earnest expectation of the early Christians on Pentecost, we would indeed have a new church and a new world.

The union of His Spirit with our spirits restores the original creation of God and more than restores it, for we are then not only spiritual beings abiding in a body of flesh and triumphant over the flesh, but we are spiritual beings welded into His spirit and thus filled with the Holy Spirit as He was filled after His baptism. This we are, not by virtue of our own strength or perfection, but by virtue of His strength and perfection. This we could never attain for ourselves. It must grieve the Lord to see man still trying to attain it after all these years: through long hours of disciplined meditation, through self-mortification and self-abuse, leaving the world and sitting in a cave and starving and denying the body . . . It is no use!

Man can attain peace of mind through the absence of desire, but what is the use of this negative peace of mind in a world full of sufferings? Man has no right to it. Man can by subduing the body teach it various tricks such as climbing up an unsupported rope, or being buried alive and surviving by suspension of animation. What is the use? These supersensory abilities do not change the nature of man. Even if a soul of high attainments can produce effects of healing or of curing—of giving more life to a person or of taking life away from him—again, what is the use? The final objective for mankind, the changing of the species, cannot be attained except with the grafting of him into the life-stream of Jesus Christ: the merging of man's spirit into His.

---

[1] *The Book of Common Prayer.*

Only by the union of man's spirit with His Spirit can the new creature, the Son of God, come into being.

How does one know then, whether or not one has been born of the Spirit? How does one know whether a human child has been born? One looks and sees him. There he is, a new creature, not perfect as yet but with the potentiality of complete manhood within him. One knows whether one is born of the Spirit because one sees the new creature, instinct with a new power and aflame with a new love.

One arises out of the old into the new, as a butterfly arises out of the chrysalis. The butterfly is a new order of being, totally different from the caterpillar that entered that chrysalis; he is no longer ugly but radiant and beautiful. He no longer crawls upon the earth but flies on swift wings—he is a totally different being, a new creature, yet all of him was potential in the caterpillar. So our God who speaks to us in all things great and small, in the farthest of stars and in the smallest of worms, preaches a resurrection sermon in His whole creation.

11. The New Creature

in Christ Jesus

This new person arising out of the old lives under new laws. "The law of the Spirit of life in Christ Jesus hath made me free from the law of sin and death (Rom. 8:2)," wrote St. Paul in his magnificent chapter on the new man—the one who walks "not after the flesh but after the Spirit (Rom. 8:1)."

One becomes a new person not because one's original nature is artificially altered, but because certain potentialities latent within us are made active. St. Paul calls this quickening of dormant or latent gifts within us the giving to us of heavenly gifts by the action of the Holy Spirit upon our spirits. "Now concerning spiritual gifts, brethren, I would not have you ignorant," wrote (I Cor. 12:1). Therefore, lest after two thousand years we remain ignorant of these gifts, let us look at his classification of them in First Corinthians 12:

We will note that these gifts fall into three classes: one that we would consider quite normal, gifts of wisdom and knowledge and faith; another that we should by this time understand: gifts of healing and the working of miracles; and a third that we have not as yet considered and that may at first startle us: super-sensory gifts of prophecy, of the discernment of spirits, of speaking with tongues and of the interpretation of tongues; and finally, the greatest and the most misunderstood gift of all, the gift of charity.

That our mental abilities of wisdom, knowledge and faith should be increased by the inspiration of the Holy Spirit is quite obvious and requires no comment. Creative people of all ages have recognized that a certain quality above and beyond mere rationalization is necessary to creative action and have waited for the "mood" or cried out for the inspiration or plaintively besought "Oh come, my muse . . ."

It is not at all strange that these natural gifts of man, quickened variously by joy and zeal and an intense interest, should also be quickened by the indwelling of the Holy Spirit.

As for the working of miracles of healing, of protection, of the transformation of personality or salvation, it is obvious that these are works of the Holy Spirit and therefore the more we are quickened by the Spirit, the more readily the Spirit can work through us to accomplish God's will.

These gifts need no clarification. But the other gifts mentioned by St. Paul are so little understood today that an avoidance of any consideration of them has dimmed our total understanding of the Holy Spirit. Therefore we may do well to consider them briefly and try to understand them as much as we can.

The gift of prophecy: this means in the Scriptures both inspired preaching and also the *foreseeing of the future*. When St. Paul refers again to prophecy in the fourteenth chapter of First Corinthians, he clearly means the exposition of the Word, or preaching. "He that prophesieth speaketh unto men, to edification and exhortation and comfort . . . (I Cor. 14:3)." All of us who teach or preach have felt this gift. Have we not often prayed "Come, Holy Ghost, our souls inspire," and have not words come to us with a clarity and power not our own, so that people have said, "I felt that God was speaking through you"?

However, the word "Prophecy" is also used in the scriptures and in everyday language to mean a *foreseeing and foretelling of the future*. "The Holy Ghost witnesseth in every city," said St. Paul when he persisted in going to Jerusalem, "saying that bonds and afflictions abide me (Acts 20:23 & Acts 21:4)." The prophet Agabus bound Paul's hands and feet with his girdle and said, "Thus saith the Holy Ghost . . . (Acts 21:10-11)." All of these and countless others had the gift of looking ahead into time and seeing certain events that were to take place.

A bit of this gift is latent in all of us, and it is nothing to fear! We have our "hunches" and would do well to heed them. Even animals at times show an amazing and instinctive perception of the future, like rats who are said to desert a ship fated to be destroyed and dogs who seem to know when a master is about to return from a trip or when he is faced with death, and to react accordingly. Many people of today are intensely interested in such phenomena and give them long names such as "extra-sensory perception." Others are frightened of such study, feeling that it is, per se, irreligious. But one who is filled with the Spirit of God sees nothing strange about such matters as extra-sensory perception, either within time or beyond time. Probably he feels no necessity of studying it from the mental plane, since it is best acquired on the spiritual plane and best maintained with a minimum of study. On the other hand, he need not be distressed by any scientific study of this matter any more than he need be disturbed by the study of psychology.

From the religious point of view, the extra-sensory gifts of discernment and of prophecy hinge on the fact mentioned before, namely that in the world of the Spirit time is not, and the future is as today. In the eyes of the Spirit of God, events that happened yesterday and events that will happen tomorrow are presently going on. Then what is more natural than for the Spirit of God to so fill our own awakened spirits that we can see into time and perceive things just a bit ahead of our noses? Again and again a bit of this gift comes to us and we in our stupidity laugh it off and run into danger because we do not heed it.

Sometimes we do heed it, acting either from a conscious seeking for guidance or from a subconscious urge. I have learned, on planning a plane trip, to look ahead into the weather and endeavor by guidance to sense prevailing winds and clouds. If I have a dim and unhappy feeling about the weather, I cancel the plane trip and go by train. Since learning to direct my attention to this matter, I have not missed an appointment by reason of weather, and on the three occasions when I cancelled a plane by hunch, or by a bit of the gift of prophecy, planes have been grounded by weather on the day when I would have flown. There is nothing strange in this. One merely looks through the eyes of the spirit in order to see a little farther into time, just as one looks through a telescope in order to see a bit farther into space.

Holy men in the Bible looked with the telescope of their spiritual eyes and saw through the years and through the centuries. Many of their beautiful or terrifying pictures of the future were seen through a glass darkly. Some were literal and some symbolic; some were written as plainly as men knew how to write, and some may have been written in a sort of holy code, understandable only to the prophets and the saints. The translation and interpretation of these prophecies is too great a subject for this book, or indeed for most Christians. But our own bits of prophecy, or "hunches", trifling though they may be, make clearer to us that this gift is not a dead phenomenon wrapped in the sanctity of the Bible and buried, but is available to us today, and it is obviously of great value in healing, in counselling and in planning our lives and our work.

We now come in St. Paul's list to one of the most perplexing of these gifts: the gift of the discernment of spirits. The first thought that occurs to us may be that this refers to things seen by psychic research; to materializations and spiritualistic guides or controls. But as we study the Bible we see that this cannot be, for such "curious arts" seem to be regarded in the Scriptures as aberrations of the real purpose of God, as things to be avoided (Lev. 20:6 & Deut. 18:10-14) and cast out (Acts 19:13-19). A certain sorcerer who nowadays would be called a spiritualist, had a medium possessing a familiar spirit, or guide, as we would say today. This girl, the medium, followed St. Paul calling aloud, "These men are servants of the most high God". Her message was true. Nevertheless, St. Paul cast out the "guide" and set the girl free (Acts 16:18). This searching for truth through "guides" or by contact with lower spirits than God's Spirit is discouraged in the Bible. Should not people seek unto their God, says Isaiah (Isaiah 8:19), rather than to those who have familiar spirits? (Or as we would say today, "guides.") Shall the living look to the dead for help?

I am not condemning those who engage in psychic research as a science. They have added to man's knowledge of the intangible and therefore a church that has been too much immersed in the flesh owes them a debt of gratitude. But psychic research has nothing to do with Christianity, and when one attempts to mix it with Christianity, then one runs into danger. Shall the living fasten their attention upon the dead? Remember—the thing upon which we fasten our attention tends to become true. Let us fasten our attention therefore on Jesus Christ, who is not dead but living forevermore, not as a discarnate spirit but as an ever-living resurrected Body!

When St. Paul speaks therefore of the discernment of Spirits we know that he does not mean cooperation with psychic entities or any kind of work on the psychic plane, but refers rather to the quickening of our perceptive powers on the spiritual plane— a very different thing.

The Bible is full of stories of the discernment of spiritual beings. Usually these are called angels. Occasionally they are called "men" but the context has shown them to be men not abiding in a body of flesh (Gen. 18:1-2). Perhaps they are angels appearing as men or perhaps they are saints who have already attained to the resurrection body. Two of the angels have been called by their heavenly names: Michael (Jude 9) and Gabriel (Luke 1:19, 26). Those who saw these heavenly beings most certainly had the gift of discernment of spirits. It is amazing beyond belief that this gift should have so completely disappeared from the church that many Christians, even when they say in church, "Therefore with angels and archangels and all the company of heaven" do not believe a word of what they are saying! If the church had lived closely enough to God so that the eyes of holy men could see those wonders that transcend the flesh, as the eyes of holy men of all ages have seen them, there would be no need of the present-day searching for proof of the everlasting life through mediums and through guides.

The Holy Spirit does not need to use a "control" in order to illumine the mind or body of man. If one will search the scriptures, one will find not a single instance of a "healer" or holy man who functions under the guidance of a control or "familiar spirit." The saints of old have been controlled by God alone and by His Spirit and have sought only Him. When angels or heavenly men acting as God's messengers have come to these saints, they have come spontaneously, at God's own bidding, not through the seeking of any man. We have no account of anyone concentrating on an angel or any kind of heavenly being and calling to him for help and trying to see him. We hear only of those who live completely for God and turn the eyes of the spirit always to Him being given at times to see angels and messengers from heaven for the purposes of illumination (Luke 1:1-19) (Luke 1:26-38) and comfort (Luke 22:43), of guidance (Ex. 3:2) and of protection (Ps. 34:7 and Ps. 91:11).

The same thing is true today. Therefore if it be given to us to see a vision of Christ or of an angel or even of someone whom we have loved and lost coming to us for our comfort, let us not be afraid. We are not becoming "psychic". We are merely seeing with the eyes of the spirit. We are not becoming psychotic either: "seeing" something that is not there! We are seeing something that *is* there and is made perceptible to us by the sharpening of our spiritual vision through the action of the Holy Spirit. Even on the physical plane, vision is not a static and universal ability! Some people see farther than other people do—A hawk sees farther than a man can see. An astronomer equipped with a telescope sees farther than any hawk.

Any bit of clairvoyance or clairaudience, therefore, that comes to us unsought is for our comfort, guidance or protection and is altogether good. It is the gift of the discernment of spirits. The Holy Spirit does not do violence to our natures, but only increases and develops in us gifts that are already potential to our natures. Some people have a natural-born spiritual sensitivity, and if they use this only in the realm of meditation and spiritual living, avoiding seances, ouija boards and automatic writing, this gift can be greatly used in God's service.

Most of us have little of this potentiality, but as we are filled with the spirit, new powers of discernment come to us, not through visions or voices, but simply through an intuitive understanding and perception of matters usually termed extra-sensory. Some "healers" are able to sense the presence in a disturbed person of an interfering spirit of evil. The one thus sensing or "seeing" the disturbing spirit does not necessarily perceive this power of evil in a picture, nor need he personalize or visualize this possessing or disturbing thing. All that he needs to do is to cast it out in the name of Jesus Christ and through His power: to exorcise it, simply commanding whatever interfering spirit this may be to depart completely from the earth-realm, never to return to it again.

This type of prayer has power, whether the trouble be possession or obsession—whether it be objective or subjective. One cannot always tell to what extent the spirit of hate or of fear or of perversion may be from without and to what extent it may be from within: merely an overgrown, obsessing thought-habit of evil. But we may remind ourselves that God is love and that all evil is from the enemy, and that the words of exorcism are the most potent sledge-hammer of suggestion known to the subconscious mind, and so we may speak the word of power without further effort at analysis.

Last in the gifts of the Spirit as listed by St. Paul is another type of extra-sensory phenomena: something like clairaudience combined with an ability to speak aloud those words sensed by the spirit.

The words are not heard in the mind but only in the spirit. The conscious mind is not apt to know what these words are until they are spoken. And lest one should doubt that these words heard by the spirit of man come from the Holy Spirit, these words are frequently in a language unknown to the conscious mind. This is the gift of tongues. It is strange that in today's interest in extra-sensory phenomena this authentic and Biblical gift of extra-sensory perception has been ignored by the intelligent. Yet perhaps it is not too strange, for together with many of the gifts of the Spirit, this gift of tongues fell into abuse and then into disuse in the history of the church long ago. However, like all the gifts of the Spirit, the power to speak with tongues has remained potential with all Christians and actual with some groups devoted to this manifestation of God's power.

When the Holy Spirit came to the disciples on the day of Pentecost, they began to speak in other tongues (Acts 2:4) as the Spirit gave them utterance. This same phenomenon is mentioned time after time in the New Testament. If we believe the Bible at all, it is hard to see how we can throw out this gift of the Spirit. Most of us, true, endeavor to explain it away by claiming that the Holy Spirit so quickened man's intelligence that their smattering of Greek or Latin or Egyptian was increased and they were more able to make themselves understood in these languages. But while this is undoubtedly one way in which the Spirit spoke through them, it is not the only way. St. Paul definitely and regretfully states in his discourse on the gift of tongues (I Cor. 14) that the language thus spoken was not intelligible to most men (I Cor. 14:2). He even intimated that some of the languages spoken had never been used upon this earth at all, but only by heavenly beings (I Cor. 13:1).

This may sound to most of us like nonsense, but if we base our faith upon the Word of God, we can hardly dismiss it and say, "The rest of the Bible I will believe but this I cannot accept." What then? Are we required to accept something that to our conscious minds seems idiotic? By no means. Every one of the gifts of the Spirit is given to us to profit withal and every one of them can be grasped by our understanding if we will but bend upon the matter the same amount of intelligent research and consideration that we are willing to give to the phenomena of science.

My own illumination began when I dared to mention this matter to a trusted friend.

"Why, Agnes, I've had the gift of tongues for twenty years," she said.

"But I've known you for ten years!" I cried, recalling many

laughing hours I had spent with this jolly and sensible person. "And I've never heard you speak in tongues!"

"Of course not. The gift of tongues is not usually for public use but only for one's private devotions," she told me. "St. Paul apparently did not speak in tongues in public, yet he said, 'I thank my God, I speak with tongues more than ye all (I Cor. 14:18).' "

"What *is* this thing?" I demanded, utterly confused.

"It is the Holy Spirit filling your spirit and sending His power through your tongue, just as He sends His healing power through your hands when you lay them on a sick person," she told me. "After all, if He can send an energy that you do not understand through your hands so that they have healing power, why can't He send an energy through your tongue, so that it speaks words that you do not understand?"

"But *why*?"

" 'He that speaketh in an unknown tongue edifieth himself,' " she quoted (I Cor. 14:4).

"How can he edify himself if he doesn't know what he is saying?"

"Oh, but he does edify himself. It is only the conscious mind that does not know what he is saying. The spirit knows and apparently the subconscious mind catches it, for one's mood changes instantly. One feels extraordinarily happy and can almost tell that the words one speaks are words of praise to God. And afterwards one's guidance is apt to come more clearly, as though the spirit had received messages from God and had imparted them to the subconscious."

"But in that case, why don't the messages come in English?"

"They do, sometimes. Haven't you ever heard yourself say while teaching or lecturing something that you did not know you knew?"

Yes, I had. Many a time. So I dropped this question and went on to the next: "Well, then, why doesn't the word always come in English?"

"I don't quite know," she replied in all honesty. "All I know is that I seem to feel more of the transforming joy of the Spirit when it comes in another tongue."

"But what if you were to stand up to teach your Bible Class," I asked, "and all of a sudden you were to let fly and speak in tongues?"

"That could not possibly happen," she replied. " 'The spirits of the prophet are subject to the prophet. For God is not the author of confusion, but of peace.' (I Cor. 14:32-33)."

Now let us consider this matter first introduced to me by the above conversation.

Why, after all, should the Holy Spirit be limited to the English language? He knows all languages of men and of angels, of those in the flesh and of those out of the flesh and of any who may live on other planets, whether or not they have ever put on flesh. He, the Holy Spirit of God, broods upon the mass mind of the earth and flashes through the universal to the individual. He touches not only the spirit but also the tongue of the individual. Thus the tongue of man speaks aloud words of praise and glory given him by the Holy Spirit. It is possible that the Holy Spirit speaks to him at times in a language he does not know in order to subdue the interference of the conscious mind and to find a more direct pathway into the subconscious. More often, true, the Holy Spirit speaks to one in one's own language, but when He does so speak, the man may not recognize that it is He, the Spirit, speaking. And even when one does recognize that he is inspired by the Holy Ghost, he may still introduce his own concepts into the message so that it is diluted by human "wisdom."

On the other hand, when one speaks with tongues he cannot but know that the Spirit is speaking through Him. His subconscious mind hears the voice of the Spirit more clearly, since it is not interrupted by the interference or "static" of his own train of thought. Thus he rejoices. Thus there is renewed within him the *feeling* of the immortal life, a feeling which no words can encompass. Thus the actual light of Spirit enters into his heart, changing its emotional quality, piercing its dark corners, overruling its predisposition to heaviness with a flow of heavenly joy and directing it into the ways of peace. "May Thy Holy Spirit direct and rule our hearts—" so we pray.[1] But usually we do not open a wide enough door for the entry of the Spirit's power. When we permit Him actually to come in and take control of thought and speech, then that wide door is opened. We speak aloud in order that the consciousness of His "ruling and directing" shall be reinforced upon the conscious mind. The words spoken with the tongue and heard with the ear seem to give a release of joy that these same words merely sensed and pent-up within us cannot give. The entire personality is then filled and

---

[1] *The Book of Common Prayer.*

flooded with heavenly light and lifted up to that state of consciousness that is in heaven. After one is so lifted, then tongues
may cease and the spirit, being made one with God's Spirit, may
dwell with Him beyond time, seeing His glory and sensing His bliss.
And in this contemplation of His eternal Being, the still, small
voice may speak to us not now in words, but in an inner knowing
that goes beyond words. From this inner knowing will flow into
all our affairs a wisdom and an inspiration that men will see.
Thus they will see our good works and glorify our Father who is
in Heaven (Matt. 5:16).

"But is this not a dangerous gift?" we may ask.

Certainly. There is a danger in all advanced knowledge and
indeed in learning of every kind. From the time when the infant
gets out of his crib and learns to walk, he is in danger of falling.
The danger of this particular gift is obvious and St. Paul has
expounded on it at some length in his first Epistle to the Corinthians (I Cor. 12 & 14). It is a danger of over-emphasis and over-
emotionalism. But as we are able to achieve a balance in other
matters, so we can achieve balance and moderation in this matter.

Am I suggesting that every Christian shall seek the gift of
tongues? No! By no means. Nor am I suggesting that every
Christian should seek the gift of discernment of spirits. Nor do I
say that every Christian should be a prophet or a preacher.
The Spirit divides His gifts to us according to His will (I Cor. 12).
In all the Bible I can find no instance of anyone praying for the
gift of tongues—only instances of prayer for the Holy Spirit,
after which they sometimes spoke with tongues (Acts 10:44-46).
The value of this discussion of the gifts of the Spirit is not that we
shall seek this gift or that gift, but merely that we shall understand all of them and fear none of them, lest by our fear we close
a door to the Spirit Himself. Rather than seeking this gift or
that one, I suggest that we follow the "more excellent way" that
St. Paul points out in the thirteenth chapter of First Corinthians.

Valuable as the gifts of the Spirit may be, so said St. Paul,
the universal gift or fruit of the Spirit which he calls charity or
Christian love is more valuable than any one of them. It is by
growing into this love of Christ that we can achieve a balance,
lest we over-emphasize any one of the gifts of the Spirit. There
are diversities of gifts, but the same Spirit (I Cor: 12:4). The
fruit of the Spirit, which is given to all of us who sincerely follow
Christ, is over and above all of the gifts and must flow through

all of them or else they have no value. This charity, which we translate most inadequately by the word "love", is more than a mere increase of human affection. Fleshly affection is a part of all life. Even animals show affection toward their young, toward each other and often toward man. Earthly love which human beings share with animals is a pale reflection of God's charity and it is good, but it is not that "more perfect way" of which St. Paul writes in First Corinthians 13. Nor does the mere increase of human love or eroticism change it into that gift or fruit of the Spirit which is God's love.

Human love breeds jealousy. It leads often to unseemly action. It is easily provoked and hurt. It seeks love in return—it tends to bind. Divine love is totally free, totally unpossessive, totally unselfish and tremendously powerful to heal and to save. Divine love, or charity, is actually *God's love working through us*. One may have no *feeling* of love, for His love may be working with such intensity that one forgets oneself utterly.

I once spent three hours fighting for the soul of an alcoholic friend. I used every kind of prayer that I knew: the prayer for the healing of the disease of alcholism in the body, the prayer of exorcism of any evil influence that might enter into the matter, the prayer for the forgiveness of sins and the healing of the memories. When I related the incident years afterwards, the woman having become a person great in prayer, someone shocked me by saying, "You must have loved her very much."

This shifted the emphasis to myself and my personal feelings, which had not entered into the matter at all. I had not been conscious of love or of any feeling of any kind. I had not been aware of myself, but only of the woman and of Jesus Christ. If I had been moved by personal, human concern I doubt whether the power would have been so freely available for her healing. My fear and worry might easily have narrowed the channel for God's power. Moreover, human love might have bound her to me, so that she sought my company and help from that time on, whereas she was never bound except to Christ. I see her occasionally, usually in order to pray for someone else. We are then together in Christ's service, and so are filled with His charity. When we are not together we are healthily unconcerned about each other.

What then is this charity that can be so personally helpful and yet so divinely impersonal—that can claim people for Christ but never for oneself? It seems to me that while St. Paul did not list it among the other gifts of the Spirit, since it is the all-inclusive and all-important gift, it is nevertheless not only a fruit of the spiritual life, but also a gift of the Spirit just as truly as is the gift of tongues. And according to St. Paul, while all the gifts of the Spirit are good, this gift of charity alone is the absolute essential. He did not say that men were to be recognized as Christians by their possession of any one of the specialized gifts of the Spirit, but by the fruits of the Spirit working within them, and above all by this that is the very hall-mark of the Spirit—Christian love.

When Christians were converted through love of Christ and faith in Him and when the Holy Spirit was passed on to them with the eager expectancy of their becoming new creatures in Christ Jesus, there was no need of an understanding laboriously achieved through study and pictures and charts. But since our faith has grown so small and our love so dim, as we state in our hymns to the Holy Spirit, ("Hosannas languish on our tongues and our devotion dies")[1], let us strive to revive our faith and brighten our love by our understanding of the actual work of the Holy Spirit within those Christians who make up the Holy Catholic Church. Let us now sum up the seven steps toward becoming a son of God (John 1:12).

1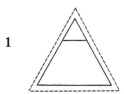

My drawings are but symbols, containing, I hope, the seed-thoughts of reality. Let us consider first the soul of the infant— that is, the total personality—as it comes from God into this world; small, complete, the conscious and the subconscious mind in embryo, inactive, but still enfolded in the light of the spirit.

Our birth is but a sleep and a forgetting:
The Soul that rises with us, our life's Star,
Hath had elsewhere its setting,
And cometh from afar:

---

[1] *The Hymnal.*

Not in entire forgetfulness,
And not in utter nakedness,
But trailing clouds of glory do we come
From God, who is our home:
Heaven lies about us in our infancy!
Shades of the prison-house begin to close
Upon the growing Boy,
But he beholds the light, and whence it flows,
He sees it in his joy;
The Youth, who daily farther from the east
Must travel, still is Nature's Priest,
And by the vision splendid
Is on his way attended;
At length the Man perceives it die away
And fade into the light of common day[1].

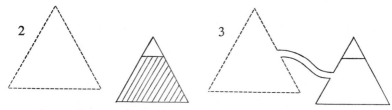

Remember now our fairy story of the shock of birth into this dark kingdom, this fallen planet, and look upon the next drawing, suggesting the partial withdrawal of the spirit and the darkening of the subconscious mind as it comes into contact with the sin of this world.

The third symbol suggests that in the rite of baptism, through the faith of parents, minister and loving congregation, and through the sanctified water charged with God's creativity, the spirit of the infant is regenerated and endued with a new power, so that it can now make a connection with the subconscious mind, sending into it messages of God's surrounding light and of Christ's over-shadowing presence and love, thus lightening the subconscious and comforting and strengthening the soul of the infant.

The fourth picture suggests the soul (total personality) of the adult, the heart (subconscious) troubled with certain sins and hurts held down by an act of will.

The fifth picture suggests a conscious acceptance of the

[1] *"The Intimations of Immortality from Recollections of Early Childhood"* by William Wordsworth.

forgiveness of Christ that opens a door into the subconscious mind, heals the memories and redeems the whole personality, as we saw in Chapter Eight.

The sixth picture indicates the transformation that takes place when the reborn Christian is filled with the Holy Ghost. The spiritual centers are then activated to the fullest extent,

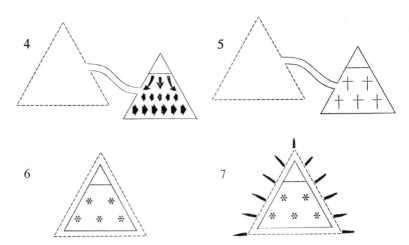

not by his own efforts but by the free gift of God's Holy Spirit. The spiritual powers latent within him are released so that not only does he bring forth the fruit of the spirit—love, joy, peace, long-suffering, gentleness, goodness, faith, meekness, temperance (Gal. 5:22,23)—but also the gifts of the spirit are given him in varying degrees (I Cor. 12:8-10)—. The spirit of man being quickened by the Holy Spirit becomes integrated with both the conscious and the subconscious minds of man, as we have studied in Chapter Ten. The conscious mind is inspired and guided, so that all work is done with more ease and effectiveness and all play is filled with more joy. And the subconscious mind is "ruled and directed" by His spirit—His spirit "directs, sanctifies and governs both our hearts (subconscious minds) and our bodies," according to the Book of Common Prayer. His spirit directs the subconscious so that we are in extraordinary ways guided more actively and perfectly to do His will. His spirit sanctifies the heart or inner being by so filling us with Himself that the impulses toward sinful and fearful and distressful thinking gradually dim away and are changed into joy. Thus the salvation wrought in us by the cross of Christ is turned into the transformation wrought by the baptism of the Holy Spirit. I have indicated this, rather childishly, by changing all the crosses, symbols of the cleansing of the Cross of Christ, into stars. They are not taken away. As long as we are in this world we will need to be under the shadow of the cross of Christ and to be cleansed by that life that flows from Him. So the crosses in my picture are still there, but they are so lit with the light of the spirit that they are turned into stars, and we feel not the sorrow of the bereaved disciples but the joy of Jesus Himself as He stood in the very shadow of the cross and said to His disciples that His joy would remain with them, so that their joy might be full (John 15:11).

I finally in chart seven indicate around the soul or the total personality of the redeemed and spirit-filled Christian, an effulgence—an enfolding light: the light of the Spirit of Jesus Christ. Could one imagine another triangle enclosing this symbol of man—a dotted triangle filling earth and heaven and glowing with the light of eternity? This might symbolize, if there were enough paper in the world to draw it, the Spirit of Christ. And the effulgence of light surrounding our picture of the new creature in Christ Jesus—the changed species—the new order of man—indicates that he is so filled with the Spirit as to be actually lifted up into the Christ Being. "That we may be very members incorporate in the mystical body of Thy Son[1]" . . .Where have we heard those words before?

This is the seventh step in the Christian life: The redeemed and spirit-filled Christian is actually no longer living in his own body alone, but in the Body of Christ; and is thus lit by the effulgence of that Holy Spirit, the Comforter who proceeds from the Father and the Son.

I believe in the Holy Catholic Church, the Body of Christ on earth, the blessed company of all faithful people, the Bride of the Lamb . . . .

Moreover, I believe that the Holy Catholic Church when it is filled with the Holy Spirit will have the same power that was seen in the early church and that was foreseen by the prophets of old. "Then shall the eyes of the blind be opened," said Isaiah, "and the ears of the deaf unstopped. Then shall the lame man

---

[1] *The Book of Common Prayer.*

leap as an hart, and the tongue of the dumb shall sing (Isa. 35:5)."

This was true while our Lord was on earth and it was also true so long as His Body, the church, remained full of His Holy Spirit. The Holy Spirit is called the Spirit of Christ (Rom. 8:9), and the Spirit of God (Gen 1:2) as well as Holy Spirit or Holy Ghost. How to differentiate the Holy Spirit from the Spirit of Christ I do not know, any more than I know how to differentiate the Son from the Father. Jesus Himself said, "If ye have seen me, ye have seen the Father (John 14:10)." But this I know, that whereas the disciples were weak and inadequate before the coming of the Holy Spirit—and this in spite of the fact that they were undoubtedlly reborn, believing Christians—after the coming of the Holy Ghost they were full of power (Acts 3).

This power could work with transcendent energy through faith and through the spoken word, as it did for the man born lame (Acts 3:1-11). It could work also with increased vigor through the body and the subconscious, as it did when St. Paul embraced the young man whose neck was broken and restored him to life and health (Acts 20:9-10). It could also work spontaneously where a sufficient number of Spirit-filled people were together. We are told that even the heathen were so aware of this that they brought forth their sick and laid them in the streets so that the shadow of Peter passing by might fall on them and restore them to life (Acts 5:15). Indeed and truly the shadow that passed over them was not only the shadow of Peter's body, but was the overshadowing of the Holy Ghost, released in a larger body than Peter's, the Body of Christ on earth—the blessed company of all faithful people.

We read in every instance of the coming of the Holy Ghost that He came to a *group of people* worshipping together. The first time He came it was to a hundred and twenty, bursting upon all of them spontaneously. But the hundred and twenty waited together for days until they had achieved sufficient unity of Christian love and sufficient longing of spirit to open the doors and make it possible for Him to come. Having once burst through, with a great rush of spiritual power, so that the room shook with the mighty wind of its vibration, so that its light was seen and felt upon the heads of every one of them (Acts 2), He came afterwards more quietly through the passing on of His power from one incandescent soul to others. And wherever He was received, His coming was followed by signs and wonders:

miracles of healing, conversion, and of guidance, and most of all the miracle of joy as of a well of water springing up to everlasting life.

When the church is sufficiently filled with the Spirit, then her power to heal and to save will be tremendously increased.

Therefore, if we desire healing it behooves us at some time on the steep ascent to heaven to lay aside praying for healing per se, as we three women did in the desert where we waited before the Lord, and to pray for the Holy Spirit to enter us and to receive us into Himself that we may be filled with power from on High. We may pray this prayer in our private petitions, and the power will shine in us in a steady and gradual way and some day when we make a close enough attunement, will burst into light within us. Or we may pray together as a group, being of one mind and in one accord, meeting together at regular intervals to pray, not for a long list of sick people, but for the Holy Spirit who can heal all those people when He is sufficiently released within the church of Christ. Or if we know someone who has this heavenly gift, we may ask that one to pray for us with the laying on of hands that we may be quickened in that gift of the Holy Ghost that we received at confirmation—but that has never come to full life within us, due to lack of faith and of desire. St. Paul wrote to Timothy, "Stir up, therefore, the gift of God that is in thee (II Tim 1:6)." And a group of Christians meeting together to pray for the Holy Spirit need not feel that they are usurping a sacrament of the Church, but merely that they are stirring up the Spirit passed on to them at that time by the authority of the Church but not sufficiently appropriated due to lack of faith, understanding—and of desire.

For in order to receive this heavenly gift, we must desire Him with the whole heart. This is the final accomplishment of His Spirit—making us once more sons of God as we were meant to be in the beginning. This is the completeness of His salvation. This is the re-establishment of the heavenly strain within us— the transformation of the personality—the changing of the species. For this, God the Creator brooded long over His fallen earth, shaping we know not what trends of destiny in the heaven and in the earth so that in the fullness of time the Savior should be born and the Holy Spirit should emerge upon this planet. For this, Jesus Christ crashed through into time and lived and loved and suffered among us, giving even the life of His body

for us, that we might be cleansed and opened to the life of
His Holy Spirit.

This is the pearl of great price (Matt. 13:45-46). Is it
strange that we must seek with earnest longing in order to open a
wide enough door that He shall enter into us? "As the hart panteth
after the water-brooks (Ps. 42:1)," so must our souls thirst for
God, for the living God, that He may give us His water of
life which is the power of His Spirit. "More than they that
watch for the morning (Ps. 130:6)," so must our souls watch
for Him, that He may redeem us and make us His children—
heirs of God and co-heirs with Christ (Rom. 8:17).

12. The Company of
the Redeemed

What if we have all three currents of God's healing power? What if we not only know the power of faith or positive thinking, not only comprehend and discern the healing energy of the Body and Blood of Christ, but also are transformed by the baptism of the Holy Spirit? Certainly we will find that our own spirits, minds and bodies are so integrated that they work together like a perfectly balanced and well-oiled machine, so that as Jesus said, the bodily energies can throw off any poison absorbed from food or drink or accident (Mark 16:18). We will find many hitherto unsolved problems of other people dissolving before us in the flow of the love of Christ. We will become aware that the Holy Spirit more and more works through our spirits and helps people whose problems we may or may not know.

However, we will still find it difficult to carry on this work alone, because the more power released through us, the more the weight of the world's sorrows descends upon us—the more people bring us troubles and look to us for help. What then?

Then we need but remember that we do not work alone. We are corporate beings, and the full power of God can never be released through an individual, but only through the Church— the Body of Christ on earth (I Cor. 12:13-27).

Of all known miracles of faith I believe that the miracle of the church, or the body of Christ, is the most surprising. It is a miracle of God's faith in man. That Jesus Christ should have turned over to human beings dully wrapped in flesh His

plan for changing the species on this earth—that He should
have concentrated His attention on the few who had the Spirit
sufficiently to understand Him (John 6:60-71)—that He should
have made a main objective of training His successors that
they might carry on His work—this is a boldness and a trust
past comprehension. Why did not God once more wipe out the
species as in the days of Noah and start again with a holy seed,
Mary and Joseph and Mary of Bethany and John the Baptist
and a few other chosen souls, as a florist might destroy a whole
field full of seed and keep only a few carrying the strain that
he desires to perpetuate? Oh wonder of love and patience, that
instead of this He came to earth and started the slow and
laborious process of cleansing His own by water and by fire
and of lifting them into Himself! Oh greatest wonder of all,
that when a group of people are knit together in Him and meet
Sunday after Sunday in His Holy Temple to worship Him, then
He Himself can be among them and there do His healing work
as He did on the streets of Galilee! The Church should be
His healing agency. The Church should be the healer—the
comforting mother—the place of peace. So it was in the beginning. The heathen brought their sick to the disciples, yes.
But for the most part it did not seem necessary for any one
person to function as a "healer" to the Christians, for the group
itself was full of the healing power of the Spirit and the presence
of Christ at the altar fed them with the bread of life and wholeness. Thus St. Paul upbraids the Corinthians at one time because
they did not "discern the body of Christ" but ate and drank un-
worthily and he adds, "For this cause many are weak and sickly
among you (I Cor. 11:30)." The power of Christ to heal, he
felt, was potentially available to the whole congregation when
they met together in true worship, making a worthy repentance
and offering worthy praise to God. Even in those early days
this heavenly state did not last long among the Christians (Tim.
4:20). But the reasons for its dimming in power were not God's
departure from the church, but the church's departure from
God. And this ideal of a healing church can still be attained
today.

There was a young man seriously injured in an airplane
crash in the last war. Not only had he wrecked his plane in training, but he had killed his instructor in so doing. How much of
his consequent depression and mental confusion was due to
injury to the brain and how much was due to shock I do not

know. Though he did not belong to our church, he came to our services. He gradually regained strength and balance of mind. "Each Sunday I get just enough to carry me through the week," he said.

But his business sent him to a distant city, and when he returned, he came and showed me the church folders of all the churches in that town. "I tried 'em all," he said, "and it wasn't there—it wasn't there."

"Jesus Christ is in every church!" I replied.

But he only shook his head sadly and repeated, "He wasn't there. Not enough so that I could feel His power, anyway."

Not enough—that is the trouble. Jesus Christ is bound to be in every church! Religion is a matter of experiencing God— and we experience God first of all in a church. The church is the spiritual mother of all our infants, giving them birth into the life of the Spirit as the human mother gives them birth into the life of the body. The church is the "upper room", where those who earnestly expect the increase of the Holy Spirit are given that increase when they are confirmed by their Bishop. The church is the Lord's table spread before them, where the bread of life is given them Sunday by Sunday or morning by morning for the cleansing of their subconscious minds and the feeding of their souls. Thus the very atmosphere of a church is bound to become instinct with power! In Chapter Two I suggested that we have a place for our daily prayers, because the atmosphere of that place would become charged with power. This is in part the result of habit, but it is more than the result of habit. Thoughts live—thoughts remain—thoughts and spoken words are vibrant in the air, as we ought to know from our radios. The very walls of a place filled with prayer become instinct with spiritual life. How much more, then, the walls of a church, where thoughts and words are constantly directed toward God and where His life is continually meditated through the sacraments?

The sacraments, especially baptism, confirmation and the Holy Communion—let us consider them as channels of healing and see if we can "discern the body of Christ" working toward our healing within them.

Those who join His holy church are cleansed first of all by water. "Sanctify this water to the mystical washing away of sin,"—so the priest or minister says when a baby is first brought into that company of the redeemed that we call the church.

The mystical washing away of sin. What sin can a three

weeks old baby have committed? Or is it fair to consider, in God's justice, that the infant has inherited an active sin of such reality that he is in danger of hell fire if he is not baptised? What do these medieval words really mean to us? They must speak to a certain reality, for ministers have often seen miraculous healings follow the rite of baptism. Many a time my husband has been called to baptise a "dying" baby and without exception, the baby has lived. Usually its healing has been rapid and perfect, as though his soul had been freed from an intolerable load. How can this be?

Behold, I show you a mystery . . . "Look, I will tell you a fairy story." Let us humble ourselves to brood by the imagination upon the soul of a small entity—or a great entity, for who knows the size of the spirit? —entering into this world for the first time. Can we imagine such an immortal being drawn down from the bright glory of eternity, entering into the atmosphere of this earth and immediately being touched with the dirty air it has to breathe, as an airplane enters into the area of dust and smoke that darkens our cities and immediately is shrouded in dimness and can no longer see the brilliance of untainted sky and shining clouds? Can we imagine such a spirit saying to its small inadequate body, "No, I don't want to stay here! I am homesick! I am too far away from God! He has forsaken me! I feel unclean and dull and miserable, and I want to go home!" (Remember, this is a fairy story. In reality, we say that babies are just sweet pink lumps of flesh . . . so we presume, for we have no way of communicating with their souls.) In the fairy story, then, can we imagine God actually sanctifying that water as we asked Him to do—changing it into the wine of heaven, as Jesus changed the water into wine at Cana (John 2:1-13)—imparting to the water a life-giving stimulant more powerful than alcohol, totally different and completely mystical? Those who have eyes to see know that water is a powerful conductor of a spiritual life-force. Those who wonder about this fact may find it out for themselves by entering into a meditative state while bathing, preferably in sunlit water, but even in a bath-tub. If they are sufficiently sensitive to feel the vibration of God's power upon them while they pray, they will feel it even more when they pray with the body immersed in water. Those who learn God's mysteries through science also know that water is the great mother, the cradle of life. And the Bible story of creation unites its voice with theirs in telling us that the first living creatures were brought forth in the ocean, God's creativity being more readily received by water than by the dense earth or the thin air.

Dare we to imagine, then, that the water when blessed by the minister becomes not only a symbol of cleanness but also a channel for the imparting of a recreating energy, as the bread and wine at the Holy Eucharist become not only a symbol but also a channel for the human-divine life of Our Lord?

Since this is just a fairy story, let us imagine it. And let us dream of a baby feeling that the dirt of the sin-enveloped earth is being washed away, so that it once more basks in the sunlight of heaven and is once more enveloped by the love of the Father and enfolded in the Savior's arms. Let us imagine that bright spirit being thus comforted and saying, "Well, I find that God is here too, and I am not so lonely now that I feel His love, so I will stay here a while with these strange new people."

I believe that the infant, thus received into the fellowship of the church, is shielded from the influence of the present evil of the world and that its soul is turned toward God. God's spirit thus becomes active within the infant, protecting and strengthening him. In this sense, he receives at baptism a portion of God's Spirit. But the fullness of the Holy Spirit, the Third Person of the Trinity, the spirit of truth and of understanding, awaits him in the church until he has been sufficiently instructed in the creed, the Lord's prayer and the ten commandments[1], to intelligently invite and understand Him, so that he can receive more of His power through the Confirmation Service.

A short time after the incident recorded in the last chapter —the time when three women, earnestly seeking, received the Holy Ghost—I attended a confirmation service, not for the first time, my husband being an Episcopal minister. As I watched the bishop laying his hands on the heads of those people and listened to the words of the prayers, it came to me with an overwhelming rush of surprise that this was a service of passing on the Holy Spirit as Paul passed on this power when he laid hands on them who had not known that there was such a thing as the baptism of the spirit and they all rejoiced and spake in tongues praising the Lord.

"Why, the Bishop is doing just what we three women did

---

[1] *The Book of Common Prayer.*

in the desert!" I thought. And there are no words great enough
to express my amazement.

I had considered this experience of ours to be extraordinary
if not unique, a time of the highest spiritual and mystical experience—yet the Bishop was doing precisely what we had done.

And there is no question that those young people whom
he confirmed did receive, through the authority of the Church
and the will of Jesus Christ, the power of the Holy Ghost. But
much of that power while conferred upon them did not become
actual in their subsequent lives. They were by no means so instantly and completely transformed as the disciples were on
the day of Pentecost, nor did they go forth from that church
doing miracles.

Why?

Because they did not expect to be transformed and to do
miracles, nor did the congregation expect it. They did not expect it because they did not understand the third Person of the
Trinity, His nature or His powers, and they did not understand
this because they were not taught it in the church. In *Lost
Shepherd* I relate a story of four young people who attended a
confirmation class in order to learn what Christianity was. They
had a need and a hunger for truth—the basic truths of God and
man, of Jesus Christ and His salvation, of the Holy Spirit and
His indwelling. But the minister taught them only the history of
the Church, the church seasons and colors, the church symbols,
the structure of the Prayer Book, and the manner of receiving
communion. That is a true story. And it is a tragic story.

Nevertheless, I believe that the church can prepare a person for the full indwelling of the Holy Spirit and can teach him
to receive God's grace and healing Sunday by Sunday through
the Communion Service. According to the Prayer Book, a person
is to be brought to the Bishop to be confirmed *as soon as he
is sufficiently instructed* in the Creed, the Lord's Prayer and the
Ten Commandments. If sufficiently instructed in the Ten Commandments, a person will know how to live according to God's
laws. If sufficiently instructed in the Lord's Prayer, he will know
how to pray. If sufficiently instructed in the Creed, he will know
that God loves him and that Jesus came into the world to die
for him and to give him the Holy Spirit. And the purpose of
this instruction is not merely to enlighten the mind, but surely
it is also to touch the heart. Surely this teaching is supposed
to bring about a change that turns one from a potential Christian,

placed by his parents and sponsors under the protection of the Church, to a reborn person convicted by the Holy Spirit of sin, forgiven by Jesus Christ of that sin and growing daily in His strength and power. The subconscious mind of the infant has been opened to the invasion of the Holy Spirit by the faith of his parents, but it is necessary for him to personally invite the conquering Jesus into himself in order that he may become consciously and actively a Christian.

In other words, in order to be a reborn Christian ready to receive the Holy Spirit, and not merely a member of some religious organization, he must be converted.

Some churches endeavor to bring about a conversion by revivals and by evangelistic services and by personal work, introducing one to the redeeming work of Jesus Christ that he may accept Him with his will and with his word. Other churches expect that this acceptance of Christ will happen automatically and in a gradual fashion through the child's Church School work, his church attendance and certain confirmation lectures enlightening him as regards the Episcopal Church, its history, its days and its rituals. Sometimes this does take place, and a person becomes a devoted and sincere Christian though he could not put the finger upon the time of his conversion. But there is a danger in this method. Just as there is the danger of over-emotionalism in revival services, so there is the danger of under-emotionalism in the ignoring of any definite acceptance of Christ. How can one look with no emotion at all upon Jesus and His cross, realize that his own sins and the sins of humanity made that necessary, repent of those sins and ask Jesus to come into him and save him? Could one escape from a burning house without emotion? Could one flee a sinking ship without emotion? Emotion is cleansing and healing, and is moreover the earnest of a real repentance.

I was converted at the age of nine through the simple and sincere words of a Presbyterian minister in a small Southern town, but even more through the Bible, which my parents taught me to read, study and understand. I could not read of the passion of Our Lord without tears. I still remember those tears. They were not of hysteria or agitation. They were gentle and healing, and they opened a door in my mind that the love of Christ could enter in and there begin a process of rebirth which to this day is going on.

One does not insist that every young person should weep

before being received into the church. But surely one can say that everyone before entering into the congregation of Christ's flock should be moved with repentance and should love Christ. How can anyone accept so great a gift without a feeling of gratitude? Yet in some churches one accepts, to all intents and purposes, not Christ but the church.

We have been looking far away, have we not? Far away. Those of you who read and turn your minds wistfully to your own church—your church that may have a form of godliness but denies God's power to heal—or your church bustling with activity but not knowing that there is such a thing as the changing of the species by the power of the Holy Spirit—how shall you transform your church into one of God's colonies from heaven? How shall you make your church a place of healing and a haven of peace?

When we want to know how to do anything, we look to Jesus. He did not burst upon His people with the full power of the Spirit—not until He had lived among them and touched their hearts with His love and prayed for them and healed them. And this is the best way for us to work within our churches. All the prayers that we say for our brothers and sisters in Christ— all the healing that comes to pass through our prayer groups or our personal visitation and work—all of this will help to bring the light and life of the Holy Spirit within the Church.

But there are other ways of filling the Church itself with God's power and with the love of Christ and with the light of the Holy Spirit—simple and humble ways that I and my friends have tried and that I will pass on to you.

First, we come to church ten or fifteen minutes early and kneel or sit in silent prayer for the power of the Spirit of Christ to fill that church. In some churches this is easy. In others it is desperately hard, for custom dictates that church members should greet each other and whisper or talk together until the service opens. Possibly a group might agree to sit together and hold this silence, closing their ears to all but the voice of God.

If the minister himself is interested in prayer, he might instruct the congregation as to the value of a period of silent meditation and adoration before the service opens and request them to try it. If he feels that some people will not be able to endure the loss of fifteen minutes' conversation, he might soften his request by asking them to keep this silence for the six weeks of Lent or for some other stated period. Surely any

Christian would be willing to try this for Jesus' sake! In the old days they would have hung on a cross for Him. But nowadays, as someone said, they no longer hang Christians on crosses— they hang crosses on Christians.

Whether or not the minister is interested in prayer, we pray for him, from the moment he enters the church, that God may fill him with power and with grace and with the love of Christ. If some who read do not approve of their ministers, then let them rejoice that theirs is the opportunity and the power to help him through prayer. But let us pray in all sincerity that God will accomplish *His* perfect will in the minister and not *our* imperfect wills. Let us see our rector increased in charity and in wisdom and in power in every good way according to the potentialities of his own nature, but let us not pray "Lord, please make him do what I want him to do."

We can imagine Christ standing behind him and speaking through him. And we can imagine Christ entering and walking down the aisles with His hands spread forth in blessing and in healing. And we can imagine the light of the Holy Spirit enlightening every mind in that church, and the love of Christ touching every heart. If we see some who especially need to be made loving by His love, then we may pray especially for that one. If we see those whose eyes are dim and whose faces are tense and heavy, then we may pray especially for the light of the Spirit to enlighten that one.

"Did you pray for me in Church?" a man once asked me on the church steps.

"Yes, I did," I admitted. "You looked very unhappy . . . ."

"I thought so! I felt terrible when I went to church—wretched and out of sorts—I didn't want to go, but my wife made me, and then all of a sudden everything cleared up and I felt just wonderful, and I thought, 'Someone has been praying for me.' "

We also pray for healing during the church service and we find that more power is available there than in any prayer group, as indeed it should be. It would be tragic if the Church itself, where the life of Christ is offered from the altar, should be so cold and dull a place that we have to do our real spiritual work elsewhere. We pray for any in the congregation whom we know to need healing. A friend of mine once sat beside a man suffering obviously from some kind of discomfort. Glancing at him my friend, whom we will call Mr. A, noticed that one of Mr. B's legs was very swollen. Therefore, he made this healing the object of his private devotions during the course of the church service. There was no change visible to him when he left the church, but the next day he met Mr. B. on the street, looking well and happy.

"How are you?" said Mr. A.

"Oh, fine, fine!" replied Mr. B. "You may have noticed yesterday that I was rather restless. I had an attack of phlebitis— not the first one I've had. My wife wasn't sure I should go to church, but I told her I usually feel better in church, so I went. Funny thing, the minute I left the church, all the pain went away and the swelling went right down. Funny thing."

"Mmm. Funny thing," said Mr. A. "Well, glad you're better. So long."

When the day comes when a Christian will awaken of a Sunday morning and say, "I feel terrible today. I'll just have to get up and go to church," then that will be the Day.

I once inquired of an old friend concerning certain headaches that she used to have.

"Oh, I don't have them any more," said she. "Hardly ever. I did have one last Sunday. But I knew that if I could only get myself to church I would be all right. It was quite an effort, but I made it. And after about ten minutes I was all right. But you know, I tried that when I was at the seashore on vacation, and it didn't work at all."

"Mmm," I thought, remembering Mr. A., "Funny thing."

When the members of a church are praying for Jesus Christ to be present and heal, then He is present to heal, which is His own desire. "Ask and ye shall receive," He said, "that your joy may be full."

But when the members of a church do not believe that God heals today, or when they are too selfish to pray for the congregation even though they may pray for themselves, then His power among them is limited. John Maillard says that he often visions Jesus standing in His own churches with His hands tied behind Him.

Sometimes we agree beforehand as to special ones either in the congregation or at a distance for whom we shall pray. Occasionally we take someone at a distance as our "special intention" for the Communion Service and prepare to pray for him with prayer and fasting in the manner set forth in *Lost Shepherd*. Some of the most amazing miracles in my experience have taken place in this way. There was a man for whom two or three of us prayed at a Communion Service and whose name my husband mentioned in the Prayer for All Conditions of Men. This young man was "dying" of bleeding stomach ulcers which had so afflicted him that for two years he had lived mainly on Pablum. We did not know him, but prayed at the request of a faithful Presbyterian friend who took the trouble to arise and go to his bedside that she might lay her hands on him while we prayed. The tale that she related to me was that the next day she met him down town and he remarked, "I had forgotten how good hamburgers and onions could taste . . ."

We did not always give the names of these special ones to the minister. We did not feel it necessary, nor did we want to over-burden the service with special requests. Sometimes, therefore, the congregation heard, "Thy servant So-and-So, for whom our prayers are requested," and sometimes they did not. There was nothing said or advertised in any way that would point to this service as a healing service. Yet many people recognized that it was so, and indeed, even many of the children knew and felt that the church itself was full of healing power.

One little girl once told another that she had an earache.

"Well, silly," was the inspired response, "go to church and say a prayer about it. That's what I always do."

Sometimes the members of our prayer group shared each others' special intentions. "How many do you have for eleven o'clock?" a friend would ask me. "I'll take one of yours if you'll take one of mine."

It took many years to build this church up into a place of power — to change it from a mere edifice of stone into a warm and comforting dwelling-place of Our Lord, lit with the light of His Spirit and filled with the sense of His presence. If we had been able to use the reserved sacrament this would have been more readily accomplished, for obviously, if the bread and the wine have really received His life and Being, their presence in the church will be both a symbol and also a channel of His Holiness and His Love.

However, though it was not expedient that the reserved sacrament should have been made available to our low-church congregation, the power gradually permeated even the walls of the building itself. I once asked a Jewish friend of mine to step into the church.

"I'd rather not," he said. "I should tell you that I have a prejudice against churches."

"I understand that," I replied, reflecting with shame that I would also have this prejudice if my ancestors had been put to death in gas chambers by Christendom . . . "But it won't hurt you just to step inside the door and I would like you to do so for a special reason."

He came inside, started and looked up at the vaulted roof. "Why, it's *here!*" he said.

"What is here?"

"The power that heals!" replied this young man whose spiritual sensitivity far exceeded my own. "The same tingling, sort of an electric power that I felt when you put your hands on me and prayed for healing!"

Yes, it was there. I could not feel it physically, but spiritually I too was aware of a peace and of a Presence, and for that reason I would make my private devotions in that church rather than in my own home. True, living in the rectory made it easy for me to do so — and doing so added to the prayer-power perceptible in the church. But many from a distance passing by stopped and prayed before they went on their way. Either the church itself or the chapel was always kept open and heated for this purpose, as in the Roman Catholic Church one finds always warmth and the light of many candles and the tenderness of many prayers. (There are some things that we can learn from each other, we who make up the Body of Christ on earth, the Holy Catholic Church.)

It may not be necessary that our organizations should be merged, since a body is not an organization but an organism. It may not be good that we should all follow the same forms, since there is no standardization in God's kingdom and we differ each from each. It would be obviously impossible for us all to worship under one roof. But surely we can love each other and learn from each other those things that are good for us, and surely our prayers can ascend together unto the throne of God and unto the Lamb!

If we will do so, the power and the Presence can be so real in a church as to be perceptible to the sensitive even when they walk by it. A woman once passed this church, driving through the town. She was in great despair. Seeing the church, she stopped on impulse and went into it. The Good Friday three-hour service was just beginning, so she took her seat, intending to stay only a few minutes.

She stayed three hours. Afterward she sought out the minister.

"What is this you have in your church?" she asked. "When I came in here, I was on my way to commit suicide. I had been depressed for a long time and the doctor had just told me that I had angina and that it was incurable. I don't know why I stopped the car and came into the church. I thought I'd stay only a few minutes, but I stayed the whole three hours as you see, and all the time my heart got better and better and I felt better in every way, and now I don't want to commit suicide at all. *What is this that you have in your church?"*

And the minister replied, "I suppose — Christianity."

I believe in the Holy Catholic Church — in a group of people so united in prayer and in Christian love and in faith that they become the Body of Christ on earth, filled with His Holy Spirit. And when this is fully accomplished, then shall come the Kingdom of God on earth, when the earth shall be filled with the glory of God as the waters cover the sea. This life of the Body of Christ is the heavenly energy that shall unite all nations into an inevitable brotherhood that pulses with the same life, the same blood-stream. This is the foundation on which shall be built the new order of life, the Holy City, the new Jerusalem. And the nations of the earth shall bring their honor and their glory into it and the Lamb shall be the light thereof.

The glory of this heavenly Kingdom is beginning to shine upon us now, awaiting the invitation of loving hearts, and when the day comes, the day of God's final victory, then there shall be no more death, neither sorrow nor crying, neither shall there be any more pain, for all the former things will have passed away (Rev. 21:4).

13. National Repentance

Brings National

Blessings

Suppose then, that our churches were filled with the power of the Holy Spirit as was the early church. Could there be anything to prevent the perfect flow of God's healing power toward us? Would there be any barrier left between us and the fulfillment of God's perfect will?

Remembering that the barrier between God and man is man's sin and not God's will, then let us ask: would there be any sin left among us as our responsibility? Yes, there would be, for as we are part of the church, so also we are part of our nation. What of the sins of the nation? Can we claim a perfect holiness and therefore a perfect power, so long as we are sharing in national sins? While we as a nation hold down the standards of living of other peoples so that we can keep our own standard high, can we claim God's protection over our vested interests? Can we say, "In God We Trust," while we serve not God but mammon? Can we as a nation turn God's holy day into a high day upon the highways and then ask Him to protect us from accidents and dangers? Can we who took up the weapon of atomic energy and destroyed cities full of unarmed and helpless people call on God to save us from the destruction of that same atomic energy?

The people of this nation are riddled with fear. Of those who come to me for help in mental difficulties, ninety-nine hundreths are tormented by fear. Fear of *what?* They do not know . . .

It is a safe guess that everyone in the United States is afraid of the destructive force that we have released through the splitting of the atom. Our very excuses expose our fear. We justify ourselves for Hiroshima by saying that it speeded the end of the war and so saved lives. But this is no excuse, for we could have speeded the surrender of Japan by answering her question: "What are your terms of peace?" We know this now, looking back. For our own men, of whom my son is one, tell us that the Japanese were surprised, amazed, overwhelmed when they found that our terms of surrender were, on the whole, merciful and just. They had expected wholesale slaughter, rape and torture. No wonder they hesitated to surrender. If we had only said to them, "Our terms of surrender will be such and such," they would have surrendered long before, as the newspapers at that time made abundantly clear. Instead of that, we insisted on "unconditional surrender," meaning, "We will not tell you what we are going to do to you."

Militarists give us many reasons for this. But I wonder whether those reasons will hold good before the throne of God. I wonder whether the robes of righteousness and the flesh of expediency with which we clothed our action in Hiroshima will be burnt away by the fire of God's truth, showing beneath them the dry bones of fear and hate and pride. Surely nothing less could cause us to do a thing so horrible, not only in its destruction of human life but also in its effect upon future generations.

We deny these things. Naturally. We are afraid. Therefore, we refuse to face truth, and the more we refuse to face it the more afraid we are. As Hermann Hagedorn most truly says, the atomic bomb really fell on America[1].

We deny the fact that the atomic-fall-out may in awful ways affect the genes of future generations. We deny the fact that this same fall-out—not the mere repercussion of an atomic explosion, but the mysterious effect that the breaking of the atom has upon the other atoms that make up this world—has produced strange variations in our weather. The newspapers tell us that there will be cyclones upon the earth as a result of hydrogen explosions upon the sun, ninety-three million miles away from

---

[1] *The Bomb that Fell on America,* Hermann Hagedorn. Association Press, N. Y.

us, and in the same issue deny that a hydrogen explosion here upon our own earth could have any effect at all upon our winds and clouds. *Yet everyone knows it.* Most of us know it consciously and the rest of us fear it in a subconscious uneasiness, and for that very reason rush violently to deny it. We have released upon this earth a degenerative power. We ourselves have set in motion the disintegration of the very fabric of life, and what the final result of this will be no man can tell.

Not only that, but by our test explosions we increase day by day this cumulative danger to future generations.

Thank God that Dr. Albert Schweitzer has had the courage to write to the peoples of many nations and tell them that these explosions should at all costs cease! There is truly *no* cause great enough to make them necessary. Dr. Schweitzer says, in his "Declaration of Conscience": "The explosion of an atom bomb creates an unconceivably large number of exceedingly small particles of radioactive elements which decay like uranium or radium. Some of these particles decay very quickly, others more slowly, and some of them extraordinarily slowly. The strongest of these elements cease to exist only ten seconds after the detonation of the bomb. But in this short time they may have killed a great number of people in a circumference of several miles.

"What remains are the less powerful elements. In our time it is with these we have to contend. It is of the danger arising from the radioactive rays emitted by these elements that we must be aware.

"Of these elements some exist for hours, some for weeks, or months, or years, or millions of years, undergoing continuous decay. They float in the higher strata of air as clouds of radioactive dust. The heavy particles fall down first. The lighter ones will stay in the air for a longer time or come down with rain or snow. How long it will take before everything carried up in the air by the explosions which have taken place till now has disappeared no one can say with any certainty. According to some estimates, this will be the case not earlier than thirty or forty years from now.

"From official and unofficial sources we have been assured, time and time again, that the increase in radioactivity of the air does not exceed the amount which the human body can tolerate without any harmful effects. This is just evading the issue. Even if we are not directly affected by the radioactive material in the air, we are indirectly affected through that which has fallen down, is falling down, and will fall down. We are absorbing this through radioactive drinking water and through animal and vegetable foodstuffs, to the same extent as radioactive elements are stored in the vegetation of the region in which we live. Unfortunately for us, nature hoards what is falling down from the air.

"None of the radioactivity of the air, created by the explosion of atom bombs, is so unimportant that it may not, in the long run, become a danger to us through increasing the amount of radioactivity stored in our bodies.

"What we absorb of radioactivity is not spread evenly in all cellular tissue. It is deposited in certain parts of our body, particularly in the bone tissue and also in the spleen and in the liver. From these sources the organs which are especially sensitive to it are exposed to radiation. What the radiation lacks in strength is compensated for by time. It works day and night without interruption.

"How does radiation affect the cells of an organ?

"Through being ionized, that is to say, electrically charged. This change means that the chemical processes which make it possible for the cells to do their job in our body no longer function as they should. They are no longer able to perform the tasks which are of vital importance to us. We must also bear in mind that a great number of the cells of an organ may degenerate or die as a result of radiation.

"Not our own health only is threatened by internal radiation, but also that of our descendants. The fact is that the cells of the reproductive organs are particularly vulnerable to radiation which in this case attacks the nucleus to such an extent that it can be seen in the microscope.

"To the profound damage of these cells corresponds a profound damage to our descendants.

"It consists in stillbirths and in the births of babies with mental or physical defects.

"We are forced to regard every increase in the existing danger through further creation of radioactive elements by atom bomb explosions as a catastrophe for the human race, a catastrophe that must be prevented.

"There can be no question of doing anything else, if only for the reason that we cannot take the responsibility for the consequences it might have for our descendants.

"They are threatened by the greatest and most terrible danger."

We must stop atomic test explosions. One hopes that by the time this book is published, statesmen will have come to that agreement for which they are so earnestly seeking, and we will have stopped . . . or else that the methods of fusion rather than fission will decrease the dangers of future explosions.

But what of the radioactive rays already released in this world and exerting, according to Dr. Schweitzer, a degenerating and decaying force that will continue increasingly to make our food and water radioactive? Do I believe that God, being Almighty, can and will save us by reconstructing the life-energy that we have destroyed? No, I do not. Unless we face the sins of the nation and repent of them. And not unless we cease from dangerous explosions. I do not believe in the automatic interference of God in the affairs of men. A man cannot throw a boomerang and say: "Why didn't God prevent it from hitting me?" But I do believe in the forgiveness of sins, not only personal sins but national sins. I do believe that if we repent and cease sinning, God can come to be our Judge and that He can save us from the very destruction that we have brought upon ourselves. Unless these sins are forgiven and this destructivity in the air is counteracted by God's power the degenerative diseases of mankind will increase in spite of all our faith, *because the causes of them are unrepented and unforgiven.*

We have considered the working of this law in personal ills. There was no use in Anne praying for her heart to get well until she was forgiven of hating her mother-in-law and until she turned that hate into love.

The same law holds true in national and world-wide issues. While there is a degenerative force running loose in the world as a result of man's sins, God's perfect healing cannot come through to us. We can still pray for wholeness, yes, and we must, not only for our own sake but for the sake of the world. Every prayer for life and every healing achieved by prayer releases God's life in the world and helps in the battle against death. But as the prayers for life increase life, so also the radioactive rays will increase death unless we learn to pray not only for ourselves, but for the sins of the world.

Our only hope or help nationally is to face our sins and be sorry for them: *our* sins, note, not the sins of our president or statesmen. In the act of repentance one considers one's *own* sins, individual or collective, not simply the sins of others. It would be a mistake to blame the decision concerning Hiroshima or concerning the testing of hydrogen bombs on any one person. Our representatives in the government act according to the mass mind of the United States. God's people waste His time and dissipate their prayer power if they fall into the common escape method of blaming or criticizing this person and that person. The United States is made up of all of us great and small, and every one of us is responsible for its mistakes. We can see them, repent of them, atone for them, and so help to turn the nation toward goodness. We can do all within our power to arouse public opinion concerning them. But merely to spend our time criticizing our statesmen dissipates our energies fruitlessly.

How then does God deal with nations, and how shall we repent for the sins of a nation? Let us look at the Old Testament, a history of God's dealing with a nation, and learn His ways.

"If my people, which are called by my name, shall humble themselves, and pray, and seek my face, and turn from their wicked ways; then will I hear from heaven, and will forgive their sin, and will heal their land (II Chron. 7:14)." God is able to heal our land. His power is unlimited, His resources infinite. The history of His people is full of times when in answer to the prayer of repentance He has intervened directly in the affairs of men and of nations and has saved His people by guidance and inspiration and even by the forces of nature: wind and fog and water and fire. He has reserves of spiritual energy locked up in the spirits of men, as physical energy is locked up in the atom. As scientists try to get through the electrons and protons and neutrons of the atom to reach the nucleus, so we should try to get through our barriers of pride and faithlessness, of selfishness and hardness of heart and to release the unknown and unused power of the Spirit that is dormant within us. This happened at Pentecost, in a small way to a handful of men, and unleashed a force that overturned the Roman Empire. Who knows how many Pentecosts there could be today, if only we would take the necessary step of admitting and repenting of our sins both personal and national, so as to get through to the center of power!

We know this by our knowledge of the ways of God. But even more emphatically we know it by guidance. Some of us who pray together have the gift of prophecy as Isaiah had it or Jeremiah—and why not? God is not dead. He is alive! Therefore, He can speak to His people today just as He always did. Countless people have told me of their feeling of imminent danger unless we repent and try as never before to find God's will. So we have gone deep in repentance for our own sins that we may be better channels for the forgiveness of national sins. Also we have repented for the sins of the nation, as all should do, for the nation is made up of all of us. "God, please forgive me for my part in the sins of this nation and through me send Thy forgiveness into the nation itself. Please spread among the people the consciousness of our own sins and unworthiness and make them turn to Thee. And please illumine the minds of our leaders, show them the mistakes they and we have made as a nation and guide them into the way of Life."

Some of us have done this, day and night, with prayer and fasting as a token of our real repentance for the nation. But still the warning comes and we know that more people must turn to the Lord and that those in our government itself must build deeper foundations of repentance and a real striving to do God's will or else the impending doom will fall upon us. Every decision of any of us made for our own profit and not for the good of all people should be repented of today—and why not, even from the point of view of common sense? What good would it do any of us to be reelected to anything if the horror of total warfare should wipe us out? And what good would it do to avoid total war if the disintegrating after-effects of atomic explosions should distort and destroy the human race? We have put ourselves in such a position that there is no other course open to us except the way of repentance. Our discovery of atomic energy is our greatest danger, as all of us know or feel. The reason is told in the law that operates just as surely as the law of gravity. Jesus Christ stated it in these words: "He that taketh up the sword shall perish with the sword," which would be in modern words: "The nation that takes up atomic energy shall perish with atomic energy." There is only one law great enough to take precedence over this law of "As ye give, so shall ye receive." That is the law of forgiveness that is in Jesus Christ.

When we have gone deep enough in repentance, then we will go high in hope. We will feel a new courage and a new power in prayer. The clouds will be lifted from our minds and the confusion gone, and we will see the steps to take toward peace. These steps may be small and may not take us far toward the Kingdom of Heaven. But every step that gives us time is of tremendous importance. For the power of prayer is being rediscovered in this nation, and is growing by leaps and bounds. There is light not very far away from us—if only this nation can be brought to its knees, the barrier will be removed. God is alive, He is real, He is here with the great gift of a Kingdom of Peace on Earth in His hands longing to give it to us. If only we will ask Him to forgive, He *will* forgive.

But why, people say, does He not just simply destroy evil out of the earth and make men be good and save us all from the suffering brought about by men's cruelty?

He is going to do so. It is in His plan. He Himself will return to be our Judge. He will come, the "weapon of His glorious majesty in His hand",[1] and will thoroughly purge the nation— and we had best be with Him and not against Him when He comes. He cannot arbitrarily force men to be good, for He has given men free will. But He can and He will, when the Day of Judgment comes, destroy all evil out of the earth, that only the good may remain.

Meantime, He can protect us from the evil. When enough of His people turn to Him in prayer, He can interpose the forces of nature between the destroyer and his victim, the forces of nature being more easily amenable to Him than the minds of wicked men. He did not protect the children of Israel by forcing Pharaoh to be kind when he wanted to be cruel. The Bible said that He "hardened Pharaoh's heart (Ex. 14:8)". He permitted Pharaoh's heart to be hard, since Pharaoh chose that it should be hard. To have autocratically softened Pharaoh's heart would have been to go contrary to His nature, by violating His gift of free will to man. However, He was not without power, and He is not without power today. He had authority over wind and waves, for they were not given free will and so could not rebell against him, and therefore He protected His people by dividing the waters of the Red Sea so that the Israelites passed over in safety (Ex. 14:21-22).

He did not save thousands on the beach at Dunkirk by sending His love to Hitler. Hitler had refused His love, thus he was cut off from the love of God by a barrier of his own choosing. But

---

[1] Collect for the first Sunday in Advent, *The Book of Common Prayer*.

God was not without resource, for He had not given free will to the wind and fog, and the wind and the fog obeyed Him. Thus through the powers of heaven and through the prayers of the faithful, the allies were shielded by fog, the sea was calm as glass, and the English escaped as the Children of Israel had escaped over the sea long ago.

Jesus Christ came into the world for the forgiveness of sins. But He set His own price on that forgiveness, and that price is repentance. Therefore, if we pray for His enemies to repent, we are praying according to law, but if we merely send them love and expect that love to turn them into sweetness and light without leading them in the way of the Cross, we are not praying according to law.

Shall we then pray for them to repent? Only if we do everything in our power to implement that difficult prayer—standing in the shadow of the Cross for them, and making for them sin-offerings as taught in the symbolism of the Old Testament. "Howbeit, this kind goeth not out but by prayer and fasting," Jesus said (Matt. 17:21). And if they will not repent we have no reason to lose faith, for since God has given man free will, He will not force repentance on him. It is easier to pray for those who do not reject prayer but desire it: for the Christians of all nations.

I once received a letter from a Russian immigrant asking, "Why do you not pray for the thousands of Russians in concentration camps, those who cry to God day and night for release?" And so I do. For years I have envisioned the power of God around His own in Russia, enfolding and protecting them, and have seen this power so increasing that their rulers must either change or be removed.

And I can pray for the Christians in China, that their faith may be increased and that they may stand firm and that the power of the Holy Spirit may so fill their churches that eventually His glory will cover their land.

But the working out of these prayers might take centuries, and the time is short. Therefore, more than all else, let us pray that Jesus Christ will soon come to be our Judge.

And while praying for Him to come, we can pray always for our own nation. In a sense it is our greater national body, as the Church is our greater spiritual body. Therefore, we may pray that more and more cells in this national body may be resurrected into cells of light: that more and more people in this country will be truly converted and will learn to pray. Also we may pray for our leaders, who honestly want to do what is right, to be guided and supported by God's Holy Spirit. And most of all we should pray that all of us, leaders and people, shall see our sins and our failures and our weaknesses and repent of them, that we may be forgiven.

While we are thus identifying ourselves with our nation and praying for the forgiveness of those national sins of which we honestly repent, we may also pray for our protection from the dangers and sufferings brought upon us by those sins: *after praying for forgiveness,* we may pray for protection.

This protection-prayer will some day be the greatest and most difficult prayer-project that anyone has ever undertaken or will undertake, for the time will come when we will need to pray for the protection of this earth from radioactive rays. If we do not believe that God parted the waters of the Red Sea and stilled the English Channel at Dunkirk—if we do not believe that the Creator has any authority in His own creation—then we can never learn to pray this prayer. But the church has always so believed, and prayers for God to intervene in the air about this earth are incorporated in the Book of Common Prayer and are used Sunday after Sunday by faithful people. These are prayers for God's power to order and control the air and clouds, wind and weather over a certain area smaller than the whole earth. So let us first consider these prayers, that we may some day learn how to pray the greater protection-prayer.

As I write, I look out of my window at a forest felled by tornado, at houses levelled to the ground or carried off into the fields. In the Old Testament this would have been called the wrath of God (Jer. 10:10). Do we believe it? Do we believe that flood and drought, cyclone and hurricane are acts of God, indicating His wrath at the sins of the nation? We do not act as though we believe it. And yet we pray that He will send us rain or sunshine as we need them, and that He will turn away from us those calamities that we "Most justly have deserved[1]." And whether or not these calamities come upon us by the will of God, one thing I do know: we can by faith and through the forgiveness of sin find deliverance from them. For instance, all one summer no rain fell in New England. The fields were parched, the gardens withered, the crops failed. Therefore we prayed in our church that

---

[1] *The Book of Common Prayer.*

God would give us "moderate rains in due season." And two of us agreed together to follow up this prayer with an act of repentance and faith. We looked upon the selfishness and pride of our well meaning nation, repented of it in the name of the nation, and said prayers of repentance for our share in it. Then, *accepting by faith God's forgiveness,* we sent our own spirits forth into the skies, as when we pray for a person we send our own spirits toward that person. Those skies were hard and brazen. Weather forecasters said that there was no moisture available and no rain in sight. However, we remembered that the ocean was near by and in faith we visioned moisture rising from it, drifting gently over the land, condensing into mist and then to rain. We put all else out of our minds and held to this imagining all day, finding occasion to be out-of-doors that we might be more fully at one with nature. The next day a gentle mist clouded the sky, though the sun could still be seen through a veil. Toward evening a light rain began to fall. The next day the rain increased to a downpour and weather analysts tore their hair in despair. We had three days of rain. On the third afternoon the rain ceased, and a friend who drove down from Maine entered my house with the blithe remark, "Oh, I prayed for the sun to come out so that I would have a pleasant day for the trip, and isn't it wonderful—it did!"

Is it any wonder that many people feel that we have no right to pray for national forgiveness and for protection from national or wide spread calamities such as drought? If they are going to pray as this woman did, with utter selfishness, they are quite right. But the trouble is not that we have nothing to do with weather or that God has no dominion over it, but that we ourselves are too selfish and short-sighted to pray for such a great matter. We have merely shifted our own unworthiness over to the innocent clouds when we say that we cannot believe in the prayer-book prayers for rain or sunshine. If we will broaden our vision and submerge those interests that are purely personal, such as desiring a pleasant ride even though the suffering plants need rain, then certainly we can assume over nature a bit of that dominion that God gave to man (Gen. 1:28).

"And it shall come to pass," said the prophet, speaking the word of God, "if ye shall hearken diligently unto my commandments which I command you this day, to love the Lord your God and to serve Him with all your heart and with all your soul, that I will give you the rain of your land in due season, the first rain and the latter rain, that thou mayest gather in thy corn and thy wine and thine oil. And I will send grass in thy fields for thy cattle, that thou mayest eat and be full. Take heed to yourselves, that your heart be not deceived and ye turn aside and serve other gods and worship them; and then the Lord's wrath be kindled against you and He shut up the heaven that there be no rain and that the land yield not her fruit; and lest ye perish quickly from off the good land the Lord giveth you (Deut. 11:13-17)."

We in our great wisdom and in the wealth of our scientific knowledge have died for the want of this ancient wisdom. We have chosen to perish in flood and to see our cattle die in drought rather than to grant to God whom we blithely call Almighty the dignity of a power to control the clouds that He has made. But what does the Bible tell us of the unfruitful vineyard of the Lord? "I will also command the clouds that they rain no rain upon it . . . (Isa. 5:6)."

Time would fail me to tell all of the Bible statements concerning this very power that we deny to God: the power to order and control the weather according to His will and according to our sins or our repentance from these sins, our faith or our lack of faith. "If ye walk in my statutes and keep my commandments and do them," God promised through the mouth of His servant Moses, "then I will give you rain in due season, and the land shall yield her increase and the trees of the field shall yield their fruit (Lev. 26:3 & 4)."

Oh fools that we are and slow of heart not to believe all that the prophets have spoken! In one breath we deny that God has an interest in our prayers concerning the weather and in another breath we speak of the eccentricities of the same weather as "an act of God." Our inconsistency passes belief. Why do we persistently refuse to see any connection between the dryness of our land and the dryness of our souls—even when brazen skies and starving cattle cry aloud of His wrath? If we believe that God has power, as the Bible says, to order and to control the clouds (Deut. 11:17 & I Kings 8:36 & Job 5:10), then why will we not admit that He uses this power according to those moral principles which we pretend to attribute to Him?

"But we have prayed for the rain to come or for the rain to cease or for protection from the tempest," we say, "and there has been no result."

Certainly. We have not fulfilled the conditions of prayer.

What then are the conditions? First, the keeping of God's

laws, as we have seen from the passages quoted above. Secondly, if we as a nation have failed to keep God's laws, then our prayer effort should be to see wherein we have failed and to repent of it. "Therefore also now, saith the Lord, turn ye even to me with all your heart and with fasting and with weeping and with mourning; and rend your heart and not your garments and turn unto the Lord . . . then will the Lord . . . pity His people." Yes, the Lord will answer and say unto His people,. "Behold I will send you corn and wine and oil and ye shall be satisfied therewith . . . Be glad then, ye children of Zion, and rejoice in the Lord your God; for He hath given you the former rain moderately and He will cause to come down for you the rain, the former rain and the latter rain (Joel 2:12-28)." "I have withholden the rain from you when there were yet three months to the harvest . . . yet have ye not returned unto me," saith the Lord (Amos 4:7-8).

"But that is a message from a bygone age," we may think. "It no longer applies to us."

Why not? God is from everlasting to everlasting (Ps. 41:13). He does not change. His laws are constant. The pull of gravity is not shifted from generation to generation. Electricity having been once created remains. And there remains also the mighty interplay of the mind of God and the mind of men and those lesser things around us, wind and water, sun and rain.

If you do not believe this, try it and see! Consider first the sins of the nations, whether they may be in any way connected with the inclemency of the weather. If we have cut down forests that nature needs in order to draw rain, then there is no use in beating on the doors of heaven unless we do all we can to awaken those in authority to the need of reforestation. If we have turned grass lands into fields and so deprived nature of the protective covering of grass that it needs, then we must seek guidance in the spirit of repentance for this sin committed in ignorance against our land, and must seek to restore nature's balance. If we have injured the forces of life by splitting the atom, then at least we need to acknowledge this before God and ask forgiveness and guidance for those in high places, that we may cease from doing so. If the more subtle sins of ignoring God and His laws have their debilitating effect on nature, then we can repent of those national failures and pray and work for their forgiveness. Whether or not our prayers are strong enough to affect governments and cattle, fields and streams, they certainly release God's power in our own souls. For when we have thus done a work of national repentance, then we feel within us the authority to pray for God's power to protect us from the forces of nature.

Even if it did not affect the creation—so I said. But I believe with all my heart that prayer *can* affect the creation. If I did not believe, I could not look down the dark vista of the future and live. If the nation repents of its use of atomic energy and ceases to split the atom, then I believe that the radioactive love of God can introduce a higher spiritual law of life into a lower physical law of death, and heal the air about this globe, turning a degenerative force into regenerative power. Thus I believe. He can give to us who pray with faith a measure of victory, a measure of protection, until the time when He shall come to be our Judge. For it is necessary, according to the Bible, that He Himself must return not as a suffering Savior but as a Warrior-Judge to set this world free from sin so that it may be forgiven. Judgment is not without pain, and in the final judgment there will be great tribulation.

We are in the midst of the latter days. I believe that we can by faith be saved out of this great tribulation, for our redemption draweth nigh (Luke 21:28). How much of this tribulation can be averted, to what extent the time can be shortened (Matt. 24:22), that I do not know. Some people will not pray for the world at all, feeling that it is of no avail, that horsemen and vials, trumpets, plagues, pestilence and famine are bound to come, according to the Scriptures. I believe also that these things have come and are coming and will come. If a modern seer were St. John on Patmos seeing in visions the destruction raining from airplanes in the sky—seeing two thousand years before it happened the awfulness of Hiroshima and Nagasaki—he too would try to describe these things in such words: dreadful horsemen racing across the sky, raining fire and destruction (Rev. 9:16-18), God's wrath poured out in vials (Rev. 16), the trumpets of awful noises from the heavens announcing doom upon men (Rev. 8).

Jesus Himself prophesied these things. But He also prophesied His coming victory over the army of darkness, His own return to glory (Luke 9:26), the establishment of His Holy Ones upon the seats of judgment that they may bring upon this earth a kingdom of peace (Matt. 19:28), the temporary chaining of the power of evil (Rev. 20:1-3),—and then its final destruction (Rev. 20:10) and the establishment upon this earth of a new Jerusalem, a Holy Community, the Lamb Himself being the light thereof (Rev.

21:23), a river of spiritual life flowing in the very midst of its
streets bringing forth varying fruits of righteousness and glory
(Rev. 22:1-3). Time and again He spoke of this His final victory,
when all evil being destroyed out of the earth, the Kingdom of this
world shall become the Kingdom of the Lord (Rev. 11:15).

He is both the Lamb of God and also the lion of the tribe of
Judah. He is both Sacrifice and Priest and King. "And I saw
heaven opened and behold a white horse; and He that sat upon him
was called Faithful and True, and in righteousness He doth judge
and make war. His eyes were as a flame of fire and on his head
were many crowns . . . and He hath on His vesture and on His
thigh a name written, 'KING OF KINGS AND LORD OF
LORDS (Rev. 19:11-16).' "

Wherefore then, should I fill my mind with thoughts of death,
pestilence and destruction and fail to obey Him and to pray for
the coming of His Kingdom? I will think of Him and dream of
Him, Forgiver of sins and Establisher of Righteousness—"One
like unto the Son of man . . . clothed with a garment down to the
foot and girt about the paps with a golden girdle. His head and
his hairs were white like wool, as white as snow; and his eyes
were as a flame of fire; and his feet like unto fine brass, as
if they burned in a furnace; and his voice as the sound of
many waters (Rev. 1:13-15)."

What mean those high exalted words? I do not know, save
that they speak of His glory, and of His glory will I dream, and
with Him will I fill my soul.

And as I rest my heart on Him and watch for His coming,
I will not fail to pray for this world in the way that He Himself
taught and commanded us to pray: "Thy Kingdom Come, Thy
Will Be Done, On Earth As It Is In Heaven."

Praying thus, I will implement this great affirmation with the
visioning of faith, and will see in my mind this earth becoming
the planet that God meant it to be, an orderly planet in which
the evolvement of life proceeds from glory to glory according to
His will, as it does in heaven. Seeing this, I will bring down my
vision to a smaller part of this planet and will see my own nation
learning God's will and doing it. And I will also see that new step
toward the brotherhood of man, the United Nations, learning more
and more to do God's will on earth as it is done in heaven. I
will see God's first experiment, His chosen people, returning to
the Lord and being forgiven and accepted back into their new
spiritual Jerusalem. Thus will I see this forgiveness of sins

spreading over the whole earth until the glory of God covers the earth as the waters cover the sea.

"Oh Zion, that bringest good tidings . . . . . . say unto the cities of Judah, *'Behold your God* (Isa. 40:9)!' "

14. The Resurrection of the Body and the Life Everlasting

What if we believe in God the Father, learn his creative laws, believe in Jesus Christ and His redemption, receive the Holy Spirit and pray for the church, the nation and the world? Shall we then, in our present life, attain to perfect wholeness? Certainly we will be renewed in vigor, energy and youth. But how long can that last?

What about death?

The answer to this question is resurrection. But what do we mean by resurrection? Most of us mean, vaguely, that when our bodies die, our souls will go to heaven—though it is noteworthy that none of us want to do so. We sing of the joy and the glory of those endless Sabbaths, but when the time comes to enter into that joy and glory we do everything in our power to resist it. We speak of the soul finding its way into eternal rest, but we feel uncomfortably that a vague bodiless spirit resting forever is not a thing to be desired.

But the stalwart words of the Apostles Creed, which we repeat Sunday after Sunday in church, say nothing about the eternal rest or about the surviving spirit going to heaven. The summed-up teaching of the church goes beyond these truths to the highest truth of all—the greatest adventure of time and eternity—and boldly states "I believe in the resurrection of the body."

That is the final accomplishment of faith and holy living. That is the ultimate goal of all our prayers for healing: a body of perfect and immortal wholeness wrought in eternity: a resurrected body.

This resurrected body is not identical with the surviving spirit. When the body of Jesus lay in the tomb, *His surviving spirit descended into Hades* and there preached to the spirits that were in prison (Pet. 3:19). His spirit was an actual being, but like the imprisoned spirits, could not manifest itself in a corporal body until after His resurrection. According to His own words, we too shall attain to some such resurrection. "I am the resurrection, and the life," He said. "He that believeth in Me, though he were dead, yet shall he live: and whosoever liveth and believeth in me shall never die (John 11:25-26)."

Those who believe on Him, even though the body does die, shall yet live, as even old Job saw long ago: "And though . . . worms destroy this body, yet in my flesh shall I see God (Job 19:26)." And those who are living at the time of the resurrection unto life shall attain to the resurrected body (Rev. 20:6) as Enoch (Gen. 5:24) and Elijah (II Kings 2:11-12)) attained to it, without going through death at all.

How shall these things be?

If we are living by faith, then a new current of life is quickening these mortal bodies (Rom. 8:11). This new current is our Divine birthright. It is a reserve of spiritual energy locked up in every cell of the body, as I have stated even from my first book, *The Healing Light.* This reserve of spirtual energy can be called upon by the prayer of faith and can supplement the natural recuperative forces of the body so that the body is renewed in strength and in youth. "They that wait upon the Lord shall renew their strength—they shall mount up with wings as eagles—they shall run and not be weary and they shall walk and not faint (Isa. 40:31)." However, this renewing must be done by a rigorous training of the mind after the pattern of faith, by a constant softening of the heart through the love of Christ, and by a disciplined and ordered spirit. It is not easy. Moreover, this renewal of life and strength adds many responsibilities to our lives because we cannot live to ourselves alone. That would be contrary to the very flow of this life, which is on the thought waves of love and which therefore demands that we make ourselves part of humanity, and work for others, for the nation and for the world, as well as for ourselves. Therefore, the body eventually becomes weary. Some of the life-force is lost by the very effort of keeping the life-force flowing. We cannot do it without the Holy Spirit.

But when one is filled with the Holy Spirit, the process of quickening is taken over from the conscious and the subconscious mind and is carried on by the Spirit Himself. Thus the effort of living according to the laws of faith is lessened to a very considerable extent. We do not need to exert our minds so vigorously in prayer, for the Spirit Himself prayeth within us with groanings which cannot be uttered (Rom 8:26). Moreover, we do not need to keep such a long prayer list, for the Spirit often prays through our spirits without direction from our minds, but according to the will of God (Rom. 8:27). We know not what we should pray for as we ought (Rom. 8:26)—we do not know at a given moment who may be in danger of sickness or trouble, calling out to us in spirit or calling out to God, therefore we cannot pray as we ought. So the Spirit often uses us according to the will of God, working through us quite without our efforts and merely through our yielded spirits. With all this work taken over by the Spirit, the rejuvenation of the body can be carried on much more effectively.

It is strange that so many of the saints have not fulfilled this glorious destiny of walking from life to Life, but have deliberately put themselves back under the law of sin and death, choosing to afflict and mortify and starve the body and thus frustrating the will of the Spirit which is to quicken that body and raise it up into everlasting life!

What then is the ultimate work that God's Holy Spirit can do within us? What is the highest of which this mortal body is capable? Can the day come when God's Spirit can so quicken this body that it shall be spiritualized and resurrected in every cell and become, while here upon this earth, a body like to the body of Jesus Christ? His resurrected body was capable of manifesting itself in the flesh (Luke 24:36-44), and yet also capable of becoming pure spirit, passing through closed doors (John 20:19), vanishing and reappearing at will (John 21:14). And this overcoming of death by life is the final victory for those who abide in Him. "The last enemy that shall be overcome is death (I Cor. 15:26)."

But whether any of us in this present life can attain to this final will of God, in which there shall be no more death, neither sorrow nor crying, for the former things have passed away

(Rev. 21:4), that is another question. It depends not only on us personally but also on the amount of spiritual power available in the whole Church, since we are one in Christ.

What then of us who are as yet too far away from the coming Kingdom to complete our spiritualization of this body while living in the flesh? Shall we in heaven itself perfect this resurrected body? Shall the spirits and souls of the righteous, after sleeping for a season that they may rest and after long survival in a life of pure spirit, once more make contact with this earth and take the next step forward, being no longer pure spirits but resurrected bodies after the pattern of Jesus Christ? The Bible points to some such event as this (Rev. 20:12-15 & II Cor. 5:2 & John 5:29 & Acts 24:15 & Rom. 6:5 & I Cor. 15 & Phil. 3:11 & Heb. 6:2 & Rev. 20:5-6) and describes it in words of terrifying and yet thrilling glory.

How shall these things be?

According to St. Paul (I Cor. 15) we plant a seed of spiritual life when we depart from this world: the soul, or spirit, that is indestructible and that lives in another rate of vibration when the body has disappeared. That seed grows as a seed planted in the ground grows. It develops in spiritual power and discernment. It learns by service. And the time comes when that seed planted in heaven shall once more clothe itself with a body—not a destructible body, but a body that is incorruptible. This spiritual body shall be recognizable. When Jesus stood before His disciples, they knew Him (John 20:19). True, He could if He so pleased draw the veil of spirit over that body so that His disciples looked on Him and did not know Him (Luke 24:15-16). But unless for His own purposes He ruled otherwise, the resurrection body of Jesus was most literally and obviously the body that His disciples knew (John 21:12). He was *not* dead after all.

And the final meaning of this statement, "I believe in the resurrection of the body" is that there shall be, in the future, *not any death at all* (Rev. 21:4)! Moreover, that astounding, overwhelming belief is the foundation of our Christian faith (I Cor. 15:14). It is the amazing truth that Our Lord told us in straight and direct words (John 11:25-26). It is the glorious vision of St. Paul, who even longed to be clothed upon with the immortal body while here in the flesh without even having to be unclothed of this mortal body by death (II Cor. 5:2). He did not quite attain his objective. But there are those in the Scriptures who did attain it, as we have noted in other chapters (Gen. 5:24 & II Kings 2:11-12).

But why should these have attained the resurrection body in this life while no one else through all the long centuries has been able to do so?

How do we know that no one else has been able to do so?

If some holy person had disappeared and not returned, as an occasional legend states, who would have believed in any other possibility other than an unknown death and a hidden grave?

But now let us come back from the realm of conjecture to what we do know, and they are the statements concerning Jesus. His own spirit, made perfect through suffering (Heb. 2:10), raised His own body from the tomb as He said that He would do (John 2:19-21). The very cells of His physical body were transformed into cells of a different order, so instinct with spiritual life that they were from thenceforth completely subject to the will of the Spirit and therefore death had no more dominion over them.

Will our spirits, when they are sufficiently powerful in the life everlasting, come back and find the actual cells of the body, long since melted into the common dust, and out of them build a new body? I do not know. I cannot feel that it need necessarily be so. The important point seems to be that the spirit, living in the life everlasting, shall at some time attain such spiritual energy that it will build itself an immortal body. Whether the spirit looks about for the grave of its former body and uses those cells or whether the spirit creates new living cells does not seem to me so very important. If I want a new dress, I may use an old, discarded dress and make it over, or I may make one out of new cloth . . . but the final result will be much the same: I will be clothed anew.

Some people feel that the only understandable way of attaining this new body is the way of Enoch and Elijah: to live with such spiritual power while upon the earth that one can attain complete mastery of the body and transform it into a resurrection body without going through the gates of death. This was St. Paul's desire, as I have said.

"But I haven't seen any resurrection bodies walking about!" said I to the friend who propounded this theory to me.

And she replied quite simply, *"How do you know?"*

Since I do not and cannot know, then why do I concern myself about the resurrection of the body?

Because it is a matter of the utmost practical importance to know that this body in which I now live will live again and will live forever! The desire for an immortal life is deeply written into our natures, and is not to be satisfied with any dismal tales of disembodied spirits floating around in heaven!

No matter what we say, the idea of living without a body does not appeal to us. As Rufus Mosely used to say, "A body without a spirit is a corpse, and a spirit without a body is a ghost, and I don't want to be either." That is why we put up such a resistance to death, a resistance that would be completely illogical if we believed what we say we believe in the burial service: "My heart is glad and my glory rejoiceth: my flesh also shall rest in hope. Thou shalt show me the path of life; in Thy presence is the fullness of joy, and at Thy right hand there is pleasure forevermore[1]." St. Paul did not fear death nor detest it, because he knew that he would live again even as Jesus lived again (I Cor. 15:55 & I Cor. 15:22-23). His whole being, physical as well as his eternal spirit, would live again and forever. Therefore he could look with calmness upon the possibility of the momentary dissollution of the body, knowing that it would be re-formed and be once more himself.

Water disappears into steam when it is boiled. The steam dissolves into vapor and is seen no more. Yet that very vapor condenses upon the window-pane and is reassembled as drops of water. Nothing is lost, only changed.

My delphiniums disappear under the action of frost into a mass of sodden decay. But those same delphiniums that have withdrawn their real life out of sight, bring it forth again when spring comes, rising again into their stalks of heavenly blue.

No flowers are really dead when they disappear under the ground. There are annuals who wrap their life into seeds and so grow again, producing a new body. *There are perennials which not only sow seeds of immortality but also reproduce the same body anew.*

All the world shouts aloud to us of the resurrection of the body! We cling to our bodies and cannot be completely consoled by the thought of an existence in an ethereal form because resurrection is a law of life—and therefore God Himself has

---

[1] *The Book of Common Prayer,* also Ps. 16:9

planted in us a craving for life that otherwise would seem to pass the bounds of reason!

There was a young girl, very dear to me, who had a fear of death. I had prayed that this fear be removed and it was alleviated, but did not entirely disappear. Once she happened to visit me when I gave a lecture on this subject to my Bible Class. "Why didn't you tell me about the flowers and the steam before?" said she. "Now I'm not afraid any more! That's what I wanted to know all the time!"

I had not told her before because I thought she was too young to understand such things or to believe them. But I learned a lesson from that young person: *it was what she wanted to know all the time.* It is what we all want to know all the time! That is why it is boldly stated in the Apostles' Creed: I believe in the resurrection of the body.

If we will but drop our foolish pretense of being satisfied with a life everlasting in which we have no such great and thrilling hope as the resurrecting of our bodies, and will let ourselves believe in that resurrection, then we will have no more fear of death.

And if we are relieved of the fear of death, then our efforts toward healing, whether for ourselves or for others, will be far more effective. Every fear that departs from us leaves more room for faith, and so adds power to our prayers. And the greatest of all fears that can depart from our souls is the fear of the dissolution of this body. Without that fear, we can look calmly upon life and upon Life and rejoice! Without it we can rightly judge when to direct our prayers toward life and when to direct them toward Life!

For if the spirit upon departing undertakes a tremendous adventure, the resurrecting of the body, then it is a matter of some importance that the spirit should be free to attend to this matter at the right time. The spirit can do a great deal toward this eternal project here in this life—far more than most of us do. Every prayer for healing whether of an abscessed ear or of a stomach ulcer or for anything—*every prayer for healing is really a prayer for the resurrection of the body. This is the final and ultimate importance of spiritual healing.* To patch the body with medicine and surgery when it falls apart is good, because it prolongs life and gives the spirit more time to be about its real business. But to keep the body well by filling it with a live and powerful spirit is far better, for it is working in Time as well as in time—it is working toward that final mastery of the body by spiritual power that will transform it entirely into a body like unto the resurrected body of Christ (Phil. 3:21).

So it is most important to keep this body alive till the spirit has accomplished as much as possible of the work of learning and living that it needs to do in this lifetime. But there comes a time when the spirit has done all it can according to the limits of our present lonely world, when Christ has not as yet come again in His full glory. There comes a time in extreme old age when the spirit can grow no more within this body, because the very flesh has dimmed its shining—the brain cells are worn out, the strain of pumping life into the flesh takes all the spiritual energy and leaves none for real growth. There comes a time also when we can no longer serve our Master with efficiency, can no longer help life about us, and might even hinder life rather than help it by remaining upon this world.

If we only believed in the resurrection of the body, this would be a happy time to us. What joy to look forward to the freeing of the spirit from this dull clay, so that it can begin a more thrilling stage of its everlasting adventure with God! What delight to think of this body starting anew in beauty and in perfection, healed of all the wrinkles and deformities of age! So I am consoled when my delphiniums die. Their bodies had grown old, stiff stalks with withering leaves and only a stunted blossom here and there where their tall spires had been. So I rejoice to see them covered at last by the life-giving snow, looking forward with eager expectation to the pale shoots that will in due time come forth from the warm earth of spring . . .so I rejoice in their death, knowing that it leads to a new and purified and strengthened life.

Why do most of us close our eyes to reality and deprive ourselves of the most exciting moment of our lives—the moment of departure? Why do most of us fight for physical life with such blind insistence that we lose all joy of immortality in a vain clinging to the flesh? Why are we so afraid to see the moment of our going that we must needs be kept under opiates and so go unperceiving into the other world?

Why do we refuse to release our spirits for their second birth?

For just as it is important to hold our spirits in this life so long as they are useful here, so also it is important to release them when they are needed on the other side.

A pregnant woman strives to hold her baby for nine months.

If there seems danger of a miscarriage, she will do anything to avert it, during the incubation period which the baby needs. But what if at the end of nine months she still refused to let the baby be born?

That is exactly what most of us do.

When the incubation period of our spirits is over and the time is come for them to be born again into another world, we cause them pain and anguish and no doubt hamper them in their spiritual growth because we refuse to let them go.

"It's fun to bury a Christian!" said a mountain minister to me. "I'm so happy thinking how happy he is!"

He knew.

But how can we tell when our time draws near, and when we should no longer work for life but for Life?

It seems to me that of all things this would be the most easy to ascertain if we will but ask with open minds, free from fear, and then listen to the inner knowledge of our own spirits!

And if our spirits tell us that the time draws near for our departure, should we not pray for the joy and power of our going, rather than clinging with blind persistence to a life from which our straining spirits have turned away? Surely there would be power in such a going as this! Surely we could pray through the very pangs of death itself, and turn them into redemptive action for the world! Surely we could say at the last, "Lord, into Thy hands I commend my spirit," and know that the spirit would be on its way rejoicing to the throne of God!

"Let me die the death of the righteous," said a holy man of long ago, "and let my last end be like his (Num. 23:10)." Why? Merely to save trouble? There is a much better reason! As one can live redemptively, so one can die redemptively. There was Israel, who prophesied upon his death bed more clearly than he had ever done before, seeing beyond the bounds of time and speaking of what he saw in words of grandeur and beauty. He gave commandments also concerning his own burial, and when he had made an end of commanding his sons, "he gathered up his feet into the bed and yielded up the ghost, and was gathered unto his people (Gen. 49:33)." Dignity and beauty was there, dignity and power, and an alien people mourned for him with great and sore lamentation, knowing him for a man who had honor of his God and knowing and honoring his God through him (Gen. 50:9-11).

All this was long ago, long ago, before Our Savior even

came into this world. Surely now that Jesus has come so far
to reach us, we should be able to go the rest of the way toward Him! Surely we should testify to His name by the dignity
and the power of our departing, as did Stephen who saw Jesus
standing at the right hand of God (Acts 7:55) and cried saying, "Lord, lay not this sin to their charge (Acts 7.60)!" Can
we not also hold our prayer-power to the end, as our spirits
struggle free, and use that foretaste of heaven for the forgiveness
of this earth?

I believe in the life everlasting.

It is a life in which I now live, and the moments of fleeting
ecstasy that I remember from childhood are bits of that heavenly joy still remaining in my childish spirit. "Trailing clouds of
glory do we come from God who is our home," said the poet
Wordsworth. And again,

> *"O joy! That in our embers*
> *Is something that doth live!*
> *That nature yet remembers*
> *What was so fugitive!*
> *The thought of our past years in me doth breed*
> *Perpetual benediction; not indeed*
> *For that which is most worthy to be blest—*
> *Delight and liberty, the simple creed*
> *Of Childhood, whether busy or at rest,*
> *With new-found hope still fluttering in his breast—*
> *Not for these I raise*
> *The song of thanks and praise,*
> *But for those obstinate questionings,*
> *Of sense and outward things,*
> *Fallings from us, vanishings,*
> *Blank misgivings of a creature*
> *Moving about in worlds not realized,*
> *But for those first affections,*
> *Those shadowy recollections,*
> *Which, be they what they may,*
> *Are yet the fountain light of all our day,*
> *Are yet the master light of all our seeing;*
> *Uphold us, cherish, and have power to make*
> *Our noisy years seem moments in the Being*
> *Of the eternal Silence; truths that wake*
> *To perish never;*

Which neither listlessness nor mad endeavor
  Nor man nor boy
Nor all that is at enmity with joy
Can utterly abolish or destroy!
  Hence in a season of calm weather
  Though inland far we be,
Our Souls have sight of that immortal sea
  Which brought us hither.
  Can in a moment travel thither,
And see the children sport upon the shore
And hear the mighty waters rolling evermore[1].

There was one who saw. When I was but a child I recognized his seeing, and have known this poem by heart as long as I remember. There is comfort in those words. But there is even more comfort in the words of the book of Revelation which also from a child I knew and loved even though it was (and is) above my understanding. "And after these things I heard a great voice of much people in heaven, saying, Alleluia; Salvation, and glory, and honour, and power, unto the Lord our God . . . (Rev. 19:1)" Much people in heaven; those who have "gotten the victory over the beast and over his image and over his mark and over the number of his name," standing "on the sea of glass having the harps of God (Rev. 15:2)"—What do I find in those strange words, I who am not a diviner of prophesies but only an ordinary person trying to learn to pray? I find the long history of a struggle and a battle and a terrible conflict, over Satan and over sin, beginning on earth and culminating in heaven. I find the prayers of the saints ascending unto the throne and making a continuing channel for God's power in heaven as they did on earth. I find the saints themselves in positions of authority and power (Matt. 19:28 & Rev. 20:4), sitting upon the thrones at the right hand of God and with Him ruling and judging the nations . . .

His servants who have served Him on earth shall continue to serve Him in heaven! And they shall serve Him with a joy that no symbol can show us, for it is beyond showing—the joy of harps and of the ecstasy of music, the joy of an ineffable beauty like unto the beauty of every precious stone hid in every mountain and of every shining pearl rocked in silence beneath the blue waves of the sea—the joy that breaks forth in an un-

---

[1] *"Ode to Immortality"* by William Wordsworth.

ending rapture of praise that cannot be still but must cry aloud before the Great White Throne evermore saying, "Holy, holy, holy . . . (Rev. 4:8)"

And lest our earth-bound souls should weary of so much constant joy, I find also distress and anguish over an earth that has fallen and has become the habitation of devils and the hold of every foul spirit (Rev. 16). And I find the fire of the Lord, His awful holiness, destroying that evil upon the earth and purging it as by fire (Rev. 16:8-9). And I see finally a new heaven and a new earth emerging from all of this struggle—not only a new heaven, notice, but also a new earth—brought to life by the power of God and the Lamb and also by the power and the prayers of those who had climbed the steep ascent to heaven and had not worshipped the Beast of evil upon this earth.

There is nothing static in this picture! We rest from our earthly labors. But our real works—our creative accomplishments and the activities of our spirits—we take with us to the heavenly realm (Rev. 14:13). Whatever we have learned to do by spiritual power, we keep right on doing as we pass over to the other side. And what radiant and unimaginable service we may render to our God and to His Kingdom as we go from strength to strength in His perfect service[2], He alone can know. "Eye hath not seen, nor ear heard, neither have entered into the heart of man the things which God hath prepared for them that love Him (I Cor. 2:9)."

And finally I see, as I search the Scriptures, a new order of life established here upon this earth . . . a holy city, a holy community and way of life, coming down from God out of heaven (Rev. 21:2). "Behold the tabernacle of God is with men, and He will dwell with them and they shall be His people, and God Himself shall be with them and be their God (Rev. 21:3)."

God who made man in His own image, after His own likeness, is not content to abandon His experiment with time or even to salvage a remnant of it and let the rest of it go to destruction. There is a remnant, true: and all the evil of it shall be destroyed, true; but when this is done, the Kingdom of Heaven shall be established upon this earth. He did not need to make man so that man could return to the spirit world

---

[2] *The Book of Common Prayer.*

whence he had come and live forever as a ghost! He already had spirits without number and heavenly messengers as a flame of fire! No, His new creation of water and the Word was an experiment of spirit transforming flesh and glorifying it and abiding in it—of spirit redeeming the very creation itself, that at present groaneth and travaileth together waiting for the manifestation of those sons of God who shall bring His Kingdom upon earth (Rev. 22 & Rom. 8:18-25)!

Why should God so care about our frail and faltering human natures that He endows them with everlasting life and preserves them in His own glory? "What is man, that Thou art mindful of him, or the son of man that Thou visitest him (Ps. 8:4)?" From everlasting man has wondered, knowing his own smallness, that God came into this world in the form of the Son of Man and took upon Himself this human life! Why?

What can one say to a Creator? If He chooses to create after a certain pattern, who are we to say, "Why?"

Shall the clay say to him that fashioneth it, "What makest Thou (Isa. 45:9)?"

He has chosen to do a daring work through us, and one that cost Him tears and anguish: He has chosen to send our eternal spirits into bodies of flesh, subject to all the temptations and ills of the flesh, and to see whether He can still work through us a Kingdom of Heaven on earth. It is His holy experiment. It is His new creation. And being a Creator with all might and all power and all love, He will not fail to bring it to pass.

It is drawing near us even now—the new heaven and the new earth—and if only we will believe Him and work with all our hearts for the Kingdom, He will soon accomplish His second break-through into time. And we will see with our eyes what St. John saw in a vision so very long ago: we will see a pure river of the water of life, the heavenly energy that heals and cleanses and resurrects, flowing in the very center and heart of life so that it is available to everyone (Rev. 22:1) We will see that heavenly energy so filling the earth that life will grow and blossom like trees on every side, and those trees of life will bring forth all manner of fruits: fruits of judgment and of justice and of healing for men and nations (Rev. 22.2) and of the love of Christ shining like a light to all the world (Rev. 22.5).

"And the nations of them that are saved shall walk in the

light of it: and the kings of the earth do bring their glory and honor into it (Rev. 21:24).

Then at long last the curse that mankind brought upon itself by the fall will be lifted and "there shall be no more curse: but the throne of God and of the Lamb shall be in it; and His servants shall serve Him: and they shall see His face; and His name shall be in their foreheads. And . . . they shall reign for ever and ever (Rev. 22:3-5)."

So the conquering Jesus will have at long last won His wandering planet back to Himself.

"Even so come, Lord Jesus!"

THE END